A Dictionary of ENVIRONMENTAL TERMS

(With Hindi Translation)

A Dictionary of ENVIRONMENTAL TERMS

(With Hindi Translation)

Harish Chandra Sharma
M.S., M.B.A., R.E.M. (USA)

CBS PUBLISHERS & DISTRIBUTORS
4596/1-A, 11 Darya Ganj, New Delhi - 110 002 (India)

ISBN : 81-239-0656-0

First Edition : 1999
Reprint : 2002

Published by S.K. Jain for CBS Publishers & Distributors,
4596/1A, 11 Darya Ganj, New Delhi - 110 002 (India)

Printed at : Asia Printograph,
Shahdara, Delhi - 110 032

PREFACE

After attaining independence, India has made tremendous economic progress. It has become one of the ten most industrialized countries of the world. Recently, the country opened its market to the world, further intensifying its economic growth. Rapid successes due to mechanization also meant generation of more hazardous and other forms of waste making environmental controls a necessity.

Indian government has instituted new regulations to control further degradation of the environment and new words are fast coming into effect. This work of compiling the nomenclature of recognized as well as new words and phrases was undertaken to satisfy a pressing need. The terms have been selected from various sources including those commonly in use, regulations of India, and also the phrases that are presently used in the pollution industry.

The new terminology that came with industrialization is in English, in a country where almost half speak in Hindi. The terms are translated into Hindi but transliterated in English. Although primarily intended to assist any person in search of an environmental word in English, this book should be of considerable value to communicate with people who know only Hindi. Another purpose in including Hindi words is to remove from the minds of all those who have an idea that Hindi is poor in word power. These pages will convince them of the richness and creative possibilities of the Hindi language, a fact the author himself realized when compiling this glossary of environmental terms.

Terms and phrases are arranged in alphabetical order. First the defined word is entered, then next to it, in brackets, transliteration of the term of Hindi translation. Following that is the meaning or definition of the terminology. Format of the entry is as follows:

Defined Term or Phrase (Transliteration of Hindi Translation)
Definition or meaning in English.

Whenever necessary, the pertinent examples and regulation of India are indicated. This should prove beneficial and useful resource for anyone considering setting up an industry in India or assist an existing industry as an environmental professional.

With a reference in the main part, there is a very useful appendix included at the end of the book. This has been done with a view that anyone considering starting an industry could get some basic information from this source. Some of the topics in appendix include: half Life of radionuclides, guidelines to set up an industry in India, classification of hazardous waste categories for labeling, list of hazardous and toxic chemicals, guidelines for occupier/generator of hazardous waste, for transportation of hazardous waste, for owner/operator of hazardous waste storage, treatment, and disposal facility, criteria for siting of industries with reference to classification of river zones, essential items in a hazardous waste manifest, consideration in siting of hazardous waste disposal facility.

A special feature of this book is the reference list from which majority of the terms have been collected. If needed, the reader could search for more information from those sources and others. It should be understood that many words or phrases have several meanings. I have indicated the meanings that are, in my opinion, directly related to environmental activities.

This book has been written in simple words to make it as interesting and easy to read as possible. Comments from the users of this glossary would be most welcome and sincerely appreciated. They will be included in the next edition of the book.

There are many that assisted me during the development of this collection. It is difficult to mention them all here but I would like to take this opportunity to thank Zak Tucker and Rose Ann Thompson who reviewed, corrected many mistakes, and offered ways to improve this collection at many places. Special thanks to Dr. Abbas Ghassemi and Dr. Rohinton Bhada who agreed to look through my manuscript and offer their invaluable suggestions and comments. However, the mistakes still remaining are all mine. It is very difficult to find words of thanks for Prof. Norris Green, as without his encouraging words on a bright December morning in 1995, I would have never started on this path at all. All I can say is thank you Professor 'Bud' Green.

My mother Dropadi Devi who passed away a few years back and my father Dharam Jit Jigyasu, who at the age of 83 is still working hard, have been and continue to be my greatest inspiration in my life. The desire to write came from my father-in-law Dr. Rajeshwar Guru, an accomplished Hindi author himself. My in-laws Dr. Rajeshwar Guru and Vidya Guru, who passed away a couple of years back, are and continue to be an inspiration to me.

Special thanks to my children, Nivedita and Rahul for making suggestions for improvements. They are my first editors in whatever I venture to write. Thanks to my aunt, Dr. Mithilesh Sharma who corrected my Hindi translations. My wife Dr. Anuradha Sharma not only corrected my Hindi translations but also suggested ways to improve the whole collection. This book is seeing the light of the day because of her patience and persistence.

This is the work of a single man. Though I have tried my best to be as complete and useful as possible, I must confess that I have only scratched the surface. For this reason, I would suggest that users of this work let me know their suggestions or corrections to improve the contents of this book. They would be most gratefully welcomed.

Harish Chandra Sharma

CONTENTS

A

A-horizon (Dharti Ke Upari Parat Ki Matti) The upper layer of soil which contains humus and most plant roots. Considerable amounts of soluble soil constituents are leached from this zone.

A-Scale Sound Level (A Dhwani Stir) A measurement of sound approximating the sensitivity of the human ear, used to note the intensity or level of sound. Measured in decibels which refers to the sound pressure level. Measured in dB or decibels. Sound level for soft whisper is 20 dBA.

Abatement (Pradushan Nivaran) A process by which pollution by any substance in any media such as air, water, or ground is reduced or eliminated. Measures to reduce or eliminate pollution could also be done through legislation.

Abatement Debris (Pradushan Kachra) Waste that has been generated from an abatement processor due to remediation activities.

Abiotic (Ajaiva) Pertaining to nonliving components of the environment. It is the non-biological transformation. The process is mainly either due to photolytic or hydrolytic. In Hindi, *Ajaiva.*

Abiotic Degradation (Ajaiva Ka Nimnikaran) It is the breakdown of a chemical by processes other than living organisms, such as by photodegradation and chemical reactions. An example is hydrolysis.

Abrasion (Apagharshan) By means of either physical or chemical forces, when a substance gradually starts to erode. Chemical reason might be oxidation, physical being by cutting. The deterioration of the substance affects the serviceability of the material. Physical condition such as pressure and temperature play a significant role during abrasion of the material. In Hindi, *Apagharshan.*

Absolute Pressure (Vishuddha Dabaav) When other forces are not taken into account. In Hindi, *Vishuddha Dabaav.*

Absolute Temperature (Vishuddha Taapmaan) Temperature at which all molecular motion ceases. It is -459.69 degrees F or -273-16 degrees Celsius. In Hindi, *Vishuddha Taapmaan.*

Absolute Zero (Param Shunya) The theoretical temperature at which all molecular motion ceases. It is zero degrees Kelvin or -273.18 degrees Celsius or -459.6 degrees Fahrenheit. In Hindi, *Param Shunya.*

Absorbed Dose (Avashoshit Maatraa) Actual amount of a chemical that has entered an exposed part or organism through physical and/or biological process. Generally a human body. If it is radiation energy, it is measured in rads. In Hindi, *Avashoshit Maatraa.*

Absorbent (Avashoshak) When one material (absorbate) is taken up and held or retained by another medium (absorbent). An example of this is soaking of oil if spilled on water by use of absorbent materials. A solid absorbent of very small particle size can absorb more as it has larger surface area. Silica gel can absorb moisture from atmosphere. Absorbent examples are cotton, fuller's earth and sawdust. In Hindi, *Avashoshak.*

Absorption (Avashoshan) The penetration or transport of atoms, ions or molecules from one substance into the inner structure of mass of another substance through biological membranes, through active transport, passive diffusion. Some chemicals have the capacity to absorb moisture from the atmosphere. Absorption of a substance in humans takes place through inhalation, skin contact or intake through mouth. Chemicals can be absorbed into the bloodstream after breathing or swallowing any substance or chemical. Also absorption of water as well as other nutrients by the roots of a tree from soil. In radiation, it is the process by which radiation imparts some or all of its energy to any material that it passes through. As an example, an Alpha particle which travel at approximately 16,000 km per second, collide with between 30,000 and 1,00,000 ion pairs per centimetre of air traveled. In Hindi, *Avashoshan.*

Abutment (Aadhaar Bheeti) Retaining walls put in place to hold back the slippage of land or unstable areas.

Abyssal (Samudra Tal) The deep areas of the ocean where there is no light. In Hindi, *Samudra Tal*.

Access Drift (Abhigam Apavaah) A tunnel or shaft which grants a passage to a geological formation part.

Accident (Durghatnaa) As per The Public Liability Insurance Act of 1991, this means an accident involving a fortuitous, sudden or unintentional occurrence while handling any hazardous substance resulting in continuous, intermittent or repeated exposure to death, of or injury to, any person, or damage to any property but does not include an accident by reason only of war or radio-activity.

Acclimation (Paristhiti Anukulan or Dashanukulan or Paryanukulan) The physiological or behavioral adaptation and adjustments of organisms to new environmental conditions such as temperatures, pH, hardness, diet. In Hindi, *Paristhiti Anukulan*.

Accretion (Sahavardhan) When the size of a particle is increased through the form of gathering or collection. It is a form of accumulation.

Accumulative Effect of a Chemical (Sanchit Rasayanik Prabhav) Effect of a chemical on a biologic system when the chemical has been administered at a rate that exceeds its elimination from a system. Sufficient accumulation of the chemical in the system can lead to toxic concentration.

Acetaldehyde (Acet Aldehyde) A colourless highly flammable, toxic liquid with a pungent fruity odour. It is miscible in water. It causes irritation of eyes and the digestive system. Used in the manufacture of acetic acid. Formula CH_3CHO.

Acetic Acid (Acetic Amla or Amliya Amla) A clear and colourless liquid with a pungent acrid odour. Moderately toxic but very dilute form is used as a food additive. Also used in the production of plastics, medicine. Formula CH_3COOH.

Acetone (Acetone) A volatile, fragrant, flammable, colourless liquid. If absorbed, it causes irritation to eyes, nose throat, and mucous membranes. It can also damage the nervous system. A Ketone, its formula is C_3H_6O. Mostly used as a solvent.

Acid (Amla or Tejaab) Any compound which is a proton donor is an acid. Generally, they are sour to taste. All acids contain Hydrogen. When reacting with a chemical, an acid releases a hydrogen ion (H+) as one of the products of ionic dissociation in water. Its pH is less than 7.0. Hard acids have a positive oxidation state while the soft acids have little or no positive charge and have easily excited valence electrons. All mineral acids are highly irritant and corrosive to human tissue. Sulphuric Acid is an example of an inorganic mineral acid while acetic acid is an organic acid. In Hindi, *Amla* or *Tejaab*.

Acid Deposition (Amliya Nikshepan) The total acid deposited to earth both in precipitation (acid rain, snow) and dry form (dry deposition). Their pH is generally less than 5.5. The depositions are generally caused by complex chemical and atmospheric phenomenon that occurs when pollutants such as nitrogen oxide and sulphur oxides emitted by industrial activity react. Due to the movement of wind, far from its original source these are deposited on earth in either wet or dry form. The wet form is popularly called acid rain, can fall as rain, snow, or fog. The dry forms are acidic gases or particulate matter. Acid rain is common in industrial areas where coal is used in large amounts. See also Acid Rain.

Acidic (Amliya) When the pH of a substance or liquid is less than 7.0 due to the presence of acid.

Acidiosis (Acidosis) A pathologic condition resulting from accumulation of acid in, or loss of base from the body.

Acid Nitrate (Amlik Nitrate) A major component of acid rain. Principle component of acid fog. Commonly known as Nitric Acid (HNP3). It dissolves in water to form acid (H+) and nitrate (NO3-). It is formed by the oxidation of nitrogen oxides.

Acid Rain (Amla Varsha) When the rain is acidic in nature. This means that it has sulfur dioxide and nitrogen oxide in it. This is due to the industrial activity in any area. Acid rain can damage plant life due to the chemical imbalance and loss of its nutrients. Fish life in water will also be effected. Many lakes are known to have become lifeless due to acid rain. Due to low pH, fish may eventually die. Forests are known to have died due to acidity in rain water. Discolouration of the Taj Mahal is partly attributed to acid rain. See also Acid Deposition.

Acid Sulphate (Amla Sulphate or Acid Sulphate) Chief component of acid rain and acid haze. Commonly known as Sulphuric Acid (H2SO4). It dissolves in water to form acid (H+) and Sulphate (SO4-). It is formed by the oxidation of Sulphur dioxide and other forms of Sulphur pollution.

Acoustic Waves (Dhvani Tarang) Sound that is generated by structures which are under stress and thus indicate high probability of failure of the same. In Hindi, *Dhvani Tarang*.

Acrylic Resin (Acrylic Resin) Copolymers of Acrylic acid. These monomers are generally colourless liquids. As they are hard, they are used as a shatterproof material, coatings for paper, wood etc.

Act (Adhiniyam) 'Act' means any of the following acts in force at this time or amended or new regulations passed by any of the regulatory agencies, notwithstanding whether by the Central, State or a Union Territory. The Acts are:

The Water (Prevention and Control of Pollution) Act, 1974, and as amended)

The Water (Prevention and Control of Pollution) Rules, 1975

The Water (Prevention and Control of Pollution) (Procedure for Transaction of Business) Rules, 1975

The Water (Prevention and Control of Pollution) Cess Act, 1977, as amended

The Water (Prevention and Control of Pollution) Cess Rules 1978

The Air (Prevention and Control of Pollution) Act, 1981, as amended

The Air (Prevention and Control of Pollution) Rules, 1982

The Air (Prevention and Control of Pollution Union Territories) Rules, 1983

The Environment (Protection) Act, 1986

The Environment (Protection) Rules, 1986

Hazardous Waste (Management & Handling) Rules, 1989

Manufacture, Storage and Import of Hazardous Chemical Rules, 1989

Manufacture, Use, Import Export and Storage of Hazardous Micro-Organism Genetically Engineered Organisms or Cells Rules, 1989

Scheme on Labeling of Environment Friendly Produces (ECO-MARK)

Restricting certain activities in Special Specified Area of Aravalli Range

The Public Liability Insurance Act, 1991

The Public Liability Insurance Rules, 1991.

Actinides (Actinide) Alpha emitting radionuclides also known as actinoid elements. Their atomic numbers range from Actinium-89 thorough Lawrencium-103.

Activated Carbon (Sakriyit Carbon) A highly absorbent form of carbon used to remove odours and toxic substances from liquid or gaseous emissions. In waste treatment, it is used to remove dissolved organic matter from waste water.

Activated Sludge (Sakriyit Avamal) A product that results when primary effluent is mixed with bacteria-laden sludge and then agitated and aerated to promote biological treatment which speeds the breakdown of organic matter in raw sewage undergoing secondary waste treatment.

Activation Energy (Urja Utpreran) The amount of energy that must be absorbed by a molecule or a molecular complex to break the bonds and form new products. It is also the amount of energy required for one particle for it to move from one energy stage to another. This is associated with phase change. In Hindi, Sakriyan Urja.

Action Levels (Prabhavit Shreni) Media-specific concentration levels for constituents derived using conservative criteria. The derivation of action levels is most often based on low risk under a very restrictive exposure scenario, but if a regulatory standard exists and is lower than the value derived by this risk-based computation, it will be used for the action level.

Activated Alumina (Sakriyit Alumina) A highly porous and granular form of Aluminium Oxide. It absorbs moisture and odours from gases. Used as a desiccant for gases and air dryer.

Activated Sludge Treatment (Sakriyit Vishtha Nirupan) A sewage treatment process in which a portion of the decomposer bacteria present in the waste is recycled to the beginning of the process. Providing the system with 'acclimatized' organisms.

Active Life of Hazardous Waste (Sakriya Haanikarak Apashisht Sthal) Active Life of a facility means period from the initial receipt of hazardous waste at the facility until the Regulatory Authorities receive certification of final closure.

Activity Data Sheets (Vivaran Pustika) Basic document describing program activities and containing budget information for the current year, budget year, and future planning years along with regulatory requirements, milestones, priorities, and accomplishments that provide management and staff with project details.

Acute Dermal LD_{50} (Teevra Twachiva LD50) A statistically derived estimate of the single dermal dose of a substance expressed as milligrams per kilogram of body weight that would cause 50 percent mortality to the test population of animals under specified conditions.

Acute Effect (Teevra Prabhav) After a single or brief exposure to a toxic or carcinogenic substance, an effect occurs and is noticed almost immediately. The effect should be evident within 14 days.

Acute Exposure (Teevra Prabhavan or Chipra Apaavaran) A single exposure to a toxic substance which results in severe biological harm or death, generally within a day.

Acute Hazardous Waste (Parisankatmay Apashisht) A waste capable of causing injury, illness, or death in the short-term.

Acute Inhalation LC_{50} (LC50 Ka Teevra Antahshwasan) A statistically derived estimate of the concentration of a substance that would cause 50 percent mortality due to inhalation to the test population under specified conditions.

Acute Inhalation Toxicity (Teevra Antahshwasan Vishaktata) The adverse effects caused by a substance following a single uninterrupted exposure by inhalation over a short period of time (24 hours or less) to a substance capable of being inhaled.

Acute LC_{50} (Teevra LC50 or Chhipra LC50) A concentration of a substance, expressed as parts per million of medium, that is lethal to 50 percent of the test population of animals under specified conditions.

Acute Oral LD_{50} (Teevra Mukhiya LD50) Single oral dose of a substance which would prove to be lethal to 50 percent of the test population under specified test conditions.

Acute Poisoning (Teevra Vishaktikaran) This is a toxic exposure which will cause severe effects in a very short duration.

Acute Toxicity (Teevra Vishaktata) Any adverse or poisonous effect caused by a toxic agent and occurring within a very short period of time following exposure. One brief exposure may cause severe biological harm or may prove to be fatal.

Acute Toxicity Test (Teevra Vishaktata Parikshan) The concentration of a substance that produces a toxic effect (or death) on a specified percentage of test organisms in a short period of time.

Adaptation (Anukulan) A genetically controlled characteristic that enhances an organism's chances to survive and reproduce in the environment in which it resides. In Hindi, *Anukulan.*

Adiabatic (Sthiroshma) The relationship between pressure and volume when a gas or other fluid is compressed or expanded without either giving out or receiving heat. Constant heat is critical.

Adiabatic Rate (Sthiroshma Dar) The rate of change of temperature due to elevation in the atmosphere. Dry adiabatic rate is about 5.5 deg F for every 1000 feet while the wet adiabatic rateis about 3 deg. F for every 1000 feet.

Administrative Record (Prashaasanik Abhilekh) A file established in compliance with the requirements set forth in pertinent regulations.

Adsorption (Adhishoshan) Bonding, adhesion, or sticking, (frequently ionic) of a substance to soil or other medium. A substance is said to be adsorbed if the concentration in the boundary region of a soil particle is greater than in the interior of the contiguous phase. The absorbed layer is generally very thin. In Hindi, *Adhishoshan.*

Advanced Air Emission Control Device (Viksit Vayu Utsarjan Niyantrak Yantra) Secondary air pollution control equipment, such as electrostatic precipitators and high energy scrubbers, used to control air discharge.

Advection (Abhivahan) The horizontal movement of mass through a medium. In Hindi, *Abhivahan.*

Aeolian Deposit (Vatoda Nikshep) Deposition of sand due to its movement which is caused primarily by wind.

Aeon (Yug) It is a geologic time and equals to one billion years. In Hindi, *Yug.*

Aerated Lagoon (Vatit Lagoon or Vatit Samudratal) A holding and/or treatment pond that speeds up the natural process of biological decomposition of organic waste by stimulating the growth and activity of bacteria that degrade organic waste.

Aeration (Vayu Mishran) When air or oxygen is supplied, added, or exposed to; generally to water. Oxygen occurs naturally in water and keeps it pure. Addition of air to water promotes biological degradation of organic matter in it. Another method of aeration is by spraying the liquid whereby air can permeate the same. In Hindi, *Vayu Mishran.*

Aeration Tank (Vayu Mishran Tanki) A chamber used to inject air into water.

Aerobic (Vayujivi) Process that takes place primarily due to the presence of Oxygen. Organisms which can stay alive or maintain activity in the presence of air are called aerobic. As an example, the process takes place in solid waste landfills. See also Anaerobic.

Aerobic Bacteria (Vayujivi Jivanu) Bacteria which needs Oxygen to live. In Hindi, *Vayujivi Jivanu.*

Aerobic Treatment (Vayujivi Pratipadan or Abhikriyanvan) Process by which microbes decompose complex organic compounds in the presence of oxygen and use the liberated energy for reproduction and growth.

Aerosols (Vayu Vilay) Solid or liquid particles small enough to remain suspended in the air for a period of time and settle out slowly under the force of gravity. Upon release, the pressure of the gas causes the mixture to be released as a fine spray or foam. High concentration of many aerosol particles are known to irritate the lungs and have been associated with respiratory diseases like asthma.

Aestivation (Grishma Nishkriyata) A condition similar to hibernation induced in some desert animals during periods of extreme heat and dryness.

Afforestation (Vanaropan) Planting of trees on land where there are no trees. This is also associated with greening of land. In Hindi, Vanaropan.

Aflatoxins (Aflataxin) Highly toxic to birds and fish, these are a group of polymer molds produced chiefly by the fungus Aspergilus flavus.

Afterburner (Adhijwalak) A burner that is located at a place so that the combustion gases are made to pass through its flame in order to remove smoke and odours. It may be attached to or be separated from the incinerator proper.

Agent Orange (Agent Orange) A dioxin used as an herbicide and defoliant containing 2,4,5-trichlorophen oxyacetic acid (2,4,5-T) and 2-4 dichlorophenoxyacetic acid (2,4-D) with trace amounts of dioxin. A highly toxic substance.

Agglomeration (Samooh) Process of particle growth that occurs through collision or contact with other spherical particles. This usually occurs when the electrical charge is neutralized. This term has similar meaning such as flocculation and coagulation. In Hindi, *Samooh*.

Agricultural Runoff (Krashiya Vaha Jal) Process of surface water moving across farmland and taking the fertile soil and other nutrients with it. One of the most serious problems associated with land losing its fertility. When pesticides and fertilizers move with the soil, this may result in the surrounding areas getting polluted.

Air (Prevention & Control of Pollution) Act of 1981 (Pavan) This Act was promulgated to provide for the prevention, control and abatement of air pollution, for the establishment, with a view to carrying out the aforesaid purposes, of Boards, for conferring on and assigning to such Boards powers and functions relating thereto and for matters connected therewith.

Air (Havaa or Pavan or Vayu) The major constituents of dry Air by volume in the atmosphere are Nitrogen 78.09%, and Oxygen 20.94%. Other gases in small quantities include Argon 0.93%, Carbon dioxide 0.032%. Gases such as Neon, Helium, Methane,

Krypton, Hydrogen, Nitrous Oxide, Carbon monoxide, Xenon, Ozone, Ammonia, Nitrogen dioxide, Sulphur dioxide and Radon are also there in trace amounts. Water vapour is also an important constituent in normal atmosphere. Air may have other elements in them which may have been emitted from human or industrial activity in that area. Density of air is 1.29 g/litre. Air by itself is noncombustible but will support combustion. In Hindi, *Havaa*.

Air Avid To increase by addition of chemicals the affinity of fine particles for air bubbles.

Air Basin (Vayu Kund) A geographical formation which gathers and contains an air current system for an extended area of land.

Air Binding (Vayu Bandhani) Situation where air enters the filter media and harms both the filtration and backwash process.

Air Changes Per Hour (Prati Ghanta Vayu Parivartan) The movement of a volume of air in a given period of time. One air change per hour means that all of the air in that structure will be replaced in a one-hour period.

Air Curtain (Vayu Pat) A device which is located below the surface of the water and has numerous small holes along its axis through which air is pumped. The rising and expanding air bubbles create a flow gradient on the water's surface and retard the spreading of any spill. The process can also be used to stop fish from entering polluted water.

Air Emissions (Vayu Utsarjan) When pollutants are released into thè atmospheric air. Stacks from industries release chemicals and particulate matter which may be harmful to humans or plants.

Air Exchange (Vayu Vinimay) Movement of air into and out of a structure by means of infiltration, exfiltration, natural ventilation and mechanical ventilation.

Air Gap (Vayu Antaraal) Open vertical gap or empty space that separates drinking water supply to be protected from another water system in a treatment plant or other location. The open gap protects the drinking water from contamination by backflow or back-siphonage. In Hindi, *Vayu Antaraal*.

Air-Line Respirator (Shvasitra) Breathable air is supplied directly to a respirator through a hose. Regulators can be so arranged to match the wearer's needs.

Air Mass (Vayu Punj) Large volume of air confined at any location with certain meteorological or polluted characteristics. Air inversion or smog are some examples. When the air mass moves, the characteristics will change.

Air Padding (Vayu Prasechan) When dry air is pumped into a container to assist with the withdrawal of liquid. The process can also be used to force a liquefied gas such as Chlorine out of the container.

Air Plenum (Vayu Plenum) When space is used to convey air in a building, furnace, or structure. Generally, it is the space above a suspended ceiling that is used as an air plenum.

Air Pollutant (Vayu Pradushak) The Air Act defines it as any solid, liquid or gaseous substance (including noise) present in the atmosphere in such concentration as may be or tend to be injurious to human beings or other living creatures or plants or property or environment. They may be in the form of solid particles, liquid droplets, gases, or in combinations of these forms. They may be emitted either directly by identifiable sources or those produced in the air by interaction between two or more primary pollutants, or by reaction with normal atmospheric constituents, with or without photo-activation. Besides pollen, fog, and dust, which generally have natural origins, the air pollutants that fall into this category include VOCs, halogen compounds, radioactive compounds, carbon monoxide, sulphur dioxide, nitric dioxide, ozone, lead, carbon dioxide, mercury and cadmium nitrogen compounds, odors, sulfur compounds, solids. In Hindi, *Vayu Pradushan.*

Air Pollution-Effects of (Vayu Pradushan Ke Prabhav) The heart may be damaged by air pollution indirectly secondary to lung disease, through changes in the haemoglobin quality with Carboxyhaemoglobin due to carbon monoxide, increased occurrence of hypertension (lead, mercury and cadmium), coronary disease and congestive heart failure due to smog, carbon monoxide, Suspended particulate matter and sulphur dioxide.

Air Pollution (Vayu Pradushan) The Air Act defines 'Air Pollution' as the presence in the atmosphere of any air pollutant. It includes oxides of sulphur and nitrogen, smog, particulate matter, dioxins, furans, carbon dioxide, carbon monoxide, heavy metals, chlorofluorocarbons (CFCs), volatile organic compounds (VOCs), heavy metals such as mercury, lead among others. They may cause respiratory diseases, asthma, and skin irritation among others. Chemical leak at Bhopal in 1984 is the largest known casualty due to air pollution incident in a chemical plant.

Air Pollution Control Area (Vayu Pradushan Niyantrit Kshetra) The Central or the State Board may declare any area or areas within the State as air pollution control area to control further emission of air pollutants into that region. Burning of certain fuel, emission of any pollutants by plants or industries may be banned in those areas. The regulatory agency may require additional monitoring of emissions by placement of control equipments in the premises.

Air Purifying Respirators (Vayu Swachhikaran Swasitra or Respirator) These types of respirators remove particles or may do selective removal of gases. They can be either full-face piece or may just cover the mouth and nose.

Air Quality Criteria (Vayu Gunavakta Manak) The levels of pollution and lengths of exposure above which adverse health and welfare effects may occur.

Air Scrubbers (Vayu Marjak) Devices in smokestacks or exhaust systems that are installed to remove most, but not all, particles before they are released into the atmosphere.

Air Sparging (Vayu Sparging) Process which involves injection of air into the lower of two horizontal wells. In the process, contaminants are forced into the uppermost well where they are removed. It is effective in difficult to reach areas such as beneath buildings, ponds, or lagoons. It is also called vapour extraction. Used mostly in the oil industry.

Air Stability (Vayu Ki Sthirta) The non-movement of air in any area of the atmosphere.

Air Stripping (Vayu Niravratti) A treatment system that removes, or 'strips' volatile organic compounds from contaminated ground water or surface water by forcing an air stream through the water and causing the compounds to evaporate.

Airborne Particulate (Vayu Mein Kan or Vayu Kan) Total suspended particulate matter found in the atmosphere as solid particles or liquid droplets.

Airshed When the quality of air in an area is uniform. If a pollutant is introduced into such an area, it will disperse uniformly in that region.

Albedo (Shviti) The amount of radiation received by any surface expressed in a percentage. It differs with region, and climatic conditions.

Alcohol (Madha Saar or Alkohal) It is an organic compound in which a hydrogen atom (H) has been replaced by hydroxyl group OH). They are generally colorless, flammable liquids. They are naturally occurring in plants and also manufactured from crude oils. Generally used as a solvent, detergent, medicines, fuels, and as plasticizers. Examples are methyl alcohol or methanol.

Aldehydes (Aldehydes) A series of organic chemicals containing carbon, hydrogen, oxygen (-CHO) groups and having strong odours. They are formed from alcohols. Used in the manufacture of plastics.

Aldrin (Aldrin) One of the most toxic chlorinated organic pesticide. Its use has been banned. Formula C12H8Cl6.

Algae (Shaival or Kai) Primitive, simple and rootless Chlorophyll-bearing plants having one or many cells and usually adapted to water. They are found in fresh as well as saline water. From a single cell, they can be very large in size. Their growth is most rapid in shallow water and with increase in temperature. Algae are harvested to be used as a food supplement. They produce over 70% of earth's oxygen. They are food for fish and small aquatic animals. India has about 5,000 different algae species. Common seaweeds. In Hindi, *Kai*.

Algal Blooms (Shaival Prasfutan) Sudden spurts of algal growth which can affect water quality adversely. It is also an indication of potentially hazardous changes occurring in local water chemistry.

Algicidal (Shaival Nashi) Substance capable of killing or controlling algae. In Hindi, *Shaival Nashi*.

Algistatic (Algistic) A substance capable of inhibiting algal growth.

Aliphatic Hydrocarbons (Aliphatic Hydrocarbon) A straight or branched-chain organic hydrocarbon. They consist a paraffin, olefin, and acetylene and their derivatives. Examples include propane, methane, and butane.

Aliquot (Asheshbhajak) A part of a substance which is a definite fraction of a whole. These are used for testing or analysis.

Alkali (Kshar) Base or salt substances such as Calcium, Sodium or Magnesium Carbonate or hydroxide. Sodium Hydroxide or Potassium Hydroxide are strong bases. pH of the substance is over 7.0. In Hindi, *Kshar*.

Alkalinity (Ksharata) It is a measure of the total measurable bases such as OH, HCO3, CO3 in a volume of wter. It is an indication of a material's capacity to neutralize acids. PH is always greater than 7.0.

Allergen (Allergen) A substance that produces adverse health effects in only a portion of the population.

Allogenic Succession (Anyantrajanik Anukraman) An ecological succession or change in a local species which is caused by influences from factors such as long-term draught or deposition of riverine sediments thus altering the local environmental conditions in that area.

Allotropic (Ap Rupi) When one substance is found in two or more different forms. They may have be significantly different in physical or chemical properties also. Example is diamond and graphite.

Alloy (Mishra Dhatu or Dhatu Mishran) When small or trace amounts of other metals or nonmetallic elements are used with a metal to increase a specific characteristics such as hardness, durability, heat resistant. Addition of Chromium and nickel markedly increases the corrosion and oxidation resistant properties of steel.

Alluvial Soil (Jalodh Mrida Mitti) New soil which may be fertile.

Alpha Partical (Alpha Kan) A positively charged subatomic partical (a helium nucleus) emitted in the decay of a radioactive element such as radon-222 when it decays to Polonium-218. It contains two protons and two neutrons similar to a helium atom nucleus, has a large mass and a very short range of about one to two inches. Its energy is in the range of 4 to 8 MeV. Indistinguishable from a helium nucleus. Alpha particles are emitted by certain radioactive materials and can be stopped by a sheet of paper. This has the weakest penetrating power of any form of radiation. Sources could be americium, plutonium, uranium.

Alpha Radiation (Alpha Vikiran) Spontaneous emission of ionizing radiation composed of alpha particles in the radioactive decay of certain nuclides. Alpha particles consist of two protons and two neutrons bound together and has a positive charge; an alpha particle is identical to the nucleus of a helium atom. It is the least penetrating of the three common types of radiation-alpha, beta, gamma-and can be blocked by a sheet of paper or outer dead layer of skin or the clothing. These particles travel at a speed of about 15,000 kilometre per second and collide with other atoms. Though alpha particles pose no direct health hazard, but if eaten or inhaled inside body, then they may harm some organs and tissues which are more sensitive than the skin.

Alternate Energy (Vaikalpik Urja) Energy sources other than oil and coal are generally termed as alternative energy. Energy sources include solar, wind, cow dung cakes, biomass, geothermal and ocean.

Aluminium (Aluminium) Silvery white metal. Most abundant metal in earth. It is a very light metal and so used in auto parts, paints, and in cooking utensils. Atomic Weight 26.98. Symbol Al.

Alveoli (Alveoli) The tiny air sacs in the lung where oxygen from air is transferred to the blood and carbon dioxide is taken in exchange.

Ambient Air (Pariveshi Vayu or Aaspaas Ki Vayu) That portion of the air, external to buildings, to which the general public has access, such as those in open air. Air present in a vicinity.

Ames Test (Amig Parikshan) A process of testing a substance for its carcinogenity by using bacteria instead of animals. The results are very rapid but may not be very accurate. It was developed by Bruce Ames in 1979.

Amines (Amines) A class of organic compounds derived from ammonia. They are basic in nature and combine readily with strong acids to form salts. Used as hardeners in plastics.

Amino Acids (Amino Amla) The basic building blocks of proteins.

Ammonia (Ammonia) A pungent, colourless, gaseous alkaline compound of nitrogen and hydrogen most commonly found in the form of a water solution. Contact with ammonia may result in irritation of the respiratory system and mucous membranes, headaches, nausea, and vomiting. Used in fertilizer, petroleum and synthetic fiber industry.

Amoeba (Ek Koshikiya Jeeva or Jeevanu) A one-celled organism. There are many types of amoeba. They respond to light and any movement in which they may be found. A few of them may cause illness in humans in the digestive tract such as dysentery.

Amplification (Pravardhan) In radiation detection equipment, the process of either gar or electronic or both in which the ionization effects are magnified to a degree making it suitable for their measurement.

Amprometric Titration (Amprometric Anumapan) A way of measuring concentrations of certain substances in water using an electric current that flows during a chemical reaction.

Anaerobic (Avaayaviya or Vaatanirapekshiya) A state when organisms have no oxygen for survival or to maintain any activity. A substance that can live or be active only in the absence of oxygen.

Anaerobic Decomposers (Avaaviya Apaghatak) Decomposition of microorganism takes place in the absence of Oxygen. They break down certain organic wastes into methane, water, and carbon dioxide.

Analgesic (Peedahaari or Peeda Naashak) A pain reducing drug such as aspirin.

Analyte (Vishleshya) A chemical component of a sample whose quantity is to be determined or measured. A pollutant in a sample is an analyte as its exact amount is to be determined through chemical or other laboratory analysis.

Anaphylaxis (Teevragrahita) Lethal allergic reaction to venom or some other foreign substance. This is caused by a previous exposure to that substance. The effect is immediate.

Anatoxin (Anatoxin) A poison that is found in mushrooms that damages the membrane and nucleus of cells.

Anemometer (Anemometer) An instrument used to measure the speed of wind.

Angle of Repose (Gharshan Kon) The steepest angle at which a material will remain still. Suggested angle of repose for a landfill is 33%.

Angstrom, A (Angstrom) A unit of length, represented by A. It is a measure of wavelength and is equal to 10-10 metre or 10-4 micron. Commonly used to express the wavelengths of electromagnetic radiation in the visible, ultraviolet and X-ray regions.

Anhydrous (Nirjal or Jal Viheen) No water present in the substance.

Anoxia (Anoksita) Lack of oxygen in the body tissues.

Anthracite Coal (Anthracite Koyala) A hard, black lustrous coal with very high in Btu or the heating value and low in sulphur and ash content. It is also referred to as a very hard coal.

Antibody (Rog Pratikarak) A naturally occurring, disease-fighting agent. It is a protein molecule that interacts with a specific or closely related foreign substances (antigen) only. The antibody is induced as a prior exposure to the antigen.

Antidote (Prativish) A substance that counteracts the effects of poisons.

Antifreeze (Pratihim) A compound that lowers the freezing point, generally to water. Glycol derivatives are used to lower the freezing point of water. These additives could be poisonous.

Antigen (Pratijan) A substance that when introduced into the body is capable of inducing the formation of antibodies and subsequently of reacting in a recognisable fashion with the specific induced antibodies. Molecular weight is over 10,000.

Antimicrobial Agent (Pratisukshmajeevi Kaarak) Substance capable of inhibiting or destroying the growth of any bacteria, virus, fungi pathogenic to man or animals.

Appellant (Apeel Karta or Punaraavedak) Any person aggrieved by and appealing against an order made by the Board.

Appellate Authority (Appeal Pradhikari or Sangathan Samiti) An Appellate Authority constituted by the Central Government.

Approved Appliances (Anumodit Upakaran or Sweekrat Upakaran) Any equipment or gadget used for the bringing of any combustible material or for generating or consuming any fume, gas or particulate matter and approved by the State Board for the purpose of any Act.

Approved Fuel (Anumodit Indhan) Any fuel approved by the State Board for the purpose of any Act.

Aquaculture (Jala Samvardhan) Water farming of fish and shellfish in a confined and controlled area.

Aquatic Ecosystem (Jaleeya Paritantra) Habitat of plants and animals living in an aquatic environment such as water or wetlands.

Aquatic Flora (Jaleeya Vanaspati) Plant life found in aquatic ecosystem.

Aquifer (Jalabhar) A body of geologic or rock formation capable of holding, yielding and/or transmitting significant quantities of groundwater under normal hydraulic gradients to a well or a spring. The aquifer could be confined or unconfined. Size of the pores, slope of the solids may determine the rate of discharge of water from that aquifer.

Aquitard An underground geological formation that is slightly permeable and yields inappreciable amounts of water when compared to an aquifer. It may funciton as a confining bed.

Arboreal Species (Vraksheeya Jaati) Animals which live on limbs or trunks of trees and plants. Example are rabbits, monkeys.

Area of Concern (Chinta Ka Vishay or Kshetra) A specific area suspected of being contaminated.

Argon (Argon) A colourless, odourless, tasteless inert gas. Used in arc welding and light bulbs.

Arid (Oosar Bhoomi or Anurvar) An area where amount of rainfall is generally less than 25 centimetres. The rate of evaporation is higher than the rate of precipitation. Desert areas are arid.

Aromatic Hydrocarbons (Aromatic Hydrocarbon) Unsaturated cyclic organic hydrocarbons characterised by the presence of the benzene-ring molecular structure. Most of the chemicals in this classification have a strong odour.

Arsenic (Arsenic or Sankhiya) A solid poisonous element that is commonly metallic steel gray, crystalline, and brittle. With oxygen, arsenic is often used as an insecticide or weed killer. It is a human carcinogen. A highly toxic substance and can cause cancer, kidney, liver disorders, and nerve damage. Atomic weight 74.91. Symbol As.

Arsine (Arsine) A colourless, flammable and extremely poisonous gas with an odour like garlic. It may be produced by action of acids on metals containing arsenic. Arsine may cause headache, heart, liver, blood, and kidney damage. Small inhalation may be fatal.

Artesian Water (Utstrut Jal) Ground water which is under pressure. When a well is drilled, the water level will rise above the ground water level due to inherent pressure in the aquifer. Also called artesian aquifer.

Artesian Well (Utstrut Koop) Wells drilled in artesian water.

Asbestos (Asbestos) A naturally occurring fibrous, toxic mineral made of silicates. It is a noncombustible, nonconducting and chemically resistant material with long and flexible fibers. Crumbling asbestos releases fibers that can become airborne and if inhaled, cause lung disease and cancer. It is used in making of insulation. Various types of asbestos include Chrysotiles (serpentinite), crocidolite (riebeckite), amosite (cummingtonitegrunerite), anthophyllite, tremolite, and actinolite. Chrysotiles are very widely used. Once widely used in construction and industry, mostly in insulation. It is fireproof, resistant to chemicals, and a very poor conductor of electricity. Its fibers can exist in very small sizes and thus can easily reach lungs of human to cause damage and even cancer. The damage to lungs or other parts of body due to asbestosis can be noticed only after 10 to 15 years or more.

Asbestos Containing Material (Asbestos Yukt Padarth or Samagri) Any material containing more than 1% asbestos. It may include cement, pipes, and clothing.

Asbestosis (Asbestos Janit Soth or Sujan) Inflammation of and damage to the lungs caused by the inhalation of asbestos particles. The main cause is dyspnea. See also Dyspnea.

Ash (Raakh) Derived mostly from incinerators and boiler plants. Fly ash, bottom ash and boiler ash are now used with cement to increase its hardness. It is also used as a road fill. Fly ash may be hazardous in nature.

Aspection (Chhavi Vividhataa) Inherent changes in an environment due to the four seasons.

Asphyxiant (Shvaas Avarodhak) Substance capable of producing a lack of oxygen resulting in cessation of life. Generally, the substance is relatively a non-toxic gas.

Asphyxia (Shvaasaa Varodh) Suffocation.

Assay (Parakh or Aamaapan) A test for a specific chemical or effect.

Assessing Authority (Nirdhaaran Karta) Any person or a body of persons as specified by Member Secretary of either the Central or a State Government Pollution Control Board.

Assimilation (Sameekaran) Compilation of nutrients by trees for its growth. The ability of a body of water to purify itself of pollutants.

Atmometer (Atmometer) An instrument to measure rate of evaporation.

Atmosphere (Vaayumandal) The area that surrounds the earth. Atmospheric air consists mostly of nitrogen and oxygen with traces of other gases such as carbon dioxide, and neon. Weight of atmospheric air is estimated to be 5.9 X 1015 tons and more than half of that weight is within six kilometres of the earth surface. Pressure exerted by the atmospheric air at sea level is 14.696 psi or 760 mm mercury. From the surface of the earth till about 9 km, it is called troposphere, over that and up to 50 km, it is called Stratosphere and up to 100 km, it is called mesosphere. Beyond 100 km from the earth's surface, it called thermosphere.

Atom (Paramanu) The smallest or ultimate particle of all matter composed of protons, neutrons and electrons, that still retains all the properties of that element. The nucleus of every atom consists of a positively charged protons and neutrons which carries nearly all the mass of the atom and is neutral, surrounded by a number of negatively charged electrons, so that the whole system is electrically neutral. In Hindi, *Paramanu.*

Atom Radius (Paramanu Ka Ghera or Ardhavyas) The closest distance to which one atom will approach another atom of any size under the circumstances specified.

Atomic Half-Life (Paramanu ki Ardha Aayu) The length of time it takes half the atoms in a radioactive substance to decay. See Half life and also Appendix A.

Atomic Mass (Paramanu Ka Punj or Samhati) The number of protons and neutrons in the nucleus of an atom. It is expressed in terms of an "atomic mass unit" or amu. It is one-twelfth the mass of one neutral atom of Carbon-12 and is equal to 1.6604×10^{-24} grammes.

Atomic Number (Paramanu Kramank) The number of protons (positively charged) and neutrons in the nucleus of an atom. The number of protons determines what an atom is chemically and identifies itself to be a certain chemical element. Appendix B lists the atomic numbers with symbol of elements.

Atomic Volume (Paramanu Aayatan) The space occupied by the atoms in 1 gramme atom of the element in question.

Atomic Weight (Paramanu Bhaar) The relative mass of an atom of a given element. The sum of the protons and neutrons in the nucleus of the atom. The basis is the atomic weight of the common isotope of carbon-12, which is taken to be exact 12. The atomic weight of hydrogen, the lightest element, is then 1.008. Hence, the atomic weight of any element is approximately the mass of an atom of that element relative to the mass of a hydrogen atom.

Atomization (Kanikaran) When a stream of water or gas impinges upon a molten metal stream, breaking it into droplets which solidify as powder particles.

Attrition (Sannigharshan) Wearing or grinding down of a substance by friction. Dust from such a process contributes to air pollution.

Autecology (Swaparisthiki Adhyayan) Study of a single species within an environment.

Authorised Person (Pradhikrit Adhikari) A person or an organisation authorised by the competent authority to collect, treat, transport, store or dispose of hazardous wastes in accordance with the guidelines to be issued by the competent authority from time to time.

Automobile (Motor Chalit Vaahan) The Air Act of 1981 defines it as any vehicle powered either by internal combustion engine or by any method of generating power to drive such vehicle by burning fuel. Pollutants emitted from an automobile include carbon monoxide, particulate matter, hydrocarbons, oxides of sulphur and nitrogen, aldehydes, and organic acids among others. Lead would be a pollutant if leaded petrol or gasoline is used.

Autoradiograph (Swa Vikirani Chitra) The record of radiation from radioactive material in an object made by placing the object in close proximity to a photographic emulsion.

Autotrophism (Swaposhit Jeevan) An organism capable of getting all its food from inorganic sources such as green plants. Autotropic organisms, largely green plants, are able to manufacture food from simple inorganic substances.

Avogadro's Law (Avogardo Niyam) States that equal volume of gases at the same temperature and pressure contain the same number of molecules regardless of their chemical nature and physical properties. The constant number is $6.023X10^{23}$. This is the number of molecules present in a volume of 22.41 L of any gas.

Axenic (Aagantuk-Heen) A culture of lemna fronds free from other organisms.

Azeotropic Mixture (Sthirkwathi Mishran) A mixture of chemicals that when combined in certain proportions, will distill at a rate maintaining those proportions. They are substances in which the gas and liquid components are in perfect harmony. The composition of both gas and liquid must be identical. The mixtures have different vapour pressures than a single constituent but exhibit a change in boiling and freezing points.

B

Background Radiation (Prashthika Vikiran Prasaaran) Naturally occurring radiation that is always present in the body or the environment. Also due to the radioactive materials naturally present. Also, it includes the radiation from the sun, the ground, the atmosphere, building materials, and the bodies of humans and animals. Typically due to the radiation results from cosmic rays that come from outer space and from radiation from the naturally radioactive elements found on earth. The main sources of the natural background radiation are potassium-40 in the body, potassium-40 and thorium, uranium and their decay products present in rocks, soils, and cosmic rays.

Backwashing (Prashta Dhulai or Pratikshipt Jal) Reversing the flow of water back through the filter media to remove entrapped solids.

Bacteria (Jeevanu) Often single cell, these microscopic organisms are one of the smallest creatures and primarily contain protein and nucleic acid. Aerobic bacteria require oxygen to reproduce while the anaerobic types thrive in the absence of oxygen in nature. Variety of organisms. Pathogenic bacteria may be disease causing in nature. Many types of bacteria are now used to cleanup hazardous spills, such as oil. They are also used as a pollution control as they metabolize organic matter in sewage spills. However, when in soil, water or air, they may cause problems to humans, animals or plant environment. They are now used in various medicines and in soils to enable the release of nutrients to plants.

Baffle (Vyarodh or Baadhaa) A flat board or plate, deflector, guide, or similar device constructed or placed in flowing water or slurry systems to cause more uniform flow velocities to absorb energy and to divert, guide, or agitate liquids.

Baffle Chamber (Vyarodha Kaksha) In incinerator design, a chamber designed to promote the settling of fly ash and coarse particulate matter by changing the direction and/or reducing the velocity of the gases produced by the combustion of the refuse or sludge.

Baghouse (Jhola or Thaila Kaksha) A container used to control particle emissions from a stack. Inside the Baghouse, the filter is a cloth or a fabric. The gas containing particles enters the Baghouse and particulate matter is trapped by the filter media.

Bailer (Bailer) A long pipe with a valve at the lower end, used to remove slurry, water, mud or cuttings from the bottom or side of a well as it is being drilled. They are also used to collect water or liquid samples from a tank.

Baling Pressuresed compacting of solid waste into blocks to reduce volume and simplify handling.

Ballistic Separator (Prakshepik Vibhajak Yantra) A machine that sorts organic from inorganic matter for composting.

Bamboo (Baans) A plant that has a very high content of cellulose fibre present in it. Abundantly found in the jungles of Assam and other northeastern states, India produces over 3 million tons from its forests. Extensively used to make high grade of paper.

Bar Screen (Baadha Pat) This device is used to remove large solid matter in a waste water treatment plant.

Barium (Barium) Silvery white metal. It burns at room temperature and so must be stored as inert gas. Almost all Barium compounds are poisonous when taken by mouth or inhaled. It has a toxic effect on the heart, blood vessels, and nerves. Accumulates in the liver, lungs, and spleen. Causes nervous system disorders, high blood pressure and heart disease.

Barrier (Baadha or Vyadhaan) Any material or structure that prevents or substantially delays movement of any substance. It could be a fence or a wall.

Barrier Coating (Vyadhan Parat or Tah) A layer of a material that obstructs or prevents passage of something through a surface that is to be protected.

Baryon (Baryon) One of a class of heavy elementary particles. It includes neutrons, protons, and hyperons.

Basal Application (Aadhariya Prayog) In pesticides, the application of a chemical on plant stems or tree trunks just above the soil line.

Base (Kshar or Khara) A chemical whose pH is more than 7.1. Turns litmus blue. When added to an acidic mixture, they neutralise it. Strong bases are toxic to skin and eyes. Example is sodium hydroxide.

Baseline Risk Assessment (Aadharbhoot Hani Anumaan) An analysis of the potential adverse health effects (current or future) caused by contaminant releases from a site in the absence of any actions to control or mitigate these releases.
Risk assessment conducted using one or more scenarios appropriate for the site that assumes no mitigating or corrective measures beyond those already in place.

Batu (Batu Resin) A resin.

Beaufort Scale (Beaufort Paimana or Maap) A measure of wind velocity on a scale from zero to twelve. Zero indicates that the wind is calm while a scale of 12 indicates hurricane weather.

Becquerel (Baikeral) The SI unit of radioactivity equal to one disintegration per second. One Picocurie equals 0.037 Becquerel.

Bedded Salt (Sanstarit Namak) Natural salt layers in geologic formations. Usually hard and mined like a rock.

Bedrock (Aadhaar Shail or Tal Shila) Generic term for rock that underlies soil or other unconsolidated superficial material.

Beehive Cokemaking (Kshatta Coke Banana) Operation in which coal is heated with the admission of air in controlled amounts for the purpose of producing coke.

Beer-Lambert Law (Beer Lambert Niyam) The absorbency of a solution of a given chemical species, at a fixed wavelength, is proportional to the thickness of a solution(l), or the light path length, and the concentration of the absorbing species (C).

Benign Tumor (Sudam Arvud) A tumor that grows only at the site of the origin and does not invade adjacent tissues. As it is localised and not malignant, it is generally treatable.

Benthic Creatures (Nitalasth or Nital Jeev Samooh) These creatures are found at the bottom of the ocean. For example: lobsters.

Benzene (Benzene)
A colourless, volatile liquid with characteristic odour. A toxic, extremely poisonous, cancer-causing flammable liquid. Used in the manufacture of many chemicals and as a solvent. Formula C6H6.

Bermed Storage (Pushta Sangrahaakaar or Bhandaar) Protection of a storage area by raised areas (berms) that has the capacity to contain spills. Berms are also horizontal cuts along slopes that provide slope stability and contain sloughing.

Beryllium (Beryllium) Lightest known white crystalline metal. It has a very high heat capacity and thermal conductivity. Highly toxic and carcinogenic metal when inhaled as an airborne pollutant. The metal is discharged from foundries, and machine shops. Mined in India, used in X-rays, computer parts and in the nuclear reactor industry. Atomic Weight 9.0121. Formula Be.

Beta Particle (Beta Kan) A fast-moving electron or positron that is emitted from unstable atoms that are becoming stable. It is identical to an electron. Has a small mass and short range of 10 feet in air per MeV of energy which is between 0 and 4 MeV. Exposure to high levels of beta radiation can cause skin burns. See also Beta Radiation.

Beta Radiation (Beta Vikiran) Beta radiation is electron particles emitted from a nucleus during fission. Their charge is negative. The mass of the particle is 5.5 x 10-4 amu or 9.130 x 10-24 gramme. Particles have charge equal to that of electrons. Though they can travel only a few centimetres, but can travel almost at the speed of light. Beta radiation can be stopped by a couple of centimetre of thick wood or a thin sheet of aluminum, glass or plastic. As they can travel only very small distances, they are unable to harm internal human organs. But if inhaled or swallowed, they may effect human organs which are more sensitive than the skin. Source could be Phosphorous-32 or tritium.

Bhopal Accident (Bhopal Durghatna) Approximately 6,500 people were killed and at least 20,000 were blinded and choking in the central city of Bhopal. This was after 27 tonnes of highly toxic methyl isocyanate gas leaked from a tank at a pesticide factory of Union Carbide India Ltd. (UCIL) during the early hours of December 3, 1984. This is the largest incident that involved leak of hazardous substance from an industry.

Bilge Oil (Jahaaj ke Pende ka Tel) Waste oil that accumulates in the lower spaces of a ship in small quantities and is usually mixed with larger quantities of water.

Bilge Water (Jahaj ke Pende ka Paani or Jal) Water that accumulates in the hull of a ship. It is usually polluted by oil and human waste.

Bioaccumulation (Jaiva Sanchayan) Toxic substances or other pollutants are stored within living organisms. They accumulate as they are slowly consumed through air, water or food. This occurs because the substances are very slowly metabolised or excreted. Due to the storage, the concentration increases and becomes greater than the source itself. It may eventually harm the living organism.

Bioassay (Jeev Parakh) Study of living organisms to measure the effect of a substance, factor, or condition by comparing before and after exposure or other data.

Bioavailability (Jeev Prapyataa or Uplabhdata) The amount of a pollutant in any medium such as air, water or soil leaves its medium and enters a human body.

Biochemical Oxygen Demand (Aavashyak Jaiva Rasaayanik Pranvayu) A measure of the amount of oxygen consumed in the biological processes that break down organic matter in water. Measured over a five-day period, the higher the BOD, the greater the degree of pollution. It is expressed as mg/L. The Water Act of 1975 limit for BOD is 150 mg/l. See also Biological Oxygen Demand.

Biocide (Jeev Nashak) Any toxic substance, such as chlorinated hydrocarbons that harm or kill organisms.

Bioconcentration Factor (Jaiva Saandrit Kaarak) Ratio of test substance concentration in the test fish to the concentration in the test water at steadystate. When bioconcentration occurs in a fish or other organism, it means the concentration of a chemical is greater than the level of the same chemical in the sorrounding.

Biodegradable (Jeev Nimnikaraniya) Capable of decomposing rapidly under natural conditions into basic elements. Breakdown generally occurs due to the presence of bacteria.

Biodegradation (Jaiva Nimnikaran) A process by which microbial organisms transform or alter through enzymatic action the structure of chemicals introduced into the environment. Basically a destruction of chemical compounds by biological actions of living organisms and eventually reducing the contaminant mass.

Biodiversity (Jaiva Vividhata) The complex and varied living organisms that live in different and complex environmental conditions. Each environmental ecosystem is different and the molecular makeup of the organisms may vary accordingly. Organised at many levels, they encompass different ecosystems, species, and genes. India is a treasure trove of bio-diversity. It has been identified as one of the 12 mega-centres of biological diversity in the world. There are about 45,000 species of plants and 81,000 species of animals in this country. Covering 10 bio-geographic zones and 25 biotic provinces, India incorporates an exceptional range of biodiversity, including all the world's major ecosystems. As one of the oldest and largest agricultural societies, India boasts an impressive variety of at least 166 species of crop plants and 320 species of wild relatives of cultivated crops. There are 350 species of mammals, 1224 species of birds, 408 species of reptiles, 197 species of amphibians, and over 15,000 types of flowering plants. Biodiversity: Refers to the variety and variability among living organisms and the ecological complexes in which they occur. Diversity can be defined as the number of different items and their relative frequencies. For biological diversity, these items are organized at many levels, ranging from complete ecosystems to the biochemical structures that are the molecular basis of heredity. Thus, the term encompasses different ecosystems, species, and genes. It also means the analysis of blood, urine, tissues, etc., to measure chemical exposure in humans.

Bioelectric Activity (Jaiva Vidyut Sakriyata) Electric phenomena generated by vegetation.

Biofuel (Jaiva Indhan) When heat is produced from sources such as manure, algae, plant crops and human excreta. This is also called biogas.

Biogas (Jaiva Gas) Heating gas such as methane produced from sources such as crops, human excreta waste and from water hyacinth in dried form. It is derived from the metabolic activity of living organisms. In India, many biogas plants using human excreta waste are in operation. The gas is used for cooking, lighting incandescent mantle lamps and providing hot water for bathing. The dried sludge, in granulated form, is used as manure as it is odourless and so can be used in flower plants indoors. First biogas plant was set up in Patna in 1982 by Dr. Bindeshwar Pathak.

Biogas Digester (Jaiva Gas Sampaachitra) Process equipment that is used to convert manure and organic waste into a methane-rich gas called biogas. The process is generally anaerobic digestion of bacteria. Extensively used to convert human waste and recover methane.

Biogeochemical Cycle (Jaiva Bhoorasayanik Chakra) Chemical element when it passes from being an inorganic matter to an organic matter and back again.

Biological Additives (Jaivik Yogaatmak) Microbiological cultures, enzymes, or nutrient additives that are produced and deliberately introduced into an oil discharge for the specific purpose of encouraging biodegradation to mitigate the effects of the discharge. The time necessary for complete cleanup is generally long but this is one way of cleaning up oil spill as it is economical.

Biological Control (Jaivik Niyantran) Control of pests through naturally occurring predators or parasites. Animals or organisms eat or kill the pests. In this case, no man-made substance is used.

Biological Control Agent (Jaivik Niyantran Karak) Any living organism introduced into the environment that is intended to function as a pesticide agent against another pest.

Biological Exposure Indices (BEIs) (Jaivik Udbhasan Suchak) Reference values intended as guidelines for the evaluation of potential health hazards in the practice of industrial hygiene. BEIs apply to eight-hour exposures, five days a week. They are not intended for use as a measure of adverse effects or for diagnosis of occupational illness. BEI is indirectly based on the dose-response animal studies used in establishing the TLV's (Threshold Limit Values).

Biological Half-Life (Jaivik Ardha Aayu) The time required for the amount of a specified element which has entered the body (or a particular organ) to be decreased to half of its initial value as a result of natural, biological elimination processes.

Biological Magnification (Jaivik Aavardhan) It is the process in which certain substances or pollutants such as heavy metals or pesticides move up the food chain. They slowly reach the rivers and lakes which are eaten by the aquatic organisms and fish. They reach animals and humans who eat the fish and birds. The concentration of the pollutant increases with each progressive food chain. See also Bioaccumulation and Bioconcentration Factor.

Biological Markers (Jaivik Ankan) Organic compounds whose carbon structure, or skeleton, is formed by living organisms and is sufficiently stable to be recognized in crude oil or the organic matter of ancient sediments.

Biological Nitrogen Fixation (Jaivik Nitrogen Yogikikaran) Conversion of atmospheric Nitrogen occurs through the use of blue-green algae or other naturally occurring bacteria.

Biological Oxidation (Jaivik Oxikaran) Decomposition of organic matter by microorganism. The process occurs in water bodies and in activated sludge wastewater treatment plants.

Biological Oxygen Demand (BOD) (Jaivik Pran Vaayu Aavashyakata) Amount of oxygen needed by bacteria to decompose a given amount of organic waste. It reflects the amount of oxygen consumed in five days by biological process breaking down the organic waste. A high value of BOD indicates that there is greater amount of pollutant. It is a measure of eutrophication.

Biological treatment of Hazardous Waste (Haanikarak Apashisht Jaivik Upachaar) Generally, biological treatment is used to consume organic waste by using bacteria of a specific type. Major industries using it include petroleum refining, industrial organic material, plastic materials, residues and paints and allied products. Some of the suggested methods are presented in Guidelines for Management and Handling of Hazardous Wastes issued by Government of India.

Biological Uptake When a hazardous substance is transferred from the environment to plants, animals, and humans. It is evaluated through analytical measurements or other indications from the affected environment. Most commonly, biological dose measurements are used to determine whether exposure has occurred.

Biomagnification (Jaiva Aavaardhan) The process of one pollutant eaten by one small species that is in turn eaten by a bigger animal species. The concentration of the pollutant will accumulate in the bigger animal species. This way, the pollutant is magnified in animals and may pass on to humans who may consume those animal species that comprise human food chain. Heavy metals are passed on this way.

Biomarker A structure which is outside the norm of a particular species is a Biomarker. This may be caused due to a pollutant or a toxic substance.

Biomass (Jivabhaar) The amount of living matter in a given area or volume. This is generally used with plants or manure or other organisms.

Biomass Energy (Jaiva Bhaar Urja) Energy derived from renewable sources. Manure, burning wood, plants or synthetic fuels made from plants. Methane gas is produced from manure in the countryside. This is the most diversified form of energy among the renewable energy sources. Wood and cakes made of animal manure are a common source of fuel for residential cooking purposes among the masses. It is one of the cheapest forms of energy.

Biome (Jeevom) A specific, mature, stable terrestrial ecosystem in which the unique and dominant plant life, weather patterns, and wild life. Examples are deserts, tropical rain forests, and arctic tundra.

Biomonitoring (Jaivik Vishleshan) Process of detecting changes in environment conditions detected by using living things or humans. Living organisms are used to test the suitability of the effluent discharge into receiving waters. As an example, presence of E-coli may indicate the presence of animal feces. It is also done by the analysis of blood, urine, tissues, etc., to measure chemical exposure in humans.

Bioremediation (Jaivik Chikitsa) When a specific type of bacteria will flourish in an atmosphere or site which has hazardous or toxic substance and alter or detoxify that substance. Generally when that toxic substance has been completely altered or detoxified, all the bacteria will perish. Mostly used in sites where the contamination is underground or in bioreactors. Generally, the technique involves stimulating organisms by adding materials such as nutrients or oxygen to increase the rate of biodegradation.

Biosensor Analytical instrument consisting of biological recognition elements such as enzymes, receptor, DNA, or microorganism which are in intimate contact with an electrochemical, optical, thermal, or acoustic signal transducer that together permit analyses of chemical properties or quantities. Indicates a potential to development in some areas, including environmental monitoring.

Biosphere (Jaiva Mandal) The world's ecosystem or the environment. India has 7 biosphere reserves in various parts of the country.

Biostabilizer The process of converting solid waste into compost by grinding and aeration.

Biota (Jeev Jaat or Jantu) All living organisms found in a particular environmental region. It includes plants as well as a fauna.

Biotechnology (Jaiva Takniki) Rules for Hazardous Micro Organisms Genetically Engineered Organisms or Cells of 1989 defines biotechnology as the application of scientific and engineering principles to the processing of materials by biological agents to produce goods and services. It is a technique that uses living organisms or parts of organisms to produce a variety of products (from medicines to industrial enzymes) to improve plants or animals or to develop microorganisms to remove toxics from bodies of water, or act as pesticides.

Biotic (Jaiviya) Matters which concern all living organisms present in the environment. The transformation is mainly due to micro-organism activities in the environment.

Biotransformation (Jaivik Roopantaran) When a chemical compound within a living system is transformed into other compounds by use of biological organisms.

Biouptake The uptake of contaminants by biological organisms such as plants and animals.

Bitterns (Bitterns) Saturated brine solution remaining after precipitation of sodium chloride in the solar evaporation process.

Bituminous Coal (Bitumen Damar or Koyala) This type of coal has a moderate heating or Btu value and is considered a soft Coal. However, it has high sulphur dioxide content in it. On heating, they yield volatile bituminous matter.

Black Body (Kaali Vastu) An ideal body which would absorb all (and reflect none) of the radiation falling upon it. The spectral energy distribution of a black body is described by Planck's equation.

Black Water (Dooshit Jal) Sewage water which carries effluent from toilets.

Bleve When a boiling liquid expands into a vapour and explodes. This is observed when liquefied flammable gas container is exposed to fire.

Blood Dyscrasia Any persistent change from normal of one or more of the blood components.

Bloom (Falta Foolta) A sudden increase of algae or other aquatic plants in a body of water. It generally signifies an introduction or increase in a pollutant.

Blowdown (Gir Jaana or Avadhaman) Cooling water discharge from a process plant boiler. This is done to remove any salts that may accumulate in the process. Salt may be harmful to the process piping.

Blowoff (Prathak Karan) When bottom water from a boiler tank is released periodically. This helps in removing solids that may accumulate from water.

Blowout (Nirdhaman) In a pressurised tank, when the pressure inside the tank increases and the safety valve fails, it may result in a blowout of the tank. This may also occur in gas or petroleum wells. The result may be explosion accompanied with fire. This term is also used in drilling when a pocket of gas is encountered which will blow out the drilling fluids thus putting a stop to further drilling. Until the gas is controlled or completely released, drilling cannot proceed.

Board (Board) 'Board' means the Central Board or a State Board. They were established by The Water Act of 1974. Each state and Union Territory was authorised to form a State Pollution Board to oversee the implementation of the various environmental Acts.

Board, Pollution Control, Functions (Board Ke Pradushan Niyantran Kaarya) The main function of the Central Board shall be to promote cleanliness of streams and wells in different areas of the States. Among others, they may also:

- advise the Central Government on any matter concerning the prevention and control of water pollution;
- co-ordinate the activities of the State Boards and resolve disputes among them;
- provide technical assistance and guidance to the State Boards, carry out and sponsor investigations and research relating to problems of water pollution and prevention, and control or abatement of water pollution.

Functions of the State and Union territories shall be similar but will be confined at the State levels.

BOD5 (BOD Panch) Biological oxygen consumed in five days by biological processes breaking down organic matter.

Body Harness (Deha Sajja or Harness) Straps on the body of a person to hold a breathing apparatus. It is part of personal protective equipment for work in a hazardous or dangerous environment.

Bog (Dal Dal) A type of wetland that accumulates appreciable peat deposits. They are generally acidic and rich in plant residue.

Boiling Point (Kwathanank or Ubaal Bindu) When heat is applied to a liquid, the point at which it starts to boil or bubbles start to form on its surface. It is the temperature of a liquid at which its vapour pressure equals the atmospheric pressure.

Boiling Water Reactor (Kwathan Jal Bhatti) In radiation, it is a nuclear reactor in which heat from the fuel rods cause the cooling water to boil. The steam from the boiling water is use to turn the turbine-generator.

Boom A floating device to control oil which floats on top of water. When the spill is large, booms can be connected to each other. The height of the boom must be more than the height of the liquid that is to be controlled on water surface.

Boron (Boron) Black hard solid that ignites spontaneously in air. Found in borax and other compounds. Used in special alloys, are nuclear power plants.

Botanical Pesticide (Vanaspatik Keetnaashi) A pesticide whose active ingredient is a plant-produced chemical.

Bottom Ash (Taliya Raakh) Ash remaining after burning of any substance in any process. It is the substance that is non-combustible material and may include toxic in them. The residue may be from burning of pulverized coal in a boiler. Bottom ash falls to the bottom of the boiler and is removed mechanically.

Bottomland (Adhastal Bhoomi) Low lying areas prone to flooding. They have a unique ecosystem of their own.

Bowen Ratio (Bowen Ka Anupaat) Ratio of sensible heat to latent heat in the earth's atmosphere. A low ratio indicates the range between low and high temperature is narrow.

Boyle's Law (Boyle Niyam) At constant temperature, the volume of an ideal gas varies inversely with the pressure.

Brackish Water (Khara jal) Water with a salt content which is higher than found in fresh water. The salt content, however, is lower than that found in sea water.

Breaching (Vichhedan Karna) Cutting a deep opening in a landform, especially by erosion.

Breakpoint Chlorination Optimum amount of chlorine required to treat water to remove bacteria.

Breakwater (Tarang Rodh) Barriers specially installed in the coastal areas so that they restrict ocean waves from human living areas.

Breeder Reactor (Paramanu Bhatti) A type of nuclear reactor used in fission reaction. It is very efficient, as it is able to handle tremendous energy released by fission of materials.

Brine (Lavan jal or Khara Pani) Refers to any liquid which has very high dissolved salt or sodium chloride content.

Brine Mud A waste material, mostly produced from well drilling or mining operation. It is composed of mineral salts and other inorganic compounds.

British Thermal Unit (BTU) (British Ushma Ikai) Measure of heat output. Heat energy required to raise the temperature of one pound of water by one degree Fahrenheit at sea level. It is equivalent to 252 calories or 778 foot-pounds.

Bromine (Bromine) Dark reddish brown fuming liquid. If inhaled, it irritates all parts of the respiratory system. It is a toxic halogen. Used as a solvent and in plastics, dyes, and pharmaceuticals.

Bronchial Tubes (Shwaas Nali) Branches of subdivision of the windpipe (trachea).

Bronchiole (Shwasanika) A minute, thin-walled branch of a bronchial tube.

Brown Coal (Bhoora Koyala) A low rank coal brown in colour. Its heating value is low and moisture content is high. Lignite is an example.

Brownfields Abandoned, idled, or under-used industrial and commercial facilities where expansion or redevelopment is complicated by real or perceived environmental contamination.

Buffer Zone (Pratirodhi Kshetra) A controlled clean area around a contaminated area for staging workers and preventing the spread of contamination during work. The purpose of creating such an area is to protect environmentally sensitive areas.

Bulk Density (Sthool Ghanatwa) The weight of an object or material divided by its volume, including the volume of a soil mass that has been oven-dried to a constant weight at 105 degrees C.

Butane (Butane) Extremely flammable liquefied, colourless hydrocarbon gas. The gas has an anaesthetic effect but is not toxic.

Bycatch Nontarget fish species or other animals such as sharks, birds or marine animals that are captured through nets or other fishing practices and then discarded, often dead or injured.

C

Cadmium (Cadmium) Silvery and lustrous malleable metal. Reacts violently with fused ammonium nitrate. Mainly used in plating, batteries and to make a metal malleable. It is highly toxic in small quantities causing indigestion, vomiting, choking, chest pain. It is mutagenic. Symbol Cd. Atomic weight 112.4.

Calcining or Calcination (Nistaapan or Bhasmikaran) The process of heating an inorganic material to very high temperature without fusing. This is done to drive off volatile or organic matter or to effect changes.

Calcium Hydroxide (Calcium Hydroxide) Also known as slaked lime. It is a white crystalline compound used in making alkalies and bleaching powder.

Caldera (Jwalamukh Kund) Depression caused by volcanic action.

Calorie (Ushmaank or Calorie) Heat required to raise the temperature of one gram of water by one degree Celsius.

Camphor (Kapoor or Karpoor) Colourless granules with a very strong aromatic odour. It is derived from camphor tree. Flammable. Used in medicine, tooth powder. In India, extensively used in religious occasions.

Cancer (Karkat Rog or Cancer) Malignant tumor or disorderly growth of cells that invades and destroys other tissues is called cancer. It spreads to other parts of the body.

Cancer Risk (Cancer Ka Khatra) Incremental probability of an individual developing cancer over a lifetime as a result of exposure to a carcinogen.

Canister (Kanaster) A container used to hold vitrified high level waste or spent fuel rods. It is usually made of welded stainless steel or an inert alloy.

Cap (Aavaran) One or more layers of clay or other highly impermeable synthetic material installed over the top of a closed landfill to prevent entry of rainwater and minimize leakage, eliminate production of leachage from the waste.

Capacitor (Sandharitra) A device for accumulating and holding a charge of electricity and consisting of conducting surfaces separated by a dielectric.

Capillary Action (Keshikakarshan Kriya) Rise of a fluid in a very narrow hairlike diameter tubes or grains of a rock. It is caused by the surface tension of the fluid and gravity.

Carbon Adsorption (Carbon ka Adhishoshan) A treatment system where contaminants are removed from ground water or surface water when the water is forced through tanks containing activated carbon, a specially treated material that attracts the contaminants.

Carbon Cycle (Carbon Chakra) Carbon is released into atmosphere as carbon dioxide when fossil fuel is burnt, breathing of animals and humans, and photosynthesis of plants. But carbon is brought back into the atmosphere through a reversal of the photosynthesis process in plants. Huge amount of carbon is stored in trees, and in the oceans. As carbon in the form of carbon dioxide increases in the atmosphere, the greenhouse effect is produced.

Carbon-14 Dating (Carbon Kaal Nirdharan) Radioactive isotope of carbon. Used by scientists to date items found in earth of 30,000 years or less through radiocarbon dating. Half life is 5,700 years.

Carbon Dioxide (Carbon dioxide) It is an odourless, colourless, heavy and asphyxiating natural gas found naturally in the atmosphere and is about one and one half times heavier than air. It normally does not support combustion. It is also produced in abundance through burning of fossil fuel and photosynthesis process of plants. One of the most serious greenhouse gases. A vital gas to all types of life. It is a natural constituent of air. However, during the pre-industrial era of 1750-1800, its concentration in the atmosphere was about 280 ppm but now it is about 358 ppm, an increase of 25%. Increase in atmospheric gas results in the warming of the earth and so melting of the polar ice which will rise the sea level. On humans, it has a mild effect on the respiratory tract.

Carbon Monoxide (Carbon Monoxide) A colourless, odourless, toxic gas produced due to incomplete combustion of fossil fuel. In trace amounts, it is a natural constituent of air. When inhaled, it effects the heart and lungs of humans. It is also a known gas in the greenhouse effect.

Carbon Regeneration Unit (Carbon Punarutpadan Ikai) Any enclosed thermal treatment device used to regenerate spent activated carbon.

Carbon Tetrachloride (Carbon Tetrachloride) A colourless liquid used in refrigerants, metal degreasers, agricultural fumigants, and as a dry-cleaning agent. Exposure to it can cause damage to the central nervous systems, liver, and kidneys. It is a known carcinogen. Formula CCl_4.

Carburetor (Carburator) A device that mixes air and gasoline in an internal combustion engine.

Carcinogen (Cancerjan) A chemical substance or agent that causes or leads to the development of cancer. Cancerous tumor or also called malignant tumors have the capacity to multiply at a faster than normal rate. Known carcinogens include benzene, heavy metals and asbestos. Carcinogens from industrial sources can be broken down into four categories:

- Petroleum products from refinery wastes, automobile service stations, petrochemical plants, metal-working plants and ships;
- Coal-tar wastes from gas plants, coke ovens, tar distilleries, tar paper plants and wood-pickling plants;
- Aromatic amino-compounds and nitro-compounds such as beta-naphthylamine, benzidine and 4-aminodiphenyl and similar nitrogen-based products from dye and rubber manufacturing, pharmaceutical plants, textile dyeing plants, plastic producers and other industries, and
- Pesticides, herbicides and soil sterilants from a large number of manufacturers and chemical firms.

Carnivore (Mansahari or Mansa Bhakshi) Meat eating animal.

Carrying Capacity (Palan Chhamata) Based on the availability of ingredients such as food and water, the number of people that an area can nourish and support indefinitely.

Casing (Aavaran) A heavy metal pipe that is lowered into a borehole during or after drilling and cemented into place. During drilling, casing provides ground support and contains contamination. It may be sealed and left in place to keep the borehole open for future use or sampling.

Cask (Peepa) A special container for shipping radioactive waste that is protective of human health and the environment.

Catalytic Converter (Utprerak Parivartak) A device attached to the exhaust system of an automobile that contain. an emissions-controlling chemical catalyst. The catalyst converts hydrocarbons and carbon monoxide to carbon dioxide and water. Due to heavy pollution of air found in cities, regulationsmay soon require installation of a convertor in all cars.

Catch Basin (Jal Grahan Chetra) A surface collection area for rain water and runoff.

Cathodic Protection Corrosion protection for a metal surface of tank or pipe caused by electrical current flowing from one or more electrodes or a sacrificial anode to the protected structure. A tank can be cathodically protected through the application of either galvanic anodes or impressed current. One way is to make the surface to be cathode of an electrochemical cell.

Cation Exchange Capacity (Cation Vinimay Kshamata) Sum total of exchangeable cations that a sediment or soil can absorb. It is expressed in milliequivalents of negative charge per 100 grams of soil or sediment.

Cationic Polymer (Dhanayanit Bahulak) A substance that contains one or move covalently linked sub units that bear a net positive charge.

Cell (Koshika) The basic and smallest structural unit of all organisms that is capable of independent functioning. All living organisms are composed of cells.

Cell, Landfill Another type of cell is a solid waste landfill section that is enclosed by soil or any other cover material.

Cell Hybridization (Koshika Sankaran) Hazardous Micro Organisms Rules of 1989 define this as the formation of live cells with new combinations of genetic material through the fusion of two or more cells by means of methods which do not occur naturally.

Cellulose (Cellulose) Colourless and odourless solid vegetable fibre with high polymer content. Paper, wood, and cotton fibres are pure cellulose. Ethers, esters, rayon are manufactured from cellulose.

Cells, Somatic (Koshika, Daihik) Body cells, usually with two sets of chromosomes, as opposed to germ cells, which have only one set.

Cementitious Friable materials that are densely packed and nonfibrous.

Centigrade (Centigrade or Shatanshik) Measure of temperature. 100 degrees centigrade is the temperature at which water starts to boil while zero degrees is the freezing point. The pressure should be 760 mm of mercury. To convert Fahrenheit to Centigrade, the formula is C=(F-32)5/9.

Centipoise (Centipoise) A unit of ciscosity which is equal to 0.01 poise.

Central Board (Kendriya Board) 'Central Board' means the Central Pollution Control Board. The Board will consist of the following:

- A full-time chairman;
- Up to five people to be nominated by the Central Government to represent that Government;
- Up to five to be nominated by the Central Government, from amongst the members of the State Boards;
- Up to three people (or non-officials) to be nominated by the Central Government, to represent the interests of the agriculture, fishery or industry or trade or any other interests;
- Two persons to represent the companies or corporations owned, controlled or managed by the Central Government, to be nominated by that Government;
- A full time member-secretary.

The Board may have association of temporary members as well as Consulting Engineers on the Board.

Central Water Laboratory (Kendriya Jal Prayogshala) The Central Government may, by notification in the Official Gazette:

- Establish a Central Water Laboratory or specify any laboratory or institute as a Central Water laboratory, to carry out the functions entrusted to the Central Water Laboratory under any Pollution Act.

The applicable rates shall be charged as specified in the Schedule for individual analysis.

Cess (Upkar) An Act to provide for the levy and collection of a Cess on water consumed by persons carrying on certain industries. The cess to be levied by local authorities, with a view to augment the resources of the Central Board and the State Boards for the prevention and control of Water pollution constituted under the Water (Prevention and Control of Pollution) Act, 1974 and as amended. It shall be payable by every person carrying on any specified industry and ever local authority. It shall be calculated as specified in the Act. Minimum of one and one half paisa for one kilolitre of water levied by the law.

Cesspool (Mala Kund) A pit constructed to receive semi-solid or liquid waste. An example is sewage. This is in places where there are no sewage systems available.

Cfm Abbreviation for cubic feet per minute, a unit of air flow rate.

Chain Breaking (Srinkhala Khandan) One way to stop a fire. The process involves breaking the chain reaction that sustains the fire.

Chain Custody (Srinkhala Rakshak) Custody transfers must be recorded for each sample. The chain custody is a record of the people who have handled the sample from collection in the field to delivery at the laboratory.

Chain Reaction (Srinkhala Abhikriya) A reaction that stimulates its own repetition. Usually associated with nuclear power plants where the neutrons that are released in one fission cause the next fission in the series to take place thus becoming a self-sustaining reaction.

Chairman of the Board (Board Adhyaksha) The Chairman of the Central Pollution Control Board will be nominated by the Central Government. The Chairman of the State Pollution Control Boards will be nominated by the respective State Governments. They will be appointed for an initial period of three years. Specific qualifications required for the Chairman and members of the Board have been specified by the Law.

Chaparral (Jhadi Van) A broad species of plant which have many stiff branches with stiff leaves making large animal travel in them very difficult. Examples include sagebrush, buckbrush.

Charles Law (Charles Ka Niyam) At constant volume, the pressure of a confined gas is directly proportional to its absolute temperature.

Chelate (Kulir) A chemical compound which has a cyclic or ring structure. It has a metallic ion in that structure. Used in chemistry lab as a titrating agent, and also in medicines. Some examples of chelating agents include amine polycarboxylic acids

(EDTA, DTPA) and polycarboxylic acids (citric acid, carbolic acid, and glucinic acid).

Chemical Canister or Cartridge (Rasayanik Kaartus) A type of air-purifying respirator. Each type can remove a particular gar or particulate matter. It is clearly marked on the canister.

Chemical Energy (Rasayanik Urja) Change in the chemical makeup of any material results in release of energy. This is due to a chemical reaction.

Chemical Oxygen Demand (Rasayanik Pranavayu Aavashyakta) Amount of nutrients and organic matter present in a body of water. It is also the amount of oxygen required to oxidise all organic and inorganic compound in water. It is similar to Biochemical Oxygen Demand (BOD).

Chemical Reaction (Rasayanik Pratikriya) When one or more chemical convert into chemically different material, a reaction has taken place. Generally, energy is either released or absorbed.

Chemical Treatment of Hazardous Waste (Khatarnak Padartha Ka Rasayanik Upchaar) They are used to facilitate the complete breakdown of hazardous waste into non-toxic gases and, more usually, to modify the chemical properties of the waste for example to reduce water solubility or to neutralize acidity or alkalinity.

Chemisorption (Rasayanik Avashoshan) When absorption of a chemical takes place by chemical bonding or valance bonding instead of physical bonding. The bonds are very strong.

Chemosphere (Rasomandal) Between 25 and 100 kilometres above the earth's surface. Mostly contains Ozone.

Chemosterilant (Rasovyandhak) A substance that controls pests by preventing its reproduction.

Chilling Effect (Dhruta Sheetan Prabhav) Cooling of the earth's surface due to the presence of particles in the atmosphere. Particles block the sun's rays reaching the earth and so facilitate the cooling of earth. See also Greenhouse effect.

Chimney (Dhunan Kaksha) The Air Act of 1981 defines 'Chimney' to include any structure with an opening or outlet from or through which any air pollutant may be emitted.

Chlorinated Hydrocarbons (Chloronikrit Hydrocarbon) A hydrocarbon substance which has chlorine as one of the chemical attached to it. They accumulate in the food chain and are generally long lasting. Examples include DDT, chloroform, and chloromethane.

Chlorinated Solvents (Chlorinikrit Vilayak) Compounds of various hydrocarbons and chlorine. Its exposure may cause cancer of liver, lungs, skin, and blood.

Chlorination (Chlorinikaran) Addition of chlorine to drinking water or to sewage water to disinfect the same or kill infectious bacteria.

Chlorine (Chlorine) A very highly reactive halogen. It is a greenish yellow gas with a pungent and irritating odour. Used as a bleach and as a disinfectant in water purification. Exposure to Chlorine may cause severe lung problem, irritation to skin, eyes, and mucous membranes, headaches, and nausea. Limit for Free available Chlorine in drinking water as per the Water Act is 0.5 mg/l. Chemical Symbol Cl. Atomic Weight 35.453.

Chlorofluorocarbons (CFC) One of the greenhouse gases created by humans from chlorine, fluorine and carbon. It is used as a lubricant, refrigerant, and as a propellant in aerosol sprays. This gas accelerates Ozone depletion. The thinning of the ozone layer can lead to plankton destruction in the Antarctic, which could effect the whole ocean food chain. The increased ultraviolet radiation that reaches earth through the depleted layer of ozone inhibiting the growth of plants. Some of the CFCs are CFC-11, CFC-12, and CFC-13 and carbon tetrachloride.

Chlorophenoxy (Chlorophenoxy) Herbicides found in domestic water supplies which cause adverse health effects.

Chlorophyll (Parnaharit) Proteins essential to all living forms of life on earth. It is the green pigment of plants and essential for photosynthesis. Used in the manufacture of soaps, detergents, cosmetics, and perfumes.

Chlorosis (Harit Rog) When plant leaves lose chlorophyll, they turn yellow. This is generally due to presence of disease, lack of nutrients or presence of air pollutants.

Choke (Shwas Rodhak) A restrictive device put in any process in order to change the velocity and pressure significantly.

Chromatography (Varna Rekha Yantra) Discovered in 1906, it is an analytical instrument used to identify components of a mixture by selective adsorption. This enables the quantification of the components separately. Liquid chromatography is used for soluble substances while gas chromatography for volatile substances. A carrier gas is used in gas chromatography for separation of the compoments which move differentially through a two-phase system. When the ratio of components are different, they move at a different rate over the stationary phase and thus producing a series of bands by which their identity is determined. The lightest gases come out the earliest while the heaviest last. The movement is due to physicochemical principles of adsorption, partition, ion exchange, exclusion, or a combination of these principles.

Chromium (Chromium) A very hard, brittle gray metal used in corrosion resistant atmosphere. It is highly toxic. It can cause skin and nasal ulcers, lung tumors, gastrointestinal effects, damage to the nervous system and circulatory system. Chemical Symbol Cr. Atomic Weight 51.996.

Chromosomes (Guna Sutra) Composed of DNA molecules, they carry the inherent characteristic of a living organisms in plants and animal species. They can be damaged due to pollutants.

Chronic Dose (Chirakalic Khurak) Typically, a small dose of any substance received over a long period of time in months or years and better tolerated by the body than an acute dose.

Chronic Exposure (Chirakalic Apaavaran) When exposure to any toxic or hazardous substance is continuous and for a long duration. It could last weeks, months or even years.

Chronic Toxicity Test (Chirkalik Vishaktata Parikshan) Method to determine the concentration of a substance in water that produces an adverse effect such as mortality, reproduction, or growth on a test organism over an extended period of time.

Ci Abbreviation for Curie, a unit of radioactivity equal to 37 billion disintegrations per second.

Cilia (Pakshamabh) These are the tiny undulating hairs that line the respiratory tract which protect the respiratory system from the tiny particulates that may be inhaled.

Cladding (Adhipattan) Two metals bonded together metallurgically. It may be bonded together by roll bonding, solder or by explosion bonding. In radioactivity, it is when an external layer of material is applied directly to nuclear fuel or other material to provide protection from a chemically reactive environment, to provide containment of radioactive products produced during the irradiation of the composite, or to provide structural support.

Clarification (Vishuddhikaran) Process used to clarify a liquid substance. Generally associated with water to settle solids and thus purify it. The process could be aided by centrifugal action or through chemically induced coagulation.

Clarifier (Swacha Kaari) A piece of equipment which is used to remove solids and fines from water. Generally, it consists of a mixing tank and a clarifier tank with inclined plates. To assist the settling of particles or flocculating together, treatment chemicals may be added in the mixing tank.

Clays (Chikni Mitti) Earthly, extremely fine-grained sediment or soft rock crystals. They may be composed of clay size or colloidal particles, having high plasticity of about 4 micron or 1/256 mm in size. When they are extremely small, clay may be irritant to nose. Used in ceramic products and oil well drilling.

Cleanup (Saaf Karana or Safai) Actions undertaken during a removal or remedial response to physically remove or treat a hazardous substance that poses a threat or potential threat to human health and welfare and the environment and/or real and personal property. Sites are considered cleaned up when EPA removal or remedial programs have no further expectation or intention of returning to the site and threats have been mitigated or do not require further action.

Cleanup Levels (Saaf Karne ka Maapan or Stir) Media specific target concentration levels for constituents that must be met by any corrective action selected. Cleanup levels are established during corrective measures studies using selection remedy criteria such as protection of human health and the environment; compliance with regulatory requirements; reduction of toxicity, mobility, or volume through treatment; long and short term effectiveness; implementability; cost; and public acceptance.

Cloning (Sama Roopta) Creation of an identical copy of a gene from a single cell. In 1997,the first cloning of a sheep was successfully done in Britain.

Closure (Samapti or Samapan or Purti) The act of securing or closing a hazardous waste facility pursuant to the regulatory requirements.

Closure Plan (Samapan Yojana) Documentation prepared to guide the deactivation, stabilization, and surveillance of a waste management unit or facility.

Cloud Seeding Artificially producing rain by seeding the clouds with silver iodide or some other chemical.

Cloud Forest (Chirmegha Van) Forests where the trees have the capability of absorbing water from clouds. These forests are denser, more moist and darker. They are covered by clouds most of the time.

Coagulation (Skandan Kriya) When a substance has the ability to fuse, unite or grow together. The process should be unchangeable. It may require another substance such as an electrolyte for the process to take place. The result is a soft or solid mass. Used in drinking water process to remove solids. Chemical substances used to enhance the coagulation process include such as lime and alum.

Coal (Koyala) A natural organic combustible matter modified over a long period of time. It mostly contains carbon. Various stages or ranks include peat, lignite, bituminous and anthracite coal. Grade depends on impurities and its heating value. Extensively found in Bihar coal mines, and in Tamilnadu. Mostly used in generation of electricity.

Coal Cleaning Technology (Koyala Safai Takniki) Most of the coal found has very high content of unwanted chemicals such as sulphur. For this reason, before the coal is put to use, the content of sulphur is lowered by either chemical or physical process.

Coal Gasification (Koyala Gaisikaran) There are several technologies available which would recover the gaseous products from coal. In a controlled process if the gaseous products are recovered, release of pollutants to the environment are thus reduced or even eliminated.

Coal Liquefication (Koyala Dravan) When liquid fuel is obtained by processing of coal.

Cobble (Upalika) Rock fragment between 64 and 256 mm in diameter.

Cocarcinogen (Saha Cancerjan) A substance capable of increasing the observed incidence of cancer if applied with a carcinogen but not itself a carcinogen.

Coefficient of Haze (Dhundha Gunank) Interference in the amount of atmospheric visibility is given by a coefficient of haze.

Cogeneration System (Sah Utpadan Tantra or Paddhati) A power system that produces both electricity and thermal energy from the same source.

Cohort Study A study that observes subjects in differently exposed groups and compares the incidence of systems. Although ordinarily prospective in nature, such a study is sometimes carried out retro-spectively, using historical data. Both the systems in the experiment must be identical in every respect except one.

Coke (Coke) It is produced by heating bituminous coal or from the cracking process of crude oil. Used in refractory furnace lining and in the production of calcium and silicon carbide.

Coke Oven (Coke Bhatti) Recovery of Iron from its ore is done in a blast furnace and the basic material used in that oven is coke. An industrial process converts coal into coke.

Coliform Bacteria (Coliform Jivanu) It is a group of bacteria that mostly inhabit the intestinal tract of humans and animals. They are also found in soil. By itself, they are not harmful to humans. But its presence indicates that water has sewage or disease organisms or pollution in it.

Coliform Count (Coliform Ganana) A measure of human or animal wastes present in a body of water. A standard plate count of over 100 means that the water is unfit for human consumption or use.

Coliform Index A rating of the purity of water based on a count of fecal bacteria in the same.

Coliform Organisms (Kolai Rupi Jeev) Microorganisms that are found in the intestinal tracks of humans and animals. It indicates the presence of fecal pollution and potentially adverse contamination by pathogens.

Colloids (Kalil or Colloids) Solids which are very small and finely divided. They disperse in a liquid which is normally negatively charged. The colloids carry an electric charge and do not dissolve in that liquid. The size of the particle is extremely small, the diameter being in the range of 0.001 millimetre or less.

Colloidal Dispersion (Kolaidi Parikshepan or Vikhandan) A mixture resembling a true solution but containing one or more substances that are finely divided but large enough to prevent passage through a semipermeable membrane. It consists of particles which are larger than molecules, which settle out very slowly with time, which scatter a beam of light and which are too small for resolution with an ordinary light microscope.

Colloidal Particles (Kolaidiya Kan) A colloid whose particles cannot pass through an Osmotic membrane.

Colloidal Suspension (Kolaidiya Nilamban) A type of colloid that has the ability to pass through a filter without changing its properties.

Combined Sewer (Samyukta Mal Prayas) When the pipes that carry the sewage are also designed to carry runoff water to the treatment plant. This occurs when there is heavy rain and the only way to control the runoff is to pass the overflow through the sewer lines in to the treatment plants. The only danger in this case is that the overflow may also contain pollutants and may cause damage to the sewage plant itself.

Combustion (Dahan) The burning or ignition of oxygen with an organic substance that results in the production of energy such as light and heat and carbon dioxide. Uncontrolled combustion may result in the release of pollutants into the atmosphere. This could be considered as the basic cause of air pollution.

Command Post (Sanchaalan Kaksha or Sanshalan Kaksha) When an accident or a hazardous waste spill occurs, a command post is established at a safe distance but in the proximity of the accident. From this place, on-scene-coordinator, responders and others make decisions for actions to be taken to control the accidental release or the emergency.

Commensal Species (Sahabhojit Jeev) Two entirely different kind of species living together as they are dependent on each other.

Comminuter (Vikhandan or Churna Kar Dena) To facilitate in the handling of solid waste, a comminuter is used to shred or pulverize the same.

Company (Company) The Water Act defines 'Company' as any body corporate, and includes a firm or other association of individuals. The company may have a director which means a partner in the firm.

Compatibility (Sangatataa) The ability of materials to exist together without adverse environmental effects or health risks.

Composting (Vanaspatic Khad Banana) This is mostly used to handle yard waste. The contaminated soil is mixed with compostable material such as leaves, municipal solid waste, sewage sludge and other organic residues prior to treatment. It then converts itself into a humus like material and can be used as a fertiliser for soil conditioning. For an efficient operation, mixing, aeration, and addition of water to keep it moist is helpful.

Composting Facility (Vanaspatic Khad Kaksha) A solid waste management facility used to provide aerobic, thermophilic decomposition of solid organic constituents of solid waste to produce a stable, humus-like material. Water is a necessary ingredient for the process to occur. The pile needs to be turned to control the temperature that builds up.

Concentration (Gaadhaapan) Amount of a contaminant in a given quantity of substance.

Conceptual Exposure Model (Sankalpanatmak Vigopan Pratiman) A conceptual model whose objects are qualitative or quantitative descriptions of sources of contamination, environmental transport pathways for contamination, and biota that may be impacted by contamination (called receptors) and whose relationships describe qualitatively or quantitatively the release of contamination from the sources, the movement of contamination along the pathways to the exposure points, and the uptake of contaminants by the receptors.

Condensation (Sadhanan or Dhanikaran) When a vapour molecule turns into a nongaseous or liquid state. The process is reverse of evaporation.

Condenser (Sandhanak Yantra)
A piece of equipment used to cool any substance. This is generally associated with cooling of steam to water.

Conditional Remedy (Dashatmak Upchar) A conditional remedy is a regulatory agency approved action that allows contamination to temporarily remain within the boundary.

Conduction (Chalan) When heat is transferred from one molecule to the neighbouring molecule. This is the way heat is transferred in solids.

Conductivity (Chaalakta) The ability of a solid or liquid to conduct electricity through its media. Metals are good thermal conductors because of their high density. It is measured in Mhos, reverse of Ohms or it is electrical current per unit area divided by the voltage drop per unit length. In water, it is a measure of free ions. The lower conductivity of water the purer it is.

Cone of Depression (Avanman Shanku or Dabav Kon) When water is heavily pumped from an aquifer, the level around the well goes down or forms a cone. Continued excessive pumping may result in lowering of the level of water table. It means the discharge is greater than the recharging of the aquifer.

Confined Aquifer (Parisimit Jalabhaar) An aquifer bounded above and below by impermeable beds or by beds of distinctly lower permeability than that of the aquifer itself; an aquifer containing confined ground water.

Connate Water (Sahaj Jal) Fossil reservoir water that has been trapped inside a rock and thus has not been in contact with the atmosphere since deposition. Normally that water is high in chloride and calcium and frequently contains more than 100,000 ppm dissolved total solids.

Conservation (Parirakshan or Sanrakshan) Preservation of any matter or substance. Generally associated with conservation of materials found in nature. See also Waste Minimization, Pollution Prevention.

Consolidated Soil (Samaahit Mrida) When a soil is subjected to an increase in pressure due to loading at the ground surface, a re-adjustment in the soil structure occurs.

Conspecific Population (Samajatiya Janasankhya) Pair of populations whose members are capable of interbreeding. They need not be living in proximity to each other.

Constituent (Avayava) Any compound or element present in environmental media, including both naturally occurring and anthropogenic elements.

Constituent of Concern Any constituent present in environmental media or on structural debris at a concentration above its action level.

Constructed Wetland (Niyamit Namiyukt Bhoomi) Engineered systems designed to simulate natural wetlands to exploit the water purification functional value for human use and benefits. Constructed wetlands consist of former upland environments that have been modified to create poorly drained soils and wetlands flora and fauna for the primary purpose of contaminant or pollutant removal from waste waters or runoff. Constructed wetlands are essentially wastewater treatment systems and are designed and operated as such though many systems do support other functional values.

Construction Permit (Nirman Karya ki Anumati) Generally it is issued by a regulatory authority as it is mandated by the same. Required to start any plant, process, or any type of new construction.

Consulting Engineer (Paramarshi Abhiyanta) For the purpose of assisting the Central Board in the performance of its functions, the Board may appoint a consulting engineer to the Board for a specified period not exceeding four months. The consulting engineer shall discharge such duties and perform such functions as are assigned to him, by the Central Board and it will be his duty to advice the Board on all technical matters referred to him by the Board.

Container (Patra or Maal Dibba) Any portable device in which the hazardous waste is stored, transported, treated, disposed of, or otherwise handled.

Container of Hazardous Waste Any portable device in which the hazardous waste is stored, transported, treated, disposed of, or otherwise handled. If the container is to be used for disposal of hazardous waste, it must be at least 90 percent full when placed in the landfill. The emptied containers should be crushed, shredded, or similarly reduced in volume to the maximum possible extent before burial in the landfill.

Containment Building (Parirodhan Bhavan) A structure used to contain any type of material. It could be either non-hazardous or hazardous substance or both. The building could be to store any material also.

Containment System for Hazardous Waste The owner or operator of a facility storing hazardous waste should have a containment system in the storage area. As a minimum, the following guidelines should be followed:

- The base underlying the container should be constructed in such a way that it is free of cracks or gaps and is sufficiently impervious to contain leaks, spills, and accumulated precipitation until the collected material is detected and removed;
- It should be designed, and operated to drain and remove liquids which may result from leak, spill, or precipitation, unless the containers are elevated or are otherwise protected from contact with accumulated liquids;
- The containment system should have sufficient capacity to contain 10% of the total volume of all the containers or the largest container, whichever is greater. Containers that do not contain free liquids need not be considered in this determination;
- Run-off into the containment system should be prevented unless the collection system has sufficient excess capacity in addition to that mentioned in paragraph (c) of this section to contain any run-on which might enter the system;
- The containment system should have sump or collection area to collect any leak, spill or precipitation. Spilled or leaded waste and accumulated precipitation should be removed from the sump or collection area in as timely manner as is necessary to prevent over flow of the collection system.

Contaminant (Parirodhan or Sanrodhan) A substance accidentally introduced into another, either in solid, liquid or gaseous form. It the accidental release is significant, it could be called a spill.

Contaminant (Sandooshak) Substance that is either generally not present or that is present in greater than normal quantities. Any physical, chemical, biological, or radiological substance or matter that has an adverse affect on air, water, or soil.

Contaminants in Water See Water Contaminants.

Contamination (Sandooshan or Milavat) A statistically significant rise in the concentration of measured parameters which are harmful to humans or nature in any substance. Also includes introduction of undesirable substances or elements into any other matter or substance.

Contingency Plan (Aapat Kaalin Vyavastha) A document setting out an organised, planned, and coordinated course of action to be followed in case of fire, explosion, or release of hazardous waste or hazardous waste constituents which could threaten human health or the environment.

Control Equipment (Niyantran Upaskar) 'Control Equipment' means any apparatus, device, equipment or system to control the quality and manner of emission of any air pollutant and included any device used for securing the efficient operation of any industrial plant.

Continental Climate (Mahadwipiya Jalavayu) Climatic conditions of an area where there is no effect to the same by conditions of the oceans. These areas must be at a significant distance from oceans and seas.

Continental Divide (Mahadwipiya Jalavibhajak) Area separated by flow of water on both sides, generally by oceans. An example is Europe and North America.

Continental Drift (Mahadwipiya Apavah) Movement of earth's crustal plates. The movement is extremely slow and this is how the various continents were formed millions of years ago.

Contingency Plan (Aapatkalin Yojana) A document setting out an organised, planned, and coordinated course of action to be followed in case of fire, explosion, or release of hazardous waste or hazardous waste constituents which could threaten human health or the environment. It must list names, addresses and phone numbers of all persons responsible for acting as emergency coordinator. The plan should list all emergency equipment at the facility, communications and alarm systems, and decontamination systems. It should also include primary routes for evacuation of facility personnel.

Continuous Air Monitoring (Santat Vayu Niyaamak) An instrument that continuously measures the level of airborne contamination of any hazardous or toxic substance and alarms when a preset level set point is reached.

Contour Farming (Parirekha Kheti or Krishi) Farming on the slopes of mountains. It is done across the slopes in various layers each of very thin width. This type of farming can be commonly seen on the slopes of Himalayas.

Contour Plowing (Parirekha Jutayi) To eliminate erosion of soil, farmland needs to be plowed along the naturally occurring contour of the land. This is a common practice in hilly regions.

Control Equipment (Niyantran Yantra) The Air Act defines it to mean any apparatus, device, equipment or system to control the quality and manner of emission of any air pollutant and includes any device used for securing the efficient operation of any industrial plant.

Control Rods (Niyantran Shalaakaa) Devices that may be used as a catalyst in any process. Also the rods used in nuclear reactors to control and regulate the chain reaction.

Control Room (Niyantran Kaksha) The covered area used to operate any process or plant from where the whole process could be controlled.

Controlled Area (Niyantrit Kshetra) Any area to which access is controlled in order to protect individuals from exposure to a hazardous or toxic substance or from radiation and radioactive materials.

Convection (Sanvahan) When heat is transferred through the movement of the molecule itself. Heat transfer that is taking place in liquids or in air. Natural convection takes place when there is a difference in temperature and/or density. This is the phenomena which is responsible for hot air to move up and cold air to move down.

Conversion (Roopantaran) When a material changes from one physical form to another. It could be due to chemical or mechanical operation.

Coolant (Sheetalak) A substance or material used to cool or remove heat in any process or reaction.

Cooling Tower (Sheetalak Minar or Gadh) Any structure which is used to remove heat from a liquid. It is generally associated with cooling of hot water in industries.

Copper (Tamba) A highly conductive metal, copper is orange in color. It is nontoxic in nature. Large quantities of this metal may cause anemia and digestive disturbances. Used in electrical wiring, plumbing, building construction, cooking utensils, and in pharmaceutical industry. Limit for copper in drinking water as per the Water Act of 1975 is 3.0 mg/l. Symbol Cu. Atomic Weight 63.54

Core (Saarbhaag or Krod) Central part of any substance. Core of the earth is about

2900 kilometres from the earth surface and is supposed to contain molten metals and gases. It also means the soil or rock sample removed during drilling of a well. In nuclear technology, it means the uranium-containing heart of a nuclear reactor from where energy is released.

Core Sample (Krod Namuna or Pratidarsh) One or more portions of a core, a cylindrical section of soil or rocks obtained by drilling. Core samples are retained for future study. It is obtained by use of a hollow drill bit when cutting is done at the circumference of the bit, freeing the center of the cut circle.

Corrosion (Sanksharan or Jang Lagna) A slow and steady degradation or destruction of a material or substance by means of chemical or electrochemical process. The process may be accelerated by presence of an acid or a base. There are two types of corrosion-chemical and electrolytic. One of the most common being the corrosion of pipes which carry water. Contact between two dissimilar metals may also result in corrosion. It can be controlled or even avoided by application of a special coating on the surface or by use of corrosive inhibitors.

Corrosivity (Sanksharkata) Any substance whose pH is either less than or equal to 2.0 or greater than or equal to 12.5 are generally corrosive substances as they are either highly acidic or highly basic. They are capable of corroding steel at a rate greater than 0.006 m/yr. or 1/4 inches per year. On contact, these chemicals are capable of burning eyes and skin very rapidly.

Cosmic Radiation (Antarikshi Vikiran) The natural radiation that comes from the sun and outer space and consists of positively charged particles, as well as gamma radiation. A part of naturally occurring background radiation on earth surface. At sea level, the average annual cosmic radiation dose equivalent is about 26 mrem and increases about ½ mrem for each 100 feet in elevation. Even food items have trace amounts of radiation in them. At higher elevations, the amount of atmosphere shielding cosmic rays decreases and thus the dose equivalent increases.

Cosmic Rays (Antariksha Kiran) Stream of energy which emanates from beyond Earth's atmosphere.

Counts Per Minute (Prati minute Ganana) In radiation, it is the number of disintegrations in a radioactive source, as detected by an instrument.

Covalent Bond (Sahasanyoji Bandh) The bond between two atoms which are sharing an electron equally between them.

Critical Mass (Krantik Dravyaman) The minimum mass of a fissionable material that will just maintain a fission chain reaction under precisely specified condition, such as the nature of the material and its purity, the nature and thickness of the tamper (or neutron reflector), the density (or compression), and the physical shape. For an explosion to occur, the system must be supercritical, i.e. the mass of material must exceed the critical mass under the existing conditions.

Criticality (Krantikta) A sustained nuclear fission chain reaction.

Crop Rotation (Fasal Chakranukram) To maintain the fertility of soil, different crops are planted in the same land. This may result in the reduced use of fertilisers and the pesticides to control pests.

Crude Oil (Kaccha Tel) Raw petroleum pumped or removed from earth. Crude oil pumped from one place will be significantly different than that pumped from another area. It is refined and its distillate products are used as energy. Some of the distillate fractions include natural gas, gasoline or petrol, kerosene, lubricating Oil.

Cryogenic (Nimnatapi) Health hazard that freezes body tissues on contact. When refrigerants are used to achieve very low temperatures.

Cryogenic Gas (Nimnatapi Gas) When a gas is stored in a container in a liquefied state. It reduces the volume of gas. The storage temperature and pressure is less than normal.

Cryosphere Area of the earth which is permanently frozen.

Cryptosporidium A protozoan associated with the disease cryptosporidiosis in humans. The disease can be transmitted through ingestion of drinking water, person-to-person contact, or other exposure routes. Cryptosporidiosis may cause acute diarrhea, abdominal pain, vomiting, and ferer that last one to two weeks in healthy adults, but may be chronic or gatal in immuno-compromised people.

Cull (Nishkrasht) Any tree or a part thereof which is large enough for making lumber but is not suitable due to some other factor other than its size.

Cullet (Toota Kaanch) Broken or crushed glass. This may be done to reduce the volume.

Cultural Eutrophication (Sanskrit Suposhan) Uncontrolled and careless release of pollutants by humans in the environment that they live and which results in the slow degradation and ultimate death of surrounding water bodies.

Cultures and Stocks Infectious agents and associated biologicals including cultures from medical and pathological laboratories; cultures and stocks of infectious agents from research and industrial laboratories; waste from the production of biologicals; discarded live and attenuated vaccines; and culture dishes and devices used to transfer, inoculate, and mix cultures. See also Medical Waste.

Cumec Measuring the flow of water. One cumec equals 35.7 cubic feet per second (cfs).

Cumulative Toxicity (Sanchayi Vishaktata) Adverse effects of repeated doses occurring as a result of prolonged action on, or increased concentration of the administered substance or its metabolites in susceptible tissues.

Curie (Curie) A unit of measure to describe the intensity of radioactivity in materials, the rate at which it decays. It is based on the radioactivity of one gram of radium and equals 37 billion or 3.7×10^{10} nuclear transformations or (3,700 crores) disintegration per second. It is named after Madame Marie Curie, the first scientist to study the radioactivity of Uranium. The SI unit for Curie is Becquerel (Bq).

Curie Temperature (Curie Taapman) It is the temperature at which a metal such as iron loses its ability of maintaining a magnetic field.

Cyanide (Cyanide) Salt containing the Cyanogen group. Most famous among them is potassium cyanide (KCN). They are extremely poisonous causing thyroid and nervous system damage. Used in electroplating process and metal extraction.

Cyclone Collector (Apakendri Sangrahitra) When centrifugal force is used to pull large particles from polluted air.

Cyclonic Flow (Apakendri Gati) Spiraling movement of exhaust gases within a duct or stack.

Cytotoxin (Koshikavish) A toxic substance that destroys Cytoplasm.

D

Dam (Baandh) A structure built to restrict or act as a barrier for flow of water. Often used to generate electricity or reduce floods downstream. Dams are gigantic construction projects and so have severe environmental effects, all of which may not be positive.

Darcy (Darcy) A unit of permeability for flowing liquid. One Darcy equals the flow of one cubic centimetre of liquid of one centipoise viscosity flowing for one second under a pressure differential of one atmosphere through a porous medium having an area of cross section of one square centimetre and a length of one centimetre.

dB-A (DBA) A measure of noise pollution. It is the ratio of measured intensity of noise to a reference sound pressure level. It is expressed in logarithmic scale. Zero dB is a threshold of hearing. TLVs (Threshold Limit Values) for noise for 16 hour per day duration is 80 dBA and for 8 hour, it is 85 dBA.

DDT (DDT) Dichloro-Diphenyl-Trichloro-Ethane. Colourless, odourless crystals, highly toxic pesticide used to control most insects. Half life of 15 years, it breaks down very slowly in the atmosphere, and accumulates in soil and vegetation. It is a Mutagen as well as Teratogen. For this reason, its use has been banned in many countries.

Decay (Kharab Hona or Sadana or Kshay Hona) The process whereby radioactive materials undergo spontaneous disintegration. A change from one nuclide, element, or state to another, releasing radiation in the process. This action ultimately results in a decrease in the number of radioactive nuclei present in the sample. The spontaneous transformation of one nuclide into a different nuclide or into a different isotope of the same nuclide. See also Decay Heat.

Decay Constant (Kshayaank) The rate of decay of a radioactive substance per unit of time. Each substance has its own constant denoted by lambda (().

Decay Heat (Kshaytaap) The heat released as radioactive elements spontaneously disintegrate. See also Decay.

Decay Product (Kshay Utpaad) A chemical element derived from another due to the process of spontaneous breakdown or reaction by itself and generally becomes more stable than the original compound or element. Decay may be natural as well as induced by the environment. See also Decay.

Decibel (dB) (Decibel) The ratio of the loudness of one sound to another expressed in a logarithmic scale. Zero dB is the threshold of hearing, quiet room has about 30 dB, normal conversation is about 60 dB.

Deciduous Forest (Patajhadi Van or Parna Pati Van) When trees in a forest lose leaves seasonally every year. This should be a regular phenomenon.

Decommissioning Permanently removing a process out of use or service. This may be a part of dismantlement.

Decontamination (Shuddhikaran) The reduction or removal of harmful and unwanted hazardous or radioactive material or contamination from the surface of or from within another material. It can be achieved by chemical or physical treatment, or by some other process.

Deferred Action (Sthagit Kriya) Actions may be deferred at a hazardous waste site where cleanup may be required but where there is no immediate risk to human health and the environment or where institutional or engineering controls currently prevent exposure to, and/or migration of, contaminants. In most cases, deferred action does not constitute a final remedy.

Deflocculating Agent A material added to a suspension to prevent settling.

Defoliant (Nishpatran) Substance intended to cause leaves or foliage to drop from trees and plants. An herbicide is generally used for the purpose.

Deforestation (Van Katai or Vanonmulan or Vananaashan) When forests are cut down due to human consumption, disease, rain or any of the natural causes. Loss of trees in the forest increases the carbon dioxide and thus to the greenhouse effect.

Degassing (Gas Nishkashan) Removal of dissolved gas from a material prior to casting.

Degradation rate (Apakshay Gati or Nimnikaran Gati) The rate at which a chemical is broken down in the environment. I could be by hydrolysis, photodegradation, or soil metabolism, the length of time that a parent chemical persists in the environment.

Deionised Water (Viaayanit Jal) Very pure water. Generally used in labs and in very special processes.

Delta (Nadi Mukh Bhumi) Low lying or sloping land in the shape of a triangle generally found at the mouth of a river in the ocean. It may be prone to flooding.

Demineralization (Akhaniji Karan) Removal of salt from water. Done to either make hard water soft or further purify water. The processes generally used are either ion-exchange techniques or flash distillation. In very sensitive lab work, demineralized water is used.

Demulsibility (Vipayasniyata) Ability of oil to separate from water with which it is mixed or emulsified. The more quickly the oil separates from water, the better the demulsibility rating.

Denitrification (Vinitri Karan) The conversion of nitrates to nitrogen gas carried out by a specialised group of bacteria. Process is more common in plants and soils and in wastewater treatment plants. Uses bacteria and ammonia is removed from wastewater as ammonia gas.

Density (Dhanatva or Sadhanata) It indicates how heavy a matter is in comparison to its volume or size. Mass of a unit volume of a substance. Expressed as grams/cubic centimetres. At normal conditions, density of Water is 1.000 gm/cm3; Air-0.001293 gm/cm3.

Deoxyribonucleic Acid (DNA) Also known as DNA. Found in the nuclei of living cells. Consists of two long chains joined by hydrogen bond. They are extremely large and complex polymer in nature and replicate themselves in living cells. Genetic information is carried in these cells which determine hereditary characteristics.

Depletion Curve (Dravya ka Apakshai) Indication of the rate of reduction of any liquid in any substance. When water is pumped from an underground source, and if the rate of pumping is more than the rate of recharge of that aquifer, the quantity of water that is being pumped will decrease.

Depressurization Occurs when the pressure inside a container is less than outside and the pressure (usually created by air) is released. In a closed structure or building with air conditioning, when the pressure inside is less, then outside air will seep in.

Depuration (Shuddhi Karan) Elimination of a test substance from a test organism.

Dermal Corrosion (Twachiya Kshay) Irreversible tissue damage in the skin following the application of the test substance.

Dermal Exposure (Twachiya Anaavrati) When skin is exposed or comes in contact with any type of pollutant or chemical.

Dermal Toxicity (Twachiya Aavishaluta or Vishaktata) When a chemical or any substance has an adverse affect on the human skin. It might be as minor as rash or major as toxic.

Dermatitis (Twakshodh) Cracked, broken, dry skin caused by exposure to health hazards that remove fat from the skin, inflammation of the skin caused by direct contact or systemic exposure to hazardous materials.

Desalination (Vilavanikaran) Process by which salt is removed from water or brine. Ocean water can become suitable for domestic use as drinking water. The process used could be distillation, electrodialysis or reverse osmosis. Removal of salts from soil by artificial means is usually done by leaching.

Desert (Registhanor Maru Sthal) An area where yearly rainfall is less than 10 inches or about 25 cms. For this reason, it is devoid of vegetation or green plants.

Desiccant (Sukhane Vala Padarth) A moisture absorbing chemical substance. Also used in instrumentation to remove moisture from air to be used in process instrumentation purposes. Small amounts of desiccants are used to keep moisture away from very delicate instruments. Silica gel, molecular sieve, calcium chloride are a few hygroscopic substances.

Designated Facility (Nirdisht Kshetra) A hazardous waste storage, treatment, or disposal facility which has received a permit from the regulatory authority. To operate the facility, the owner should make sure that the facility will have minimum impact on the environment and human health including site closure, and reclamation. Owners should have appropriate site plan for safe storage and disposal. They should maintain all records and have a contingency plan to handle emergency situations.

Desorption (Vishoshan) The process of absorbed particles leaving the surface of another substance or the adsorbent. It is opposite of adsorption.

Destratification (Vistaran or Vistaravinyas) In a lake or a reservoir, when the temperature is constant at all depths by mixing it vertically, it is termed as destratfication. This eliminates the different aquatic species that are found at different temperatures in any water reservoir.

Destroyed Medical Waste Medical waste that has been ruined, torn apart, or mutilated through thermal treatment, melting, shredding, grinding, tearing, or breaking, so that it is no longer generally recognized as medical waste, but has not yet been treated. It does not include compacted medical waste. See also Medical Waste.

Desulphurization (Vigandhakan) Most of coal found has high amounts of sulphur in it. Removal of sulphur through physical or chemical means is called desulphurization. This is done to reduce pollution when the coal could be put to use.

Detection Level (Abhigyan Star) The minimum concentration of a substance that can be measured with a 99% confidence that the analytical concentration is greater than zero.

Detection Limit (Abhigyan Seema) The lowest concentration of a chemical compound that can be detected using a particular instrument or analytical method. Detection limits vary widely among detection methods and compounds.

Detention Time (Samrodh Samay or Kaal) In a process, the time a substance will remain at a particular place. During incineration of waste, the time the waste will remain in the heater at a specified temperature is its detention time. Similarly, when water is left in a tank for its solids to settle, the time allowed for the purpose is its detention time.

Detergents (Saabun or Prakshalak) Synthetic washing agent that helps to remove dirt and oil. Some contain compounds which kill useful bacteria and encourage algae growth when they are in wastewater that reaches receiving waters.

Detoxification (Nir Aavishikaran) The process of removing poisons or toxins. It is a metabolic process whereby a parent substance is changed to a daughter produce that has lessened toxicity.

Detritus (Malaba) Freshly dead or partially decomposed remains of plants and animals.

Deuterium (Deuterium) An isotope of hydrogen with a mass of 2 units. Its nucleus contains one neutron and one proton and is about twice as heavy as the nucleus of normal hydrogen, which has only one proton. Deuterium is extracted from water that always contains 1 atom of deuterium to about 6,500 atoms of ordinary or light Hydrogen. Also called as Heavy Hydrogen. This may be the fuel for fusion process to produce electricity. Chemical formula is D.

Developmental Toxicity Adverse effects caused on the developing child that result from exposure to a chemical substance.It results from prenatal expcsue to toxicants experienced by mothers. The effects could include structural malformations, low birth weight, metabolic or biological dysfunction. The systems manifest as the child grows.

Dew Point (Osaank) When air is saturated with moisture or if the humidity of air is 100%. The state in which air can hold the maximum amount of air. A gas which is saturated with a condensable component or liquid.

Dewater (Vijal) Removal of water. In wastewater treatment plants, the drying of the sludge is called dewatering.

Diatomaceous Earth A chalk-like, almost pure Silica material. An extremely friable and soft white rock. Used as an abrasion or as an insulating material. Used to filter out solid waste in wastewater treatment plants, as an active ingredient in some powdered pesticides.

Dielectric Material (Paraa Vaidyut Padarth) Material that does not conduct direct electrical current. Wood and ceramic materials are good dielectric material.

Diesel Engine (Diesel Engine) An engine which uses diesel as a fuel. The fuel is ignited with the heat from the compression of a fuel-air mixture by the piston rather than with a spark, as in a gasoline engine with spark plugs.

Dietary LC_{50} Statistically derived estimate of the concentration of a test substance in the diet that would cause 50 percent mortality to the test population under specified conditions.

Diffraction (Vivartan) The bending of waves around the edges of objects.

Diffusion (Prasaar or Failaav) Spontaneous mixing of different gas molecules or movement of particles throughout the air from areas of high concentration to areas of low concentration, tending to distribute the particles or molecules more uniformly. The rate of diffusion is dependent on factors such as concentration, pressure, and temperature.

Digestion (Paachan) Biochemical decomposition of organic matter. When digestion of sewage occurs, it results in partial gasification and thus removal of some of the pollutants present in it. In solid-waste conversion, a unit in which bacterial action is induced and accelerated in order to break down organic matter and establish the proper carbon to nitrogen ratio.

Dike (Tatbandh or Baandh) An embankment or ridge of either natural or man-made materials used to prevent the movement of liquids, sludges, solids, or other material.

Dioxin (Dioxin) A group of substances which contain dioxin as one of its constituents. It is a carcinogen, teratogen and a mutagen. Dioxin is so poisonous that one drop in 10,000 gallons of water makes it a dangerous concentration. They cause severe weight loss, liver problems, kidney problems, birth defects and death. The most well known dioxin is Agent Orange used widely in the Vietnam War. Dioxin is formed during manufacture of chemicals such as PVC, certain types of wood preserving, oil refining, metal smelting and incineration lead to dioxin emission. One dioxin is TCDD or 2,3,7,8 tetrachlorodibenzo-paradioxin.

Director (Nideshak) Under The Water Act, in relation to a firm, 'Director' means a partner in the firm.

Discharge, New (Naya Nikas) Under The Water Act, 'new discharge' means a discharge which is not, as respect to the nature and composition, temperature, volume, and rate of discharge of the effluent substantially a continuation of a discharge made within the preceding twelve months (whether by the same or different outlet). A discharge which is in other respects a continuation of previous discharge made as aforesaid shall not be deemed to be a new discharge by reason of any reduction of the temperature or volume or rate of discharge of the effluent as compared with the previous discharge.

Discharge of Hazardous Waste (Khatarnak Upashisht Ka Nikas) The accidental or intentional spilling, leaking, pumping, pouring, emitting, or dumping of hazardous waste into or on any land or water.

Disease Vector (Rog Vahak) Rodents, flies, and mosquitoes capable of transmitting disease to humans.

Disinfectant (Keetanu Nashak) Substance capable of killing or inactivating pathogenic microorganisms. Substances added to water to disinfect the same include chlorine, ozone, and chloramines.

Dispersants (Chitarana) Chemical agents that emulsify, disperse, or solubilize oil into the water column. Also promotes the surface spreading of oil slicks to facilitate dispersal of the oil into the water column.

Disposal Well (Niptan Kuan or Samapan Kuan) When fluid waste is disposed of through pumping it underground through a well. This is done to prevent surface contamination.

Disposal facility (Nipatan Vyavastha Kendra) A facility or part of a facility at which hazardous waste is intentionally placed into or on any land or water and at which waste will remain after closure.

Dissolved Oxygen (Vighatit Pran Vayu) The amount of oxygen which is dissolved in water, or the oxygen freely available in water, vital to fish and other aquatic life and for the prevention of odors. DO levels are considered a most important indicator of a water body's ability to support desirable aquatic life. Secondary and advanced waste treatment are generally designed to ensure adequate DO in waste-receiving waters. Thus it is a measure of the ability of water to support aquatic life. Dissolved oxygen is essential for the biochemical oxidation of ammonia to nitrate in natural water. When sewage or any other pollutant is discharged into water, it may result in reduction of oxygen in water. Insufficient amount of oxygen in water may result in increased microbial activity and thus release of methane, sulphur dioxide into the atmosphere.

Distillation (Aasavan) Process that involves evaporation and recondensing the liquid as a purified liquid. The condensed vapours are the pure product and the residue may be discarded as it will contain most of the impurities. Used in separation of various fraction of gasoline, such as petrol, and kerosene from crude petroleum oil drilled from ground. Also used to remove salt from seawater.

DNA (DNA) See Deoxyribonucleic acid.

Doffing (Utaarna) The process of taking off protective clothing.

Domestic effluent (Gharelu Nissari or Gharelu Apagami Dhara) Treated domestic sanitary sewage and treated laundry wastewater.

Dose (Maatraa or Khuraak) Quantity of a substance absorbed in a part of the body or in an individual.

Dosimeter (Maatraa Maapi) An instrument for measuring and registering the total accumulated dose of (or exposure to) ionization radiation. There are many types of dosimeters such as thermoluminescent, finger ring, and electronic among others.

Dosimetry (Maatraa Miti) The theory and application of the principles and techniques involved in the measurement and recording of radiation doses and dose rates.

Drag Coefficient (Karshan Gunank) A measure of the 'slipperiness' of a vehicle to air resistance. Designing a vehicle with a small drag coefficient makes it more streamlined, reduces its aerodynamic drag, especially at high speeds, and improves its fuel efficiency.

Drainage Basin (Apavaah Kshetra or Jal Nikaas Droni) A geographical region drained by a river or stream. The area of land from which a stream of river or pond gets its water.

Drainfield (Apavaah Kshetra) Area into which water from a wastewater treatment plant or a septic system discharges its water.

Drawdown (Jalaavatalan) Lowering of the water table due to withdrawal of groundwater from a well. With increase in population, many towns are pumping water from the underground water tables thus the level of water in them is going down.

Dredging (Tala Maarjan) When soil is removed by digging or scooping from the bottom of a body of water such as ponds, lakes, and rivers. Process mostly used to deepen the level of water for passage of ships in harbours.

Drill Cuttings (Vedhan Katàran) Rock chips cut by a bit in the process of well drilling and removed from the hole in the drilling mud in rotary drilling or by the bailer in cable-tool drilling. Drill cuttings collected at closely spaced intervals provide a record of the strata penetrated.

Drilling Mud (Vedhan Pank or Kichad) A carefully formulated material of heavy suspension, usually in water but sometimes in oil. Generally used in rotary drilling to drill deep wells. Commonly consists of bentonitic clays, chemical additives, and weighting materials such as barite. The mud is used to lubricate and cool the bit, to carry the cuttings up from the bottom, and to prevent blowouts and cave-ins.

Drip Irrigation (Tapkan Sinchai or Boondiya Sinchai) Water is supplied directly to the roots of the plants in small and limited quantities. This is common in areas which lack water such as deserts.

Dry Ice (Thos Carbon dioxide) Solid carbon dioxide used for cooling purposes.

Duckweed (Kasapat) A type of free-floating aquatic plant that has flowers. Grow very rapidly in shallow water such as a pond.

Duff (Aalepan or Duff) Partially decayed organic matter fallen from trees and so found around them.

Dump (Kshepan Bhoomi) Indiscriminate and unauthorised dumping of solid waste or garbage. Historically it is the practice of finding an open hollow space and dump solid waste to bring it to level with surrounding areas. This leads to contamination of ground water and the environment.

Dye Penetrant Testing (Rang Vedhan Parikshan) A nondestructive method for finding discontinuities that are open to the surface of the metal. A dye is applied to the surface of metal and the excess is rinsed off. Dye that penetrates surface discontinuities will not be rinsed away thus marking these discontinuities.

Dyspnea (Kashta Swaas) Difficulty in breathing, shortness of breath.

E

E-coli (E-coli) Technical name is Escherechia coli. It is an anaerobic bacteria. Presence in water is used as an indication of the presence of pollutants.

Earth (Prithvi or Bhoo or Bhoomi) Estimated to be about four and half billion years old, the fifth of the nine largest planet in the solar system. Two-thirds of its surface is occupied by salty ocean water. Equatorial radius is 6378 kilometres and circumference is 40,075 km.

Earth Day (Bhoo Divas) First started in 1970, it is celebrated in late April. It is to preserve the Earth as we know and to teach people how to respect the nature that we live in so that future generations can enjoy earth as we do today. However, World Environment Day is observed on June 5.

Eastern Ghats (Purvi Ghat) Along the eastern coastal plains of India, they stretch from Orissa through Andhra Pradesh to join the Western Ghats in Tamil Nadu at Doddabetta, touching the Bay of Bengal in some places. The lower slopes of the Bastar hills in Madhya Pradesh too are, in a sense, part of this ecosystem. The Ghats are from zero to 2,000 metres above sea level. Their geomorphology is varied and typical of pre-Cambrian formation and evolution in the hills. Nearer the coasts there are the Quatenary formations too. The Charnockite and Khondalite series run through from Orissa upto the Cuddapah-Kurnool system and the former dominate the southern region of Andhra Pradesh and Tamil Nadu. The northern section starts in Orissa's Garjhat hills. The southern region ends in the South Arcot district of Tamil Nadu. Forest types include tropical dry deciduous which are teak bearing, moist deciduoushave bearing sal trees, evergreen, scrub and savannah. Red Sanders forests, as well as the southern and northern mixed dry deciduous forests. There are 2,000 flowering plants or angiosperm and a few gymnosperms found on the ghats. Animals include the tiger, elephant, and gaur, sambar and black buck. More than 33 tribal communities like Samanthas, Bagathas, Jathapus, Kondadoras, Savaras, Yanadies reside in the area. Some of the most famous temples include Puri Jagannath (Orissa), Simhachalam Narasimha, Annavaram Satyanarayana, Tirupati Balaji (Andhra Pradesh), Tiruttani Subramanya, Sholingur Narasimha, Tiruvannamalai Arunachala and the Tiruchi Rockfort Ganapati (Tamil Nadu).

Ecesis When a species not found in an area makes that place its permanent home and starts its own reproducing cycle there successfully.

Ecological Barrier (Paaristhitik Vyavadhan or Baadhaa) A barrier, mostly manmade, which prohibits further movement of a pollutant to that area. The barrier could be in the form of a wall, road, or a fence.

Ecological Indicator (Paaristhitik Suchak) A characteristic of an ecosystem that is related to, or derived from, a measure of biotic or abiotic variable, that can provide quantitative information on ecological structure and function. An indicator can contribute to a measure of integrity and sustainability.

Ecological Integrity A living system exhibits integrity if, when subjected to disturbance, it sustains and organizes self-correcting ability to recover toward a biomass end-state that is normal for that system. End-states other than the pristine or naturally whole may be accepted as Anormal and good.

Ecology (Paaristhitik Vigyan) Made up of Greek words, 'oikos' meaning 'household' and 'logy' meaning 'study of'. The total study of living beings or organisms and effect on the surroundings. Also the interaction or the dependency between organisms and their setting and effects on each other.

EC_{50} (EC50) Concentration of a chemical in water that is calculated to induce shell deposition 50 percent less than that of the controls in a test batch of organisms during continuous exposure within a particular exposure period.

Ecological Engineering (Paaristhitiki Abhiyantriki) Study of the environment. Includes ecology, environment, bioengineering, natural habitat and the human environment.

ECOMARK (Paaristhik Chinha) Under the Scheme on Labelling of Environment

Friendly Products, a scheme to provide accreditation and labelling for household and other consumer products which meet certain environmental criteria along with quality requirements of the Indian Standards for that product. The label shall be ECOMARK. Any product which is made, used or disposed of in a way that significantly reduces the harm it would otherwise cause the environment could be considered as Environment Friendly Product. As per the Government directive passed on February 20, 1991, the objectives of the scheme are as follows:

i. To provide an incentive for manufactureres and importers to reduce adverse environmental impact of products;
ii. To reward genuine initiatives by companies to reduce adverse environmental impact of their products
iii. To assist consumers to become environmentally responsible in their daily lives by providing information to take account of environmental factors in their purchase decisions;
iv. To encourage citizens to purchase products which have less harmful environmental impacts; and
v. Ultimately to improve the quality of the environment and to encourage the sustainable management of resources.

There are three stages leading to the award of the "ECOMARK". 16 product categories have been developed. Bureau of Indian Standards (BIS) assesses and certifies products according to criteria set by the Technical Committee. BIS also handles the licensing of logo, enforcement rules, and collection of fees. BIS charges fees for testing and licensing of awards. The program allows for a 60-day public review period of draft criteria for product categories.

Ecosphere (Asahaaya Shwasan Mandal) Earth which contains life on land, in surface waters, and in the air.

Ecosystems (Paaristhitik Tantra or Paritantra) A specific and self-contained area in which all species, plants and animals interact with each other and are interdependent upon each other as well as the environment in which they live. The system is complete in itself. They are interdependent upon each other in that confined area.

Ecotone (Ecotone or Sankramika) A transition zone between two or more distinct ecosystems. It is the boundary between two ecosystems. The separation could be due to water or other boundaries.

Ecotoxicity The toxic effects on environmental organisms other than humans.

ED_{50} (ED50) The dose of a particular substance that, administered to all animals in a test, elicits an observable and specific response in 50% of the animal population.

Effluent (Apagaami Dhaaraa) Waste or a pollutant, in any form and from any source discharged into the environment through a pipe or a stack is an effluent. Generally, effluent has pollutants, returned flow from confined sites, and may be a discharge of heat. Source could be smokestacks of industries, sewage from wastewater treatment plants, discharges from chemical plants or from landfill. Limits imposed by The Water Act of 1974 for small-scale industries are as follows:

Sl. No.	Parameters	Concen. Not to Exceed
1.	Total Concn. Of Mercury (Hg) In final (Combined effluent)	0.01 mg/l
2.	pH	5.5-9.0
3.	Suspended Solids	250 mg/l
4.	Biochemical Oxygen Demand	150 mg/l
5.	Temperature	Shall not exceed 5 deg. C above the ambient temp. of the receiving body.
6.	Free available Chlorine	0.5 mg/l
7.	Oil and Grease	10 mg/l
8.	Copper (Total)	3.0 mg/l
9.	Iron (Total)	3.0 mg/l
10.	Zinc	5.0 mg/l
11.	Chromium (Total)	2.0 mg/l
12.	Phosphate (As P)	5.0 mg/l
13.	Bio-assay Test	90% of test animals after 96 hours with 1:8 dilution.
14.	Sulphide (as S)	2.0 mg/l
15.	Phenolic Compounds (as C6H5OH)	5.0 mg/l
16.	HexavalentChromium (as Cr)	0.1 mg/l
17.	Nickel (as Ni)	3.0 mg/l
18.	Cadmium (Cd)	2.0 mg/l
19.	Chloride (as Cl)	9000 mg/l
20.	Sulphate (as SO4)	1000 mg/l
21.	Cynides (as CN)	0.2 mg/l
22.	Ammoniacal Nitrogen (as N)	50 mg/l
23.	Lead (as Pb)	0.01 mg/l
24.	Total Metal	10.0 mg/l

Eight-Hour Time Weighted Average (Aath Ghante Ausatan) Cumulative effect of a substance when a person is exposed continuously for an 8-hour work day.

Electrical Energy (Vaidyut Urja) A form of energy produced by the flow of electrons. Produced from dams built on water, steam, and nuclear power plants.

Electrocoating (Vidyut Tah or Vidyut Aavaran) Deposition through the use of electricity of a metallic or nonmetallic coating onto the surface of any item.

Electrode (Vidyut Dagra) A conductor which is used to establish electrical contact with a nonmetallic part of a circuit.

Electrodeposition (Vidyut Dharohar) Precipitation of a material on an electrode when electricity is passed through the solution. The thickness of the coating can be controlled in this process. The material on which the coating is required is suspended in the solution.

Electrodialysis (Vidyut Apohan) When electricity is used to remove dissolved material from a liquid. The substances must be able to ionize in the solution. Used to purify or desalinate water. In medicine, a method to purify blood. Similar to an electrostatic precipitator.

Electroless Plating (Vidyutheen Parat or Aavaran) When a coating of material is deposited from an autocatalytic plating solution without application of electrical current. Due to a chemical reduction process.

Electrolysis (Vidyut Apaghatan) When an electric current is passed to assist in the decomposition of water. The process is controlled by the amount of the electricity passage. Hydrogen is produced from water by this way.

Electrolyte (Vidyut Apaghatya) Any substance which dissolves in a solvent and can conduct electricity. When one material ionizes in liquid. Sulphuric acid and Sodium Chloride are electrolytes as they ionize in a solution.

Electromagnetic field (Vidyut Chumbakiya Kshetra) Combined electrical and magnetic field given out by electric appliances such as power lines.

Electromagnetic Spectrum (Vidyut Chumbakiya Varna Kram) Diverse configuration of radiation energy arranged either by wavelength or by frequency.

Electrons (Vidyudanu) The smallest existing particle with a negative electric charge which revolve around the atomic nucleus. An electron is made up of three basic types of particles. The positive electron is called a Proton and a negative electron is called a nectron. The number of electrons in an atom of any element is the same as the number of protons in the nucleus. Electrons are arranged in from 1 to 7 shells around the nucleus. The outer shells may not always be filled. Electrons may be removed from the atoms of many elements by heat, light, or electric energy. Mass 9.1x10-28 gram.

Electron Volt (EV) (Vidyudanu Volt) It is an extremely small amount of energy imparted to an electron when it is moved through a potential difference of one volt. It is equivalent to 1.6 X 10-12 ergs.

Electroplating (Vidyut Se Mulamma Chadana or Vidyut Lepan or Vidyut Parat) The process of applying a thin layer of one material to any surface. The substance that is to be coated on is generally immersed in a bath or solution and through use of electric current, the other material is applied as a coating. The material that needs to be coated is generally a cathode. Anode must be an electric conductor.

Electro Refining (Vidyut Parimarjan or Vidyut Shodhan) Purifying metals by electrolysis using an impure metal as the anode.

Electrostatic Precipitator (Sthir Vaidyut Avakshepitra) By the induction of a generally negative electric charge, the particulate matter from an industrial effluent air stream is removed or made to stick onto a metal plate. The particulate matter is then removed from the plates by either gravity or by any mechanical means. They can be solid or liquid particles.

Element (Ansh or Tatva or Mul Tatva) The smallest unit of an element is an atom. All matter is composed of the element. All atoms have same properties. Hydrogen, nitrogen, oxygen, copper are some examples of naturally occurring elements. Elements can be separated into isotopes. Elements beyond uranium are artificially created. Appendix B lists names and atomic numbers of elements.

ELF (ELF) Extremely low frequency electromagnetic wave less than 300 hertz. Distributed by distribution lines, substations, and transmission lines. Routine occupational exposures should not exceed 25kV/m.

Embryo (Bhruna) An early stage of the development of the unborn offspring in which cell differentiation proceeds rapidly along with the formation of the manor organs. Young sporophytic plant before the start of germination.

Embryotoxic (Bhruna Vaishic) The harmful effects of a chemical or a substance on a developing embryo. The substance is poisonous to a developing fetus.

Emergency Plan (Aapat Kaalin Yojana or Vyavastha) An occupier who is generating hazardous waste as per Schedule of Hazardous Wastes (Management and Handling) Rules, 1989 should draw an emergency plan for on-site storage and transportation of his waste. The plan must list names, addresses, and phone numbers (office and home) of all persons responsible for acting as emergency coordinator and this list must be kept up to date. The plan must include a list of all emergency equipment such as fire extinguishing systems, spill control equipment, communications, alarm systems, and decontamination equipment which are required and available. This plan must be approved by the regulatory authorities. See also Spill Prevention Control Plan.

Emission (Utsarjan) The Air Act defines 'Emission' to mean any solid or liquid or gaseous substance coming out of any chimney, duct or flue or any other outlet and released into the atmosphere. It also includes auto emissions.

Emission Rate (Utsarjan Dar) Amount of pollutant released by a source in a specific amount of time.

Emulsion (Mishran) When a suspended material and the material it is suspended in are both liquids, they are in colloidal suspension. The particle size of the dispersed medium is very small. It is also the stable dispersion of two immiscible liquids in the presence of an emulsifying agent. There are two types of emulsifiers. They are proteins or carbohydrate polymers and long-chain alcohols and fatty acids.

Encapsulation (Parisamputan or Samputikaran) The sealing of a substance with the container in place so that the contents are not degraded or disturbed in any way. The sealing container can be made of steel, plastic or other suitable material of sufficient thickness and strength to resist physical damage that may be inflicted on the sealed substance from any source. Encapsulation also means containing of a material in its place by means of either water or other means so that material is not released into the atmosphere.

Endangered Species (Sankataapanna Jeeva Jaati) Animals or plants that are at risk of extinction in a very finite time because of habitat loss, food loss, or threatening toxics or pollutants.

Endothermic Reaction (Ushmaashoshi Abhikriya) When additional energy is essential for a reaction to take place or when the system takes heat or any form of energy to occur. It can also be defined as when kinetic energy is transferred into mass energy.

Energy (Urja) The ability to do work. Chemical, mechanical, nuclear are among the various forms of energy. Energy resources include nuclear power, hydroelectric power, wind power, coal, oil, shale. In Hindi, *Oj* or *Urja*.

Energy Conversion (Urja Roopantaran) Changing of one form of energy into another. It may mean generation of electrical energy from water through dams built on rivers and falls.

Energy Efficiency (Urja Dakshta or Kshamata) The amount of energy which is used for any purpose.

Engineered Barriers (Abhiyantriki Baandha) Features of a disposal site constructed of materials designed to isolate waste from the environment and comply with applicable regulations.

Enriched Uranium (Samradhitta Uranium) A result of the process of enrichment when uranium has more uranium-235 than natural uranium.

Entropy (Utkram Maap) The second law of thermodynamics is also called the law of entropy. It states that all systems move from order to disorder. A kind of energy that cannot be converted to another form. The entropy of the world is always increasing.

Environment (Paryavaran) Natural environment includes water, air, and land and the inter-relationship that exists among and between water, air and land, human beings, other living creatures, plant, micro-organisms, and property. Though this excludes economic and other types of environment, economic impacts are very severe. The Tata Energy Research Institute (TERI), in its study GREEN India in 1997, stated that the availability of fresh water in India has declined by 75%. The study also concluded that due to environmental degradation, 10% of national income eroded. It is feared that India is losing at least 10% of its national income due to environmental degradation. the area covered by soil degradation has increased by nearly 600 lakh hectares; and though the area covered by forest has increased by 4%, half of it is covered by low crown-density or degraded forests. In Hindi, *Paryavaran.*

Environment (Protection) Act of 1986 (Paryavaran Adhiniyam) Enacted to provide for the protection and improvement of environment and for matter connected there with. Empowers the government to take all such measures necessary for the purpose of protecting and improving the quality of the environment and preventing, controlling and abating environmental pollution. This Act specified limits on the release of individual hazardous and toxic substances, physical height of the stack by the industry such as sugar industry, thermal power plants, and also limits of emissions from vehicles. Guidelines to set up an industry have been specified and are in Appendix C.

Environmental Amendment-42nd To Indian Constitution (Bharatiya Samvidhan

Mein 42 Van Paryavaraniya Sanshodhan) The 42nd amendment to the constitution says, 'The State shall endeavour to protect and improve the environment and safeguard the forests and wildlife in the country'.

Environment Friendly Product (Paryavaran Anukul Utpad) See ECOMARK.

Environmental Impact Assessment (EIA) (Paryavaran Par Pratighat) A very useful tool to make a decision on a proposed major project. This document analyses both positive and negative impacts of the proposed action. This consists in establishing quantitative values for selected parameters which indicate the quality of the environment before, during, and after the proposed action. EIA serve as a valuable tool for identification, prediction, and evaluation of impacts arising out of proposed Hazardous Waste Management Program which include identification, assessment, and remediation of abandoned hazardous waste sites. It should cover scoping, assessment of baseline status, identification, prediction, and evaluation of impacts on major components of environment.

Environmental Impact Statement (Paryavaraniya Sanghat Ka Kathan) A report that documents the information required to evaluate the environmental impact of a project.

Environmental Pollutant (Paryavaran Pradushak) Any solid, liquid or gaseous substance present in such concentration as may be, or tend to be, injurious to environment.

Environmental Pollution (Paryavaraniya Pradushan) Any pollutant or undesired substance introduced by humans, generally in small amounts into the environment.

Environmental Restoration (Vatavaran Ka Punarsthaapan) Cleanup and restoration of a site previously contaminated from either production or accidental releases or disposal activities to its original condition. It may involve activities such as stabilizing contaminated soil, treatment of ground water, decommissioning of process buildings, removal of drums, cleanup of sludge.

Environmental Sink (Paryavaraniya Kund) Holding reservoir of a particular element, chemical or compound. Trees and oceans are sinks for carbon for the universe.

Environmentalists (Paryavaran Vaadi) Activists who work to preserve the environment from further deterioration.

Enzymes (Kinvak or Prakinva) Complex proteins which are specific to a particular reaction. Formed in living cells and are essential to many biochemical processes.

Epidemiology (Jaan Padik Rog Vigyan) It is the study of medical science dealing with the incidence, distribution, and control of disease in a population. Often done by comparing two groups of people who are alike in all respect, except for one, such as exposure to a chemical or the presence of a health effect. The investigators try to determine if any factor is associated with the health effect.

Epiliminon (Adhisar) The warm, relatively less dense top layer of water in a stratified lake. Mixing will occur either through the movement of winds or due to current in water itself. This is the area of most activity.

Epiphytes (Adhipadap) Plants that grow on other plants, usually trees, but are not parasitic.

Equivalent (Tulya or Samakaksha or Samaan) A measure of the quantity of an acid or base. One equivalent of a substance is the amount that either produces or combines with one gram of hydrogen ions. For example, one equivalent of acid sulphate is 49 grams; one equivalent of carbonate is 30 grams. One equivalent of a base will exactly neutralise one equivalent of acid.

Erosion (Apardan or Bhooksharan) The carrying away of rocks and soil particles and the transportation of the same through natural means such as water or air. Natural erosion is slow and takes place over a very long periods of time. Size of soil or rock moving due to natural means is very small. On the other hand, if the process is speeded by human actions such as extension of farming, road building, or logging operation, then the partical size may be larger.

Erythrocyte (Raktanu) Also known as a red blood cell. A type of blood cell that contains a nucleus in vertebrates and has a haemoglobin the the cytoplasm.

Escherechia Coli (E-coli) See E-coli.

Ester (Ester) Reaction between an acid and an alcohol results in an ester organic compound. Most common esters are polyesters, used to make fabrics and plastics.

Estuary (Velasangam or Muhana or Nadi Mukh) Coastal area that is adjacent to the sea and so its level will vary as per the ocean waves. It is often a river mouth, which is marsh like and brackish and may be supporting rich supplies of life. Rich in nutrients and play a vital role in maintaining sea as well as birds and wild life. Salt content of the ocean water is diluted by fresh water from inland sources such as nearby or adjacent rivers.

Etching (Niksharan or Rasayanik Utkiran) Chemical solution bath or rinse designed to produce a desired rough surface finish on a metal.

Ethanol or Ethyl Alcohol (Ethyl Alcohol) A clear, colourless, highly flammable liquid with a strong odour and bitter taste. It is highly intoxicating. Ethanol can be produced from corn also when it can be blended with motor fuel. It may cause mutations while high concentrations may damage the fetus. It also causes headache, nausea, and can irritate the eyes, nose, mouth and throat, may damage the liver and affect the nervous system. It is very widely used as a solvent, in resins, fats, fatty acids, cosmetics.

Ethylene (Ethylene) Nontoxic, colourless, highly flammable gas with a sweet odour. Used in welding and in manufacture of plastics. Formula C_2H_4.

Eutrophic Lakes (Suposhi Jheel) Shallow, murky bodies of water with concentrations of plant nutrients causing excessive production of algae.

Eutrophication (Suposhan) Process occurs when phosphorous or phosphates, nitrogen or nitrates, or organic nutrients such as sewage are added to a river or a lake, causing an algae bloom. Results in the lake becoming low in oxygen. Slowly, the lake dries out. This process also takes place if human excreta is disposed into the lake in large quantities. When the lake or pond is at its last stages, large quantities of algae bloom is noticed on the surface water. May also be caused due to rain water runoff from agricultural lands where fertilizers had been added to the soil for irrigation purposes and thus supplying unwanted nutrients to the lake. Because of the proliferation of algae, the amount of dissolved oxygen drops resulting in the death of fish and other aquatic life present in the body of water.

Evaporation (Vashpan or Vashpikaran) When a liquid starts to vapourise. The rate depends on the temperature and pressure of the liquid at its surface. Water starts to evaporate at 100 degrees centigrade at normal pressure.

Evapotranspiration (Vashpotsarjan) Discharge or loss of water from the earth's surface to the atmosphere by evaporation from lakes, streams, and soil surfaces, and by transpiration from plants.

Exclusion Zone (Apavarjit Kshetra) The area at a hazardous waste site where the actual sampling or handling of potentially hazardous materials occurs, and the potential for contact with contamination is greatest. The exclusion zone excludes all but essential personnel from entry. Prohibitions in the exclusion zone include individuals without the required health and safety training and appropriate Personal Protective Equipment (PPE).

Exfiltration Movement of air out of a building through cracks and interstices in the building.

Exosphere (Bahir Mandal) The space that is considered outside of the earth's atmosphere, over 1,000 kilometres away.

Exothermic Reaction (Ushmakshepi Abhikriya) During a chemical reaction, heat is released into the atmosphere. Also called heat of reaction. Burning of wood is an exothermic reaction.

Explosives (Visphotak) Chemicals which may explode under the effect of flame, heat or photo-chemical conditions or which are more sensitive to shocks or friction than dinitrobenzene. Explosives produce a substantial instantaneous release of gas and heat spontaneously or by contact with sparks or flame.

Exposure (Prabhavan) Human contact with a physical, chemical, or biological agent or substance through dermal adsorption, inhalation, or ingestion.

Exposure Concentration (Hazard Quotient) Level shown to cause ecological effect. If the calculated hazard quotient is greater than or equal to one, there is a strong potential for adverse ecological effects.

Exposure Point (Prabhavan Bindu) A location of potential contact between a receptor and a chemical or physical agent.

F

Fabric Filter (Kapde Ki Chhanni) Use of fabric as a filtering medium. Generally to catch dust particles from stack gases, filter press, or rotary vacuum filters in industries.

Facility (Kshetra or Karkhana) The hazardous Wastes (Management and Handling) Rules of 1989 defines it as any location wherein the processes, incidental to the waste generation collection, reception, treatment, storage and disposal are carried out.

Facultative Bacteria (Vikalpi Jeevanu) Bacteria that can survive in the presence and even in the absence of oxygen.

Fallout (Avapat) Release of radiation particles due to a nuclear explosion. Special forms of fallout include 'Dry Fallout', 'Rain Out', or 'Snow Out'.

Fallow (Parati Bhoomi) Farmland not planted for a season or similar time so that the soil can replenish nutrients taken out by previous crops.

Fathometer (Gaharai Maapak Yantra) An instrument to measure the depth of water in a well. The device utilises high frequency sound waves generated by a small energy source. The sound waves are beamed toward water which reflect it back. The time for the wave to travel and return are converted to a distance to the water table.

Fauna (Jeev Jantu) Animals living in any given area at any time and in harmony. The area has to be defined. Mammal fauna comprises 372 species, with 63% found in

Assam. India's 1,228 bird species represent about 13% of the world's total and reptilian and amphibian fauna include 446 and 204 species respectively, with concentrations in the Western Ghats. Faunal endemism varies substantially from 3.5% in mammals and 14% in birds to 32% in reptiles and 62% in amphibians. Among the larger animals, 173 species of animals , 101 of birds, 15 of reptiles, 3 of amphibians and 2 of fish are considered endangered. Mammal fauna comprises 372 species, with 63% found in Assam. There are 269 species of birds found in Mumbai alone.

Feasibility Study (Sambhavyata Adhyayan) A study conducted by the primary organisation to develop and evaluate options for remedial action. It emphasises data analysis, implementability of alternatives, and cost analyses, as well as compliance with mandates to protect human health and the environment as prescribed by regulatory standards and laws. Generally, this study is performed concurrently with the remedial investigation (RI), using data gathered during the remedial investigation. The RI data are used to define the objectives of the response action, to develop remedial action alternatives, and to undertake an initial screening and detailed analysis of the alternatives.

Fecal Coliforms (Mal Coliform) Water contains many organisms which are harmless. However some other organisms may be pathogens. Some of the organisms associated with the intestines of warm-blooded animals that are commonly used to indicate the presence of fecal material and the potential presence of organisms capable of causing human disease. Presence of fecal coliform bacteria in water is indicative of the presence of recent discharge of human or animal feces and possible contamination by pathogens.

Feedback Loop (Punarniveshan Prakriya) Process or chemical reaction that serves to increase itself. For example, if the earth is warmed too much, solar ice will melt, and release lock-up frozen carbon. The released carbon increases the greenhouse effect, and thus the earth's temperature, melting more ice, and thus releasing more carbon.

Feedlot (Bharan Kshetra) An enclosed or fenced area where animals are kept and fed. As animals are confined to an area for their feed, their excrement can thus be controlled. This is one way of controlling manure runoff or discharge into the environment.

Feldspar One of the most common type of mineral and may form up to 60% of the earth's crust. A mineral composed primarily of aluminium, silica, and any of the metallic elements such as sodium, potassium, or calcium. Slightly softer than quartz, hardness on the MOHS scale is 6.0.

Feral Animal (Vanya Pashu) An animal that was once domestic but is now considered a wild animal.

Fermentation (Kinvan) Biological breakdown of a substance induced by a living organism, yeast, or fungi. Alcoholic beverages, curd and buttermilk are made due to fermentation.

Fertility Rate (Prajanan Dar) Average number of children that women bear in their lifetime.

Fertilizer (Khaad or Urvarak) Substance that has nutrients necessary for plant and animal growth. The substance could be man-made or naturally occurring. Generally, a fertilizer may contain nitrogen, phosphorous, potassium, called NPK mixture. Plants need 16 elements for their growth. Oxygen, hydrogen, and carbon are available to the plants in abundance. But other elements may become necessary and those are supplied in the form of fertilizers.

Fetotoxic (Garbhadhan or Bhrun ke Liye Vishaila) Poisonous to a developing fetus.

Fiber (Resha or Tantu) Cotton and timber produce fiber which is used in production of clothing and paper. The main characteristic of a fiber is that the ratio between its length and to the diameter is very large. Natural fibers from wood are used to make paper.

Fibrous Root System (Reshiya Jada Tantra) A plant which has a thick mat as a root, which can hold on to soil and thus control movement of soil and water. Grass has strong fibrous root system. Used to control runoff.

Field Duplicate (Sama Roopiya Kshetra or Mrida) A second specimen collected as near as possible to one already included in the sample. In channel sediment sampling, field duplicates come from the same sediment catchment as another specimen.

Field Sampling Plan (Kshetriya Pratidarsh Yojna) (See Sampling and Analysis Plan)

Filtration (Chhanane Ki Kriya or Nisyandan) Removal of particles from air or water by means of passing the substance through a porous media or filter that screens out the particles. The porous media or filter is of a specific size to remove the required particulate matter. The filter media could be sand, synthetic material or fabric.

Filtration, Biological (Jaivik Nisyandan) Instead of a solid or synthetic material, the filter media in this case is a biological film which absorbs fine colloidal particles. Biochemical products are released in this type of filtration.

Firn (Purani Barf or Kan Him) Old and compacted snow which has not become glacier ice. If that snow survives a few more seasons, then it will become ice.

Fissile (Vikhandya) Capable of being split by interaction with a low-energy neutron. The most common fissile isotopes are Uranium-235 and Plutonium-239.

Fissile Material (Vikhandiya Padaarth) A specific set of nuclear materials, such as Uranium-235 and Plutonium-239, that may be used in making a nuclear explosive for a weapon. Does not include fissile materials present in spent nuclear fuel or irradiating targets from reactors.

Fissile Waste (Vikhandiya Apashesh) Waste that contains nuclides that can undergo nuclear fission.

Fission (Vikhandan) The process whereby the nucleus of a particular heavy element splits into two nuclei of lighter elements of equal parts, with the release of substantial amounts of energy. When a neutron strikes the nucleus of a Uranium-235 atom causing it to split apart, releasing energy as heat, fission products and two or more neutrons. This causes additional Uranium-235 nuclei to fission. Eventually, when enough nuclei are split and enough neutrons are released, the reaction perpetuates itself in a chain reaction. One ton of nuclear fuel can provide about 100,000 times more electric power than that provided by one ton of coal. Nuclear fission is used to generate electric power.

Fission Products (Vikhandan Utpad) The atoms formed when Uranium is split in a nuclear reactor. Fission products are usually radioactive.

Flammability (Jwalan Sheelataa) Any substance capable of causing fire through friction, absorption or moisture or spontaneous chemical changes that when ignited, it burns. Gives off intense heat and will produce smoke. Flash point of such chemical is either less than 600 C or 1400 F. Flammable liquids are petroleum products. They will ignite if they come in contact with other products such as oil or grease.

Flammable Chemicals (Jwalansheel Rasayan) Chemicals which are in the gaseous state at normal pressure and mixed with air become flammable. The boiling point of such chemicals at normal pressure is 20 degrees C or below. Highly flammable liquids are those chemicals whose flash point is lower than 23 degrees C and their boiling point at normal pressure is above 20 degrees C. Flammable liquids are those chemicals which have a flash point lower than 65 degrees C and they remain liquids under pressure. Particular processing conditions, such as high pressure and high temperature, may create major accident hazards.

Flammable Liquid (Jwalansheel Drav) A liquid whose flash point is less than 1000F.

Flammable Solid (Jwalansheel Thos) A solid capable of instantaneous combustion in an open atmosphere. Ignition point is very low. Care needs to be taken when stored in the open.

Flash Point (Jwalan Ank or Jwalan Bindu) Lowest temperature at which a liquid gives off enough vapour to ignite in the presence of an ignition source at the surface of the liquid.

Flat Water (Thahara Hua Pani or Gati Heen Jal) A body of water which is not in motion or is very still all the time. Water in a confined pond is an example.

Floatation (Plavan) A process of allowing solids to float on a surface.

Floating Boom (Plavan Pat) Barrier of certain type of equipment that is used to contain a floating nonmiscible substance spill on the surface of water.

Flocculation (Urnan) A mixing process that causes particles to collide and enhance agglomeration or collection of smaller floc particles into larger, more easily settleable particles. Basically a joining of small particles forming clumps. Occurs naturally through biological or chemical action in lakes and rivers and is used in water purification. The process may be enhanced by gentle stirring or by any mechanical means. As the joining of particles is very loose, they can also be separated easily by stirring.

Floe (Barf Ki Tairti Chaadar or Him Vaah) A mass of ice not attached to any land surface. Their thickness may be small. Its width may be just a few metres.

Flood Plain (Jal Plaavit Maidan) Lowlands that are susceptible to floods and have one percent (called 100-year flood plain) or greater chance of recurring in any given year. From areas where electricity could be produced, dams are constructed to control floods in many areas. In other areas, walls or any other structures are constructed to control the flooding of the area. Five hundred year flood plain has the probability of a flood once every 500 years or 0.2% probability.

Flora (Pedha Paudhe or Vanaspati) Plants living in an area at any time. Indian flora comprises about 15,000 flowering plants (6% of the world-wide total), an estimated 33% of which are endemic; roughly 1,500 plant species are threatened. Areas rich in endemism are the North-East, the Western Ghats and the North-Western and Eastern Himalayas: however, the Andaman and Nicobar Island contribute at least 200 endemic species to the endemic flora.

Flue Gas (Dhuan Kaksha) Gases emitted from a process or manufacturing plant through a chimney or a stack. The contents of the gas are generally harmful to the environment and humans. The gas may contain fine particulate matters and sulphur dioxide, nitrogen oxides, carbon dioxide and other pollutant gases also.

Flue Gas Desulphurisation (Dhuan Kaksha Se Gandhak Nikasan) Removal of sulphur dioxide from industrial emissions of flue gas through the sack by employing solvents such as lime stone.

Fluoride (Fluoride) A compound containing fluorine and another element. Substance derived from a naturally mined mineral and added to water to prevent tooth decay. Its particulates are highly toxic and irritant. Excess fluoride causes blue skin, mottled teeth, bone cancer, kidney disease, and fluorosis-a disease that causes soft and deformed bones in infants.

Fluorine (Fluorine) Lightest of the halogens, it is a thick greenish-yellow gas. Has a suffocating odour, highly corrosive and toxic. Compounds containing Fluorine are used to prevent tooth decay, in etching of glass, and refining of fuel for nuclear reactors. Symbol is F. Atomic weight is 19.0.

Fluorosis Ingestion of fluorides which may result in poisoning. This is also a known disease in some of the fruit and vegetable plants stopping their growth.

Fly Ash (Dhuan Kaksha Ki Raakh) Very fine ash produced in a plant and that goes up the chimney with the smoke. They could be dust, soot or any other kind of suspended particles. As the particles are very fine, their diameter is in the range of one to 200 microns. Fly ash is often considered toxic. It may be non-combustible. To control the emission of fly ash, various precipitators or mechanical collection devices are installed.

Focussed Data Validation A technically based analyte-, sample-, and potentially data use-specific process that extends the qualification of data beyond method or contractual compliance and provides a level of confidence that an analyte is present or absent. This validation process may focus on the data needed for a given decision, which can include review of raw analytical data such as chromatograms or mass spectrometer.

Fog (Kohara) When water is suspended in air, fog is formed. Clouds rest at or near the surface of earth thus reducing the visibility. It generally occurs in winter seasons. This phenomena is caused by the heat of the sun reaching the surface of earth during the day but radiating the same heat back in the night. The cooling effect creates fog.

Food Chain (Aahar Shrinkhala) Plants and animals can take up toxic and other pollutants from soil, water, and other food items and thus bioaccumulate them in themselves. With each food chain, the toxic and other pollutants can get concentrated and harm the consumers of food which may include animals as well as humans. This accumulation is more common with very stable chemicals such as PCBs.

Forest (Conservation) Act, 1980 (Van Sanrakshan Adhiniyam) The Act is 'to control diversion of forest land for non-forestry use'.

Forests (Van) They range from evergreen tropical rain forests in the Andaman and Nicobar Islands, the Western Ghats, and the north-eastern states, to dry alpine scrub high in the Himalaya to the north. They contain trees such as Indian rosewood and teak. Clumps of bamboo occur in south-western portion of the country. In Mizoram and Manipur where the rain fall exceeds 2300 mm per annum, there is a heavy cover of forests.

Forest Cover of India (Bharat Ke Vanaachhadit Kshetra) Based on LANDSAT Imagery, 1993, of the 77,008 million hectares of recorded forest, there are 64.0107 million hectares of actual vegetation, 25.0275 million hectares of open vegetation, 38.5576 million hectares of dense vegetation, 41.492 million hectares of reserved forest, 23.308 million hectares of protected forest, 12.208 million hectares of unclassed forest and 0.4256 million hectares of mangrove vegetation. Indian flora comprises about 15,000 flowering plants (6% of the world-wide total), an estimated 33% of which are endemic; roughly 1,500 plant species are threatened. Areas rich in endemism are the North-East, the Western Ghats and the North-Western and Eastern Himalayas: however, the Andaman and Nicobar Island contribute at least 200 endemic species to the endemic flora. India has an area of 75.23 million hectares which are notified as forests. Out of this, 40.61 million hectares are classified as reserved and 21.51 million hectares as protected. Unclassified forest area is spread over 13.11 million hectares. About 19.47% of the total geographic area is under actual forest cover. According to the State of Forest Report, 1993, the forest cover of the country is 6,40,107 sq. km.

Forging (Gadhana) Deforming of generally hot metal with compressive force into desired shapes. Dies are used when a specific shape is required.

Formaldehyde A colourless, strong-smelling gas that strongly promotes smog formation. Can cause irritation of the eyes, lungs, and skin and is a probable human carcinogen. Found in glues, paints, surface coatings. Formula HCHO.

Fossil Fuel (Jeevashma Indhan) A naturally occurring combustible substance formed from remains of ancient plant or animal matter under severe atmospheric conditions.

Requires millions of years for them to become a fuel for human consumption. Presently, the primary energy source for humans. Examples are coal, oil, and natural gas. Shale is a fossil fuel. However, it does not have much use at this time.

Fossil Water (Jeevashma Jal) Water under the ground which has been stored for millions of years in impermeable rocks. When this water is pumped out, it can not be recharged again.

Fraction, Petroleum Oil (Vikhandit Petrol) When crude oil is refined, fraction of various weights is recovered. At the top, lighter molecules come out as petroleum gas. After that, slightly heavier oil in the form of petrol for planes, and then cars. Kerosene is recovered. At the bottom, paraffin, naphtha, and asphalt is removed. The top portion could be considered as the purest form and the bottom will contain many impurities. Almost all fractions have use in almost all types of industries.

Freon Various non-flammable gaseous and liquid fluorinated hydrocarbons used as refrigerants and propellants for aerosols. They are non-corrosive. Many of them contain both chlorine and fluorine.

Fresh Water (Shuddha Jal) Naturally occurring water which has very little salinity and so could be used by humans. They account for only 3 percent of the total water on earth. The other 97 percent being sea water. 80 percent of fresh water is locked up in the ice caps and glaciers. Of the remaining fresh water, 97 percent is held underground water in aquifers. Fresh water is produced from evaporation of sea water and that evaporated water coming down as rain water. The Tata Energy Research Institute (TERI), in its study GREEN India in 1997, stated that the availability of fresh water in India has declined by 75%.

Fresh Water Classification (Shuddha Jal Ka Vargi Karan) Fresh water has been classified into four divisions:

- A-I - Drinking water source without conventional treatment but after disinfection. Point from where the river originates upto first designated notified dam/weir.
- A-II - Drinking water source with conventional treatment followed by disinfection. River stretch below first designated/notified/weir upto A-III/A-IV Class of waters.
- A-III - Fish and Wild life propagation.
- A-IV - Agriculture, industrial cooling and process.

Friable (Churnasheel or Suchurnya) The ease with which a material or substance breaks or crumbles.

Friable Asbestos (Churnasheel Asbestos) Any material that contains more than one percent asbestos and which can be crumbled, pulverized or reduced to powder by hand pressure when the substance is dry.

Frond (Taal Patra) Lemna leaf-like structure.

Frost Heave (Tushar Jal) When water is present in soil and it freezes, the soil moves upwards. It adversely affects soil, rocsk, and pavements.

Fuel (Indhan) A substance which is capable of releasing energy or perform any kind of action, mechanical or heat. Wood for fuel is a major product from Indian forests. Petroleum products, natural gas, coal, wood are some of the forms of energy.

Fuel Assembly In nuclear plants, it is a structure composed of about 240 fuel rods, which contain uranium pellets. Fuel for a nuclear power plant is loaded in the reactor core in the form of fuel assemblies.

Fuel Rods (Indhan Ki Chhadi) In nuclear plants, they are 12 feet to 14 feet long rods that hold fuel pellets.

Fugitive Dust (Kshanajivi Dhul) When a dust, mist or vapour contains a toxic pollutant and are emitted into the environment through a stack.

Fugitive Emissions (Aashulopi Utsarjan) Air pollutants that enter into the atmosphere from sources other than a stack or a chimney. The examples include dusts, vapours, or fumes.

Fullers Earth (Multani Mitti) A nonplastic type of clay which is hygroscopic in nature. Chemical composition is aluminium magnesium silicate. Used as filler in rubber products, oil well drilling mud, and as an absorbent of oil spills.

Fumigant (Dhumak) A gaseous pesticide. Affect the respiratory tract. Used to kill pests, insects, and rodents.

Fungicide (Fufund Nashi or Kavak Nashi) A chemical or any substance that inhibits the growth or kills fungi, such as molds and rust. They are fast acting.

Fungus (Fafund or Kavak) A plant that lacks chlorophyll and lives off other living organisms. Some grow in soil, others attach themselves to decaying trees and other plants whence they obtain nutrients. Some are pathogens while others stabilize sewage and digest composted waste. Decomposers and do not need light to grow. Most are multicell organisms. There are about 20,000 species of fungi in India. Examples include mildews, yeasts, mushrooms.

Fusion (Sandhi or Sangalan) A combining of atomic nuclei, resulting in the release of an enormous amount of energy. The process is exactly opposite of that in Fission. Raw materials needed for this reaction to occur are water and lithium. Fusion also means blending of metals together by melting. This operation uses heat.

Fusion Point (Sangalan Bindu) The temperature at which a solid substance becomes a liquid.

G

Gaia (Greece Bhoomi Devi) Greek goddess of earth.

Galvanizing (Jasta Chhadana or Mulamma Chhadana) Coating of steel or other ferrous metals products with a thin layer of relatively pure zinc.

Gamete (Yug Mak) It is either of the two germ cells, Sperm or Ovum which participate in the fertilization and development of a new organism.

Gametocide (Yug Mak Nashi) A substance used to selectively kill plant sex cells. This is one way of controlling the pollens of plants.

Gamma Radiation (Gamma Vikiran Prasaran) Electromagnetic radiation released from the nucleus of some radionuclides during radioactive decay. Have no charge and no mass but a very high penetrating power which ranges from 10 keV to 9MeV. Range is very large, up to several hundred feet in air. Gamma rays are generally more energetic than X-Rays. Gamma/X-rays are best shielded by very dense materials, such as lead, thick concrete, or steel. Sources could be X-Ray machines, cobalt.

Gamma Ray (Gamma Kirane) A type of radiation that has high photon energy and short wave length. These rays can be stopped by lead. Physically, gamma rays are identical with X-rays, the essential difference being that X-rays do not originate from atomic nuclei, but are produced in other ways.

Ganga Project (Ganga Pariyojana) Setup in 1985, the purpose of the directorate is to formulate, implement, and monitor the Ganga Action Plan, an ambitious scheme to restore the water quality of the river Ganga.

Gas Chromatograph (Gas Varna Rekha Yantra) A sophisticated analytical instrument that identifies the molecular composition and concentrations of the various chemical constituents in water, soil, and gas samples. The process involves volatilizing of the sample into a carrier gas stream. This mixture then passes through thin tubes containing packing material. Each component moves through the packed tubing at a different rate and thus comes out at different times. As they come out, they are detected by various ionization detectors. There are various types of detector tubes for specific components to be detected.

Gas Exchange (Gas Vinimay) Adding oxygen to water to remove carbon dioxide and hydrogen sulphide. The process is also called aeration. It is used to purify water and occurs in natural systems.

Gaseous Diffusion Plant (Gasiya Prati Sangalan San Yantran) A plant where uranium hexafluoride gas is filtered and percentage of uranium is increased.

Gasohol (Ethanol Nirmit Petrol) Mixture of petroleum with ethanol which has been derived from agricultural products.

Geiger Counter (Geiger Counter) An electronic instrument used to detect and measure radiation, especially gamma rays given out by radioactive substances. The instrument consists of a tube filled with gas which responds to radioactive rays.

Gene (Vansh) Unit of heredity. The smallest segment of DNA, containing instructions for the development of a particular inherited characteristics. There are over 10,000 genes in each cell of a human body.

Gene technology (Vanshavali Vigyan or Vansha Vishayak Takniki) The application of the gene technique called genetic engineering, include self cloning and deletion as well as cell hybridisation.

Genetic Engineering (Vanshavali Abhiyantriki) The technique by which heritable material, which does not usually occur or will not occur naturally in the organism or cell concerned, generated outside the organism or the cell is inserted into said cell or organism. The formation of new combinations of genetic material by incorporation of a cell into a host cell, where they occur naturally (self-cloning) as well as modification of an organism or in a cell by deletion and removal of parts of the heritable material.

Genetic Toxicity or Genotoxic Toxic effects that result from damage to DNA and altered genetic expression.

Geologic Repository (Bhuvaigyaniya Sangrah) A system which is intended to be used for the disposal of radioactive wastes in excavated geologic media.

Geologic Time (Bhuvaigyani Samay or Kaal) The time scale used to date any rock or substance. It is assumed that the age of the earth is about 4.5 billion years. 700 million to 4500 million years ago is termed as Precambrian while between 280 million and 570 million years back, it is termed as Paleozoic era.

Geologic Time Frame (Bhuvaigyani Samay Kaal) The following are the various time frames in the formation of earth.

Era	Age in years
Cenozoic (Recent life)	15,00,00,000 years
Mesozoic (Intermediate)	50,00,00,000 years
Paleozoic (Ancient Life)	2,00,00,00,000 years
Precambrian	3,50,00,00,000 years

Geothermal Energy (Bhutapiya Urja) Energy derived from the hot water and chemicals which are in the earth's magma or hot water, steam and hot rocks found beneath the earth. These sources are generally found in volcanic and earthquake-prone locations. They are very hot, in the range of 150-300 degrees C.

Germicide (Roganu Nashi) Any substance or compound intended to kill disease causing microorganisms.

Germination (Ankurit Hona or Ankuran) Active growth of an embryo. In plants, it is the growth of a mature seed.

Geyser (Dharti Se Garam Pani Ka Shrot) Hot water coming out of earth often rising to a height of a few metres. With a roar, they come out in intervals. They may be coming from the Magma of the earth and so may contain many hazardous chemicals.

Giardia Lamblia Protozoan in the feces of humans and animals that can cause severe gastrointestinal ailments. It is a common contaminant of surface waters.

Glacier (Himnad) A large body of ice which can move independently. They are formed when snow does not melt for many years. Their movement is extremely slow.

Global Warming (Vishwa Ka Tapna or Garma Hona) Gradual increase of the earth's temperature due to heat trapped by atmospheric pollutants. Caused by the greenhouse effect as it traps the heat around the earth. Suspected greenhouse gases include carbon dioxide, methane, nitrogen oxides, and chlorofluorocarbons (CFCs). If global warming continues, it could melt the polar ice, resulting in the increase of level of the oceans and thus disturbing the entire existing ecosystem. Estimated that the earth's temperature has increased by 1 degrees F in the past 100 years.

Glove Box (Dastana Peti) Filtered and ventilated enclosures that allow workers to handle hazardous materials without having direct contact with the contents. Work is done inside the boxes through the use of gloves attached to the box.

Grain Size (Kana Ka Aakaar) Size of a soil particle, basis for soil textural classes.

Gray Water Household waste water, except from the toilet. This water can be directly used for irrigation, and other noncritical uses.

Greenhouse Effect (Poudhadhar Prabhav) The sun is the only external source of heat and light for earth and reaches the earth along with solar radiation. As the earth is cooler than the sun, it traps some heat and emits the rest of the solar radiation back to the atmosphere. But the infrared radiation in the earth's atmosphere are trapped by gases such as carbon dioxide, methane, ozone, chlorofluoro carbons also known as CFCs, among others. These gases enhance the greenhouse effect. Because radiation from the sun is short-wave radiation and so can travel unimpeded to the earth. But the radiation from the earth is infrared radiation and that are trapped by the greenhouse gases. Results in the warming of the earth. During the pre-industrial period of 1750-1800, amount of carbon-dioxide was estimated to be about 280 ppm. It is estimated that the atmosphere contains about 358 ppm of carbon dioxide. Since 1957, amount of carbon dioxide in the atmosphere is being measured at Mauna Loa, Hawaii. It has continuously increased since that time. Current concentration of methane in the atmosphere is 1.72 ppm and that of nitrous oxide is 310 ppb.

Greenhouse Gases (Poudhadhar Ki Gas) In the atmosphere, carbon dioxide, methane, chlorofluorocarbons (CFC), nitrous oxide, and other greenhouse gases mostly produced by burning of coal, oil and gas, allow sunlight through but retain infrared radiation. Earth emits infrared radiation back toward space. Since the industrial revolution began, carbon dioxide concentrations in the atmosphere have risen from 280 to 358 parts per million. Since the late 1800s, mean global temperature has risen between 0.3 to 0.6 degrees centigrade. Oceans which expand when warmed, rose up to 25 centimetres. Computer models project further temperature increases of between 1 and 3.5 degrees centigrade by the year 2100, possibly the most abrupt climate change in thousands of years. These are due to the greenhouse gases.

Grizzly Screen Screen made of heavy fixed bars, used to remove oversized stones and stumps. The screen may be slanted to let heavy particles to fall down by gravity.

Ground Subsidence (Dharti Ka Dhaskan or Dharti Ka Utaar) When the earth's surface sinks. This is a common occurrence noticed in landfills, after underground mining or areas of bedrock composed primarily of limestone.

Ground Water (Sthaliya Jal or Bhouma Jal) Water below the surface of land which is in a zone of saturation. Through pumps, this water is mostly used for drinking and agricultural purposes. It moves slowly among the pores, cracks, and aquifers between the soil and rock. When moving water encounters any pollutant, it can move making it harder for the removal of the contaminant as it would have moved from the original location and thus harder to track. Also leachate from landfills may percolate down to the moving ground water.

Grout (Tal Chhat) A cement-like substance used to solidify and immobilize waste for disposal or to stabilize disposal trenches.

Gunnite A type of liner used in modern day solid or municipal waste landfills.

H

Habitat (Aavaas Sthal) The place where human and animal population lives as their needs for survival are available in that surrounding. It could be in forests, oceans, mountains or flat land. Proper place for each type of animal or species is essential for its continued survival.

Half-Life (Ardha Aayu) The time required for the concentration of a substance to be reduced to half of its original concentration or its effect on the environment. In radioactive substances, it refers to the length of time it takes for half of the atoms in a given quantity of a radioactive isotope to decay or disintegrate. The half-life is constant for each radioactive substance and is independent of its amount or condition. It could be as low as a fraction of a second to millions of years. Effective Half-Life is equal to:

$$\frac{\text{Biological Half-Life} \times \text{Radioactive Half-Life}}{\text{Biological Half-Life} + \text{Radioactive Half-Life}}$$

After a period equal to 10 half-lives, the radioactivity has decreased to about 0.1% of its original value. The half life of Pu-239 is 24,360 years while that of DDT is 15 years in the environment. See Appendix A for half life of some of the elements.

Halogens of Halides Fluorine, chlorine, bromine, iodine, and astatine are called halogens. Their chemical structure is very similar but they are completely different from elements in other groups of the periodic table. Any compound containing them is generally very toxic. Chemically, they are very active-combine violently with alkali metals to form salts. They are among the most ractive of all elements.

Halon A polymer associated with ozone depletion in the universe. It contains bromine and has a long atmospheric lifetime. Inert to almost all chemicals, resistant to low as well as high temperatures. Do not absorb moisture, have very high impact strength, excellent dielectric properties, very low coefficient of friction, and are self extinguishing. They are mostly used for fire fighting purposes.

Handling The Public Liability Insurance Act of 1991 defines 'Handling' to mean that in relation to any substance, means the manufacture, processing, treatment, package, storage, transportation, use, collection, destruction, conversion, offering for sale, transfer, or the like in relation to any substance.

Hardness (Kathorta or Bhari) In water, it refers to the bicarbonates, chlorides, and sulphates of calcium, magnesium and sodium. Hard water does not taste good, and when used with soap, will not produce lather. It will scale on pipes. Hardness is measured as parts per million (PPM) of calcium carbonate (CaCO3). In rocks and solids, it is the resistance to scratching.

Hardness Scale (Kathorta Maap) For rocks and solids, the Mohs scale is from 1 to 10 and is as follows:

Talc	1
Gypsum	2
Calcite	3
Fluorite	4
Apatite	5
Orthoclase	6
Quartz	7
Topaz	8
Corundum	9
Diamond	10

Hard Water (Kathor Jal or Bhaari Pani) Water which contains salts of calcium and magnesium. This water does not form lather with soap.

Hazard Quotient (Jokhim Ank or Jokhim Prapti) The ratio of a single substance exposure level over a specified time period (e.g., subchronic) to a reference dose for that substance derived from a similar exposure period.

Hazardous Air Pollutant (Khatarnak Vayu Pradushak) A substance that may cause either mortality or an increase in serious irreversible, or incapacitating reversible illness to humans, plants, or animal when released to the environment.

Hazardous Chemical (Khatarnak Rasayan) 'Hazardous Chemical' defined in the environmental regulations and it refers to:

- Any chemical which satisfies any of the criteria laid down in the Part I of Schedule and is listed in Column 2 of Part II of the notification issued by the Department of Environment, Forest, and Wildlife, New Delhi on the 27th November 1989 under S.O. 966 (E)
- Any chemical listed in Column 2 of Schedule 2
- Any chemical listed in Column 2 of Schedule 3.

Hazardous Chemicals (Khatarnak Rasayan) Chemicals that are hazardous because they are flammable, explosive, corrosive, reactive, radioactive, infectious or toxic and pose a substantial or potential hazard to human health and safety or to the environment when improperly managed. Clearly, not all hazardous chemicals are toxic.

Hazard Ranking System (Jokhim Srenikaran Vyavastha) Evaluation of the potential relative risks to public health and the environment from releases or threatened releases of harmful substances. Based on the actual or potential release of hazardous substances from a site through air, surface water, or ground water which may affect public health or the environment.

Hazardous Substance (Khatarnaak Padaarth) 'Hazardous Substance' means any substance or preparation which, by reason of its chemical or physico-chemical properties or handling, is liable to cause harm to human beings, other living creatures, plants, micro-organisms, property or the environment. A hazardous substance can cause cancer, organ disease, birth defects, hyperactivity among humans and other living matter.

Hazardous Wastes (Management and Handling) Rules, 1989 Rules enacted under this apply to the hazardous wastes as specified in various acts. These rules do not apply to waste water and exhaust gases which are covered by other regulations. These rules cover the collection, reception, treatment, transport, storage, and disposal of hazardous wastes. Also includes packaging, labelling, records maintenance, spill control, and accident reporting of the same. 18 categories of hazardous wastes have been identified and are listed in Appendix D. Also 434 chemicals have been specified as hazardous and toxic and are listed in Appendix E.

Hazardous Wastes (Parisankatmay Apashisht or Jokhim Vale Kuchde Padarth) Any waste other than radioactive wastes which by reasons of physical and/or chemical or reactive or toxic, explosive, corrosive or other characteristics causing danger or likely to cause danger to health or the environment, whether alone or when coming in contact with other waste or environment. These substances may contribute to an increase in serious irreversible, or incapacitating reversible illnesses. They are also specified in any of the Acts or Schedules.

Hazardous Waste-Guidelines for Occupier/Generator (Generator Hetu Khatarnak Apashisht Nirdesh) Some of the guidelines issued by the regulatory agencies are as follows:

- A maximum of 100,000 kilograms or a truck load, whichever is less, can be stored on-site for a maximum period of 90 days. May be extended under unforeseen circumstances;
- Must be stored only in closed specified containers in the designated protected area;
- Occupier/generator should send a copy of the manifest to the authorities as soon as the waste is shipped for ultimate treatment and disposal;
- Dispose of only in the notified disposal facilities;
- To inspect the on-site storage areas for proper storage. See also Appendix F.

Hazardous Waste-Guidelines for Transportation (Khatarnak Apashisht Ke Parivahan Hetu Nirdesh) Some of the guidelines are as follows:

- To register the authorised transporters for transportation of hazardous waste;
- To ensure that the occupier/generator transport their hazardous waste only in the specified transport vehicles;
- To train the drivers and helpers of the transport vehicles to handle the wastes under emergency situations; See also Appendix G.

Hazardous Waste-Guidelines for Storage, Treatment and Disposal Facility (Khatarnak Apashisht Ka Bhandaran, Upachaar Aur Nipataan Vyastha Hetu Nirdesh) Some of the guidelines from the regulatory agencies are as follows:

- To issue license after having satisfied with their technical, financial and managerial capabilities;
- To allow such facilities on the approved sites;
- To inspect the facility during construction and operation and also closure of landfill facility;
- To inspect for proper storage facilities and containment systems;
- To identify and establish standards for Principal Organic Hazardous Constituents (POHC) for stack emissions from incinerator;
- To monitor stack emissions, effluent and ground water quality regularly;
- To approve Emergency/Contingency plan of the waste management facility;
- To inspect the facility after any incident for appropriate measures taken in order to avert such incidents;
- To check the records of the facility periodically;

- To ensure copy of the manifest, indicating proposed treatment and disposal scheme to be followed, reaches the authorities after receiving the hazardous waste from the occupier/generator. The copy of the manifest should be linked with the copy of the manifest sent by the occupier/generator.

See also Appendix H.

Hazardous Waste Substance (Khatarnaak Apashisht Padarth) Substances that are not radioactive. It could be in solid, liquid, sludge or any form. When released into the environment, because of its quantity, concentration, or physical, chemical, or infectious characteristics they may cause, or significantly contribute to, an increase in mortality or an increase in serious, irreversible, or incapacitating reversible illness. May also pose a substantial present or potential hazard to human health or the environment when improperly treated, stored, transported, or disposed of, or otherwise managed. Characteristics they may have include toxicity, corrosivity, reactivity or ignitability. Examples include PCBs, chemicals, asbestos, acids, metals, and pesticides.

Hazardous Waste Active Life (Khatarnaak Apashishst Ki Sakriya Aayu) Active life of a facility means period from the initial receipt of hazardous waste at the facility until the Regulatory Authorities receive certification of final closure.

Hazardous Waste Sites (Khatarnaak Apashisht Sthal) A place for collection, reception, treatment, storage and disposal of hazardous wastes which has been duly approved by the competent authority of the state in which it is located.

Hazardous Waste Containers (Khatarnaak Apashisht Dibba or Patra) Containers must be made of or lined with materials which will not react with, or are otherwise compatible with the waste to be stored, so that the ability of the container to contain the waste is not impaired. Each container should be clearly marked with 'Hazardous Waste' markings in English and the respective local language. The storage area should be fenced properly and a sign 'Danger' should be placed at that site. Hazardous waste cannot be temporarily stored for over 90 days, a maximum quantity of 10,000 kilograms or a truck load, whichever is less.

Hazardous Waste Major Groups (Khatarnaak Apashisht Ke Pramukh Samooh) As defined by the environmental regulations, the major groups of industries that generate hazardous waste include inorganic and organic chemicals, petroleum refineries, iron and steel, non-ferrous metals (smelting and refining), leather tanning and finishing, and metal finishing.

HDPE High density polyethylene material used as liners for hazardous and non-hazardous landfills.

Health and Safety Plan (Swasthya Evam Suraksha Yojana) For the safety of workers, before starting any work at a known hazardous waste site, it is essential that a health and safety plan be developed. The plan should include such information as site characterisation and hazard analysis, description of the conditions for the use of personal protective equipment, medical surveillance of site personnel, environmental monitoring equipment operation, site control during investigation, decontamination procedures, emergency response procedures, and confined space entry procedures.

Heat of Adsorption (Adhishoshan Ushma) Heat released during adsorption process.

Heat of Fusion (Ushma San Galan) The quantity of heat required to change one gram of a substance from the solid state to the liquid state.

Heat of Vapourisation (Vashpan Ushma) The quantity of heat required to change one gram of a substance from the liquid state to the vapour state at the boiling point of the substance.

Heavy Metal (Bhari Dhaatu) Metals which have very high atomic weight or very high density. Some of the heavy metals are mercury, lead, silver, zinc, cadmium, chromium, arsenic, and aluminium among others. Most of these metals are known to be very toxic even in very small quantities. By forming hydroxides, these metals can be removed from water. They do not biodegrade easily.

Heavy Water (Bhari Jal) Deuterium oxide contains two atoms of deuterium and one atom of oxygen. When normal hydrogen isotope in water is replaced by heavy hydrogen or deuterium increasing its molecular weight by 2. It is mostly used in nuclear reactions as it absorbs alpha particles.

Hector (Hector) It is a metric unit of land area.

Hematite (Lohe Ka Khanij Ke Roop Mein Dharti Se) Mineral or iron ore which contains about 70% Iron. Formula $Fe2O3$.

Hemoglobin (Rakta Kan) A red protein pigment which carries oxygen in the blood stream. It transfers oxygen from the lungs to the tissues and carbon dioxide from the tissues to the lungs.

Hemolytic Anaemia (Hemolytic Anaemia) A decrease in blood concentration of haemoglobin and the number of erythrocytes. This is due to the inability of the mature erythrocytes to survive in the circulating blood.

Henna (Mehandi) Dried leaves used to colour hands. It is used in dyeing of hair and in medicines.

HEPA Filter High Efficiency Particulate Air Filter. An extended surface filter with a high rate of particle removal. Used to trap at least 99.97% of all particles 0.3 micron diameter or larger.

Hepatotoxicity Toxicity of the liver and associated bile duct and gall bladder.

Herb (Jadi Buti) Any type of flowering plant that does not develop any woody tissue. Most of them used as a medicine.

Herbicide (Shaak Nashi) Chemical, either organic or inorganic, used to destroy or kill unwanted weeds or to inhibit plant growth and so are toxic to those plants. Can be used to selectively kill a particular species of plant or overgrowth. Applied or sprayed in the target area. Excessive usage or application at a wrong site may potentially harm nontarget species or animals and humans.

Herbivore (Shakahari) Animal that eats only plants.

Heritable Effect (Vanshagat Prabhav) An effect that appears in the future children of the individuals exposed to a hazard.

Hibernation (Sheet Nishkriyata) During cold weather, some animals become dormant. During this period, their metabolism slows down considerably and the animal normally sleeps during this time. This is necessary for survival to that animal species as vegetation for their feed is not available.

High Efficiency Particulate Air (HEPA) A filtering system capable of trapping and retaining at least 99.97 percent of all monodispersed particles 0.3 microns in diameter or larger. HEPA filters are used in the removal of fine particles such as Asbestos.

High Level Waste (Ucchastariya Khatarnak Kachada) When the concentration of a pollutant is very high in a waste. Associated when the hazardous nature is high.

High Level Radioactive Waste (Ucchastariya Vighatanabhik Kachara) Highly radioactive material from the reprocessing of spent nuclear fuel. May include spent nuclear fuel, liquid waste, and solid waste derived from the liquid. These items decay slowly and remain radioactive for hundreds of thousands of years. Must be handled by remote-control instruments from behind protective shielding to protect workers. Unless concentrations are high enough, permanent isolation is required.

High Temperature Gas-Cooled Reactor (HTGR) A nuclear reactor cooled with Helium.

Holarctic Species Plants and animals found in the northern portion of North America or Europe near the northern ice cap.

Holocene (Holecene) Geologic time indicating the present period or the period since the last ice age.

Homolog Group of isomers that have the same degree of alogenation.

Homothermalism (Samataapi Jeev) Organisms that can maintain a constant temperature even in an ever shifting temperature environment. It is also called warm-bloodedness. Animals and humans are examples.

Hormone (Antahastrav) Chemical substance secreted by cells of endocrine glands, which carry signals to influence the activity of other cells or organs. Chemical neurons and act as messengers, dispersing through the blood streams. Growth must be controlled as uncontrolled growth could result in cell abnormalities and may result in severe diseases.

Host Rock The geologic medium in which the waste is placed. Serves as a host for other rocks or for mineral deposits.

Hot Spot Region in a contaminated area in which the level of contamination is somewhat greater than in neighboring regions in the area.

Humid (Nam or Aadra) Presence of water moisture in the atmosphere. Climate generally characterized by a large quantity of rainfall.

Humus (Khaad Mitti) Organic material such as leaves, grass or dead animals and plants that has decomposed resulting in humic acid or fulvic acid and humin. Adds nutrients to the soil and provides buffering capacity, metal binding capacity, soil stability, and water holding ability.

Hurricane (Toofan) Also called cyclones. High winds moving in a circular pattern around a zone of calm air in the centre of at least 120 kilometres per hour.

Hybrid (Sankar) When two or more different varieties or genetically dissimilar plants are combined, the product may be similar to both of them in some qualities but its overall qualities may be different. Hybrid crops may not be suitable to a particular area as normal crops and may require more care may be required to sustain their care.

Hydrate (Jalayojan) When water combines with another substance. Example is hydrate of lime.

Hydraulic Conductivity (Drava Chaalit Chalakta) A coefficient of proportionality describing the rate at which water can move through a medium which is permeable. The rate or speed with which water can flow between the pores of the media.

Hydraulic Gradient (DravaChaalit Anupaat) The change in depth and pressure of water table with a change in distance in a given direction. The water will always flow downwards and where the pressure is lower. The slope and pressure gradient is essential to determine the gradient.

Hydrocarbon (Hydrocarbon) Organic compounds containing only hydrogen and carbon, such as methane. They could be straight chain, branched chain or contain rings such as in benzene. There are two types of hydrocarbons-aliphatic, which are straight chain and aromatic, which are unsaturated and have hexagonal ring structure.

Hydrochloric Acid (Namak Ka Tejab) A colourless, fuming pungent liquid. A water solution of hydrogen chloride is a strong and highly corrosive acid. Toxic and can cause skin, nose, and mucous membrane irritation, ulcers, coughing, and bronchitis.

Hydrofluoric Acid A colourless, fuming liquid. A water solution of hydrogen fluoride. Very toxic and highly corrosive to skin.

Hydrogen (Udgen or Hydrogen) The lightest of the elements, a flammable and explosive gas without odour or colour. Hydrogen is the most abundant element in the universe. Atomic weight 1.01. Symbol H.

Hydrogeologic Unit Any soil or rock unit or zone which by virtue of its porosity or permeability, or lack thereof, has a distinct influence on the storage or movement of groundwater.

Hydrologic Budget Measurements of the relative amounts of water moving through the various subcycles of the hydrologic cycle.

Hydrology (Jala Vigyan) The science dealing with the properties, movement, and effects of water on the earth's surface, in the soil and rocks below, and in the atmosphere.

Hydrolysis (Jal Ghatan) A chemical reaction in which the degradation or displacement of a contaminant by chemical reactions involving water or an aqueous solution. When water is one of the substance involved, hydrogen ions may be produced.

Hydrophilic Substance (Jalaragi Vastu) Any substance which has a very strong affinity towards water.

Hydrophobic Contaminants Compounds that do not have a strong affinity for water. They have strong aversion for water.

Hydroponic (Jala Samvardhan) Growing plants using a nutrient-rich liquid instead of soil. Generally associated with plants which grow in water.

Hydrosphere (Jala Mandal) Free water found in earth. It can be in any form such as ice, snow, water, and clouds.

Hydroxyl Radicals (OH) Atmospheric molecules which reduce methane, carbon monoxide, and tropospheric ozone. These radicals are suspected to result in the increase of higher greenhouse gas levels.

Hygroscopic The specific characteristic of a substance to absorb moisture from air. Some of them are silica gels, and molecular sieves.

Hyperpnea (Ati Shwasan) A state in which deep, rapid breathing occurs.

Hyperthermia When a person is exposed to work in very high temperatures for a long time, he may develop very high body temperature. If the temperature continues for some time, damage to the nervous system is possible. Most often occurs during summer months or when individuals are fully suited and work continuously for a long period of time.

Hypocotyl Portion of the axis of an embryo or seedling situated between the cotyledons or seed leaves and the radical.

Hypolimnion Water at the bottom of a thermally stratified lake which is generally low and lack Oxygen.

Hypoxia A partial reduction in the oxygen concentration supplied to cells or tussues.

I

Ice Age (Him Yug) Referred to as the Pleistocene period which is between 2 million years to 12,000 years back. During that time, the earth was mostly covered with ice.

IDLH-Immediately Dangerous to Life or Health A level to which a healthy human could be exposed to a contamination or a chemical without carrying any irreversible health effects or any other impairment. These values have been developed so that when a respirator fails, a worker has 30 minutes time for him to reach a safe and clean place. These values are very important when clean up of a contaminated site is being carried out.

Igneous Activity (Agneya Gatividhi) The movement of hot, molten rock.

Igneous Rock (Agneya Shail or Chattan) A rock formed by the crystallization and solidification of magma (or lava), either within the crust or on the earth's surface. They are generally long and wide.

Ignition Point (Jwalan Bindu) The temperature at which a substance starts dissipating heat and catches fire even in the absence of an ignition source.

Immediately Dangerous to Life and Health (IDLH) See IDLH.

Immunotoxicity (Prati Raksha Aavidhaluta) Toxicity of the immune system. It results as adverse effects on the functioning of the immune system that result from exposure to a chemical substance. Altered immune function may lead to the increased incidence or severity of infectious diseases or cncer, since the immune system's ability to respond adequately to invading agents is suppressed. It may take several forms such as hypersensitivity, immunodeficiency, and untcontrolled proliferation (leukemia and lymphoma). Some chemicals that may cause this are PCBs, dieldrin, and dioxins.

Impermeable Layer (Apaargamya Jhilli or Abhedhya Parat) Any substance such as rock through which water or any other liquid can pass either with great difficulty or cannot pass.

Impervious Solid Surface (Apraveshya Thos Satah) Solid surfaces which are nonporous and thus are unlikely to absorb any liquid within a short period of time. Such surfaces are those of metals, and glass.

Impoundment (Avaruddha Jal) When a body of water is forcibly confined in a place. It could be through the construction of a dam, dike or any other barrier.

Impregnation (Bhar Dena) The process of filling pores with another substance in order to change its properties. Also to fertilise or cause to become pregnant.

Impurity (Ashuddhi) A chemical substance which is unintentionally present with another chemical or substance. Also called contamination.

Incineration (Bhasmikaran) A process through which a substance or material can be completely destroyed. Residue should not contain any combustible material. The process must be very highly efficient. The greater the efficiency of operation, the cleaner the air emission from that unit. Treatment technology using combustion with ranges in temperatures from 1200 to 2000 degrees centigrade. Under controlled conditions, burning at high temperatures destroys hazardous waste and reduces the volume of waste. By products are fly ash – exhausted through the stack and bottom ash which requires proper disposal. By products may be hazardous in nature. Hazardous waste regulations require a destruction and removal efficiency (DRE) of at least 99.99 percent of each POHC of the wastes. The efficiency is calculated by using the following equation:

$$DRE = \frac{(Win - Wout)}{Win} \times 100\%$$

Where POHC = Principal Organic Hazardous Constituents

Win = mass feed rate of one POHC in the waste stream feeding the incinerator;

Wout = mass emission rate of the same POHC present in exhaust emissions prior to release to the atmosphere.

Incinerator (Bhasmak) Any enclosed device using controlled flame combustion that neither meets the criteria for classification as a boiler nor is listed as an industrial furnace. Also see Incineration.

Incipient LC_{50} (Prarambhi LC50) Calculated from experimentally derived mortality data, that is lethal to 50 percent of a test population when exposure to the test substance is continued until the mean increase in mortality does not exceed 20 percent in any concentration over a 24 hour period.

Incompatible Waste (Asangat Apashisht) A waste which is unsuitable for :

(a) Placement in a particular device of facility because it may cause corrosion or decay of containment materials (e.g., container inner liners or tank walls); or

(b) Commingling with another waste or material under uncontrolled conditions because the commingling might produce heat or pressure, fire or explosion, violent reaction, toxic dusts, mists, fumes or gases, or flammable fumes or gases. Seven groups of non-compatibility have been specified and the potential consequences are as follows:

Group 1-Heat generation, violent reaction.
Group 2-Release of toxic substances in case fire or explosion.
Group 3-Fire or explosion, generation of flammable gas.
Group 4-Fire, explosion, or heat generation of flammable or toxic gases.
Group 5-Fire, explosion or violent reaction.
Group 6-Generation of toxic hydrogen cyanide gas.
Group 7-Fire, explosion or violent reaction.

Incubation Period (Ushmayan Avadhi or Kaal) The interval between the body's infection by an organism and the manifestation of the infection's first symptoms; the period in which an infection is not recognizable.

Indicator Species (Soochak Jaati) Species of plant or animal that is dependent on specific, critical factors in the environment for its survival and is often very sensitive to environmental changes. Its disappearance or reduction in numbers is used as a general sign of environmental degradation or destruction.

Indoor Air (Bhitari Vayu) The air which is within the interior of a house or a building. Indoor air pollutants include suspended particulate matter, and smoke - nicotine, hydrocarbons. In an industrial setting, the pollutants may include unprocessed sewage. Air borne allergers, fungi, viruses and bacteria, extremes of temperature and humidity, passive cigarette smoke, stoves and use of generator sets run òn kerosene, petrol or diesel are the sources of indoor air pollution. Strongly discouraging cigarette smoking, use of electric invertors in place of generators, keeping generator set at higher places, and providing adequate air filters should be recommended for control of indoor pollution.

Industrial Activity (Audyogic Gatividhi) 'Industrial Activity' means:

- An operation of process carried out in an industrial installation referred to in Schedule 4 involving or likely to involve one or more hazardous chemicals and includes on-site storage or on-site transport which is associated with that operation or process, as the case may be; or
- Isolated storage; or
- Pipeline.

Industrial Classification (Audyogic Vargikaran) Under the National River Action Plan, industries have been categorised into three groups: Red, Orange and Green.

- 'Red' stands for the highly polluting industries like distilleries and fermentation industries, sugar and fertilisers, pulp and paper industries, basic drugs and pesticides, oil refineries and tanneries among others. They are covered under the Central Action Plan.
- 'Orange' industrial category include cotton spinning and weaving, automobile servicing and repair stations, hotels and restaurants, flour mills (excluding domestic Aatta Chakki), malted food, and fish processing among others.
- 'Green' category industries include those in the small scale, cottage/village category and also those industries that do not generate process effluents or emissions. They include Aatta-chakkies, rice millers, steeping and processing of grains, mineralised water, dal mills, supari (betelnut) and masala grinding, chilling plants and cold storage, apparel making, handloom weaving, shoelace manufacturing, and gold and silver thread zari work. See also National River Action Plan. For siting of industry, see Appendix I.

Industrial Effluent (Audyogic Nikas) Industrial wastewater which has been treated to remove pollutants. It may include process wastewater, utility wastewater, cooling or heating water from a process of an industrial complex.

Industrial Furnace (Audyogic Bhatti) An enclosed device in a manufacturing process that uses thermal treatment to accomplish recovery of materials or energy.

Industrial Plant (Audyogic Karkhana) The Air Act defines industrial plants as any plant used for any industrial or trade purposes and emitting any air pollutant into the atmosphere. For siting of industry, see Appendix I.

Inert (Akriya) Substance or chemical that is very stable and will not react with any other element very easily. Examples of inert gases are helium, neon, and argon.

Infectious Agents (Sankramak Jeev Karak) Viruses, bacteria, and microorganisms that can cause disease or other adverse health impacts to humans. Capable of multiplying in body tissues. For example, human blood and blood products, discarded needles and scalpels or other medical instruments which have been used on a patient.

Infectious Waste (Sankramak Apashisht) Any substance or material which has come into contact with or has been used with a substance where an infectious agent may have been present. This may include the presence of human tissues, specimens, pathological specimens, patients, excreta, secretions, blood, or surgical operating instruments. Generally these conditions are found in hospitals, and places where patients have to visit and get treated.

Infiltration (Antah Syandan) Penetration of water through the cracks into controlled areas. Movement of air into a building through cracks and interstices in the building. Water which can enter through pores or crevices. Sewage water capable of penetrating clean water lines.

Influent (Antarvahi) Stream of water which is recharging an aquifer, reservoir or a pond. Occurs when rain water reaches ground.

Infrared (Avarakta) Electromagnetic radiation of wavelength between the longest visible red (7,000 Angstroms) and about 1 micrometre. Associated with solar radiation, often called heat wave. They are used in spectroscopic analysis, medicine, and photography.

Infrared Incinerator (Avarakta Bhatti) Any enclosed device that uses electric powered resistance heaters as a source of radiant heat followed by an afterburner using controlled flame combustion and which is not listed as an industrial furnace.

Inhalable Particles (Antah Shwasaniya Kan) Very small particles, in the range of micrometres, that can bypass nose filtrations and be deposited along the respiratory tract.

Injury (Chot or Kshati) As defined by The Public Liability Insurance Act of 1991, 'Injury' includes permanent total or permanent partial disability or sickness resulting from an accident.

Inner Liner (Astar) A continuous layer of material placed inside a tank or container which protects the construction materials of the tank or container from the contained waste or reagents used to treat the waste. Can synthetic or clay or a combination of both of them.

Inoculum (Nivesh Dravya or Sanrop) Bacteria or fungi injected into compost to start biological action. It is also a medium that contains organisms, usually bacteria or a virus, that is introduced into cultures or living organisms.

Inorganic Chemical (Akarbanic Rasayan) Any chemical compound which generally does not have hydrocarbons and their derivatives or does not have carbon as one of its constituents. The exception is carbon dioxide.

Insecticide (Keetnashi) A pesticide or a chemical substance which is used to prevent, control, or inhibit the establishment, reproduction, development, or growth of insects that are harmful to humans or substances essential to humans. These substance can be used to protect plants, humans, and animals. Toxic to humans in varying degrees. For this reason, should be used with care.

Insectivore (Keetbhakshi) An animal that eats insects.

In Situ (Swasthan) When a substance is in its original position or area. Generally associated with underground substance. Greek word which means in place.

In Situ Treatment (Swasthan Upachar or Nirupan) This process generally uses naturally occurring physical, chemical and biological reactions within the soil; oxidation of contaminants with chemical agents; and washing or flushing of soil to remove contaminants.

In Situ Vitrification (IVS) (Swasthan Kaanch Banana) An innovative approach to stabilization of transuranic contaminated waste. Involves conversion of contaminated soil into durable glass and crystalline matrices.

Inspirable Particulate Mass Hazardous particulate materials when deposited anywhere in the respiratory tract.

Interference In analytical process, it is when a chemical or physical entity whose influence results in a decrease or increase in the response of an analytical method or other measurement system relative to the response obtained in the absence of the entity. Interferences in chemical analysis may often be mitigated by changing sample preparation methods or conditions, or by changing analysis methods or conditions. In a cleanup site, it is the material that is a hinderance in the cleanup process.

Interim Remedial Action (Antarim Upachaari Kriya) An early response action that is identified and implemented at any time during the study or design phase.

Internal Combustion Engine (Aantarik Dahan Engine) An engine powered by the heat from an explosion of a mixture of gas and air. The most common automobile engines of this type operates on four cycles: intake, compression, ignition, and exhaust.

Internal Radiation (Aantar Vikiran) Radiation emitted from a source that has been taken into the body as a result of the inhalation, ingestion, or implantation of a natural or man-made radionuclides in body tissues.

Intertidal Zone (Antar Kshetra) The zone of a beach that lies between high and low tide.

Intrinsic Remediation (Taatvik Upachaar) The result of several natural processes, such as biodegradation, abiotic transformation, mechanical dispersion, sorption and dilution that reduce contaminant concentrations in the environment.

Inversion (Viparivartan) When a layer of relatively cool air is held in its place by a layer of relatively warmer air, thus inverting the normal tendency of air to decrease in temperature with altitude. This occurs due to the night time cooling of ground surface through radiation. If inversion continues for several days, there is concentration of pollutants in that area and may prove to be harmful to humans. Inversion spreads the polluted air horizontally.

In Vitro (Patre) When the testing or action is conducted outside an organism, but inside a test tube or culture dish.

In Vivo (Jive) When the testing or action is done or conducted inside an organism itself.

Iodine-131 (Iodine – 131) A radioactive material with a half-life of eight days.

Ion (Aayan) An atom or a group of atoms that has a positive or negative electrical charge. The number of electrons and protons determines the overall electrical charge of the atom. Ions with a positive charge are called cations and the negative charged ions are called anions. These ions are entirely different than their predecessor element. Electrolytes form ions as they enable the solution to conduct electricity.

Ion Exchange (Aayan Vinimay) A reversible reaction between an ion exchanger which is a solid and a water solution. Generally a batch process and may be reversible.

This process is used in the softening of water, removal of iron from wine, and recovery of valuable metals from wastes.

Ion Generator (Aayan Janitra) A device which produces and disseminates highly charged particles into the air.

Ionization (Aayani Karan) Removal of an electron from an atom by imparting energy and thus creating a charged (negative or positive) particle. Used in electroplating industry.

Ionization Radiation (Aayanan Vikiran) Radiation that has enough energy to remove electrons from the atoms of elements that it passes through, thus forming ions.

Iron (Loha) Highly reactive malleable and ductile metal. One of the earliest metals known to humans. It is the most widely used metal today. In trace amounts, it is an essential ingredient to animal and humans. Atomic weight: 55.847. Chemical formula: Fe.

Irradiated Food (Kiranit Bhojan) Use of radiation, to kill insects and other bacteria in food. The food is radiated for a very short time. This process enables food to be stored at normal room temperature for a long time.

Irradiation (Kiranan) Exposure to radiation of wavelengths shorter than those of visible light such as gamma, X-ray, or ultraviolet. Used for the destruction of bacteria in milk or other foodstuffs, and for medical purposes, and the sterilization of medical instruments and bandages, and vulcanization of rubber.

Irruption (Antarvedhan) Sudden and unexpected growth of any type of plant or animal in a confined area which may harm the environment. This might indicate environmental degradation.

Isobar (Samadaab Rekha) Connection of points where the pressure is the same.

Isolated Storage (Alag Godaam or Ekaki Bhandar) 'Isolated Storage' means storage of a hazardous chemical, other than storage associated with an installation on the same site specified in Schedule 4 where that storage involves at least the quantities of that chemical set out in Schedule 2 of the Manufacture, Storage and Import of Hazardous Chemical Rules, 1989.

Isomers (Samaa Vayav) Molecules with the same number and kinds of atoms, same formula but are different substances and structures. In some cases, two molecules with the same formula have the atoms linked together differently. They may have the same molecular weight but will have different properties. For example, HClC=CHCl. It could be cis- and trans-1,2 dichloroethylene.

Isotherm (Samataap Rekha) A line connecting areas of the same temperature. They are used to indicate climates on maps.

Isotope (Samasthaanik) One of two or more types of atoms having the same atomic number but different mass number. This means that they have the same number of protons, but different number of neutrons. Properties of isotopes may be different. A single element may have many isotopes such as hydrogen which has three isotopes. Hydrogen isotopes are protium, deuterium, and tritium.

J

Jar Test (Jar Parikshan) A test that is carried out in an analytical lab. It stimulates a water treatment plant's coagulation/flocculation units with differing chemical doses, mix speeds and settling times. Enables one to estimate the minimum or ideal coagulant dose required to achieve certain water quality goals.

Joint Boards (Samyukta Board) The State Boards, if they so choose, may form Joint Boards. 'Joint Boards' may be constituted by an agreement between-
two or more Governments of contiguous states or
by the Central Government (in respect of one or more Union territories) and one or more Governments of State contiguous to such Union territory or Union Territories). The board will be in force for such period as may be specified in the agreement to provide the constitution of the board. All states now have Boards. They were formed after the enactment of The Water Act of 1974.

Joule (Joule) The unit for work and energy. It equals to one Newton expended along the distance of one metre.

K

Katabatic Wind (Katabatic Vayu) A wind that is formed due to the flow of cold air that is flowing downhill. When a sloping land surface cools by night-time radiation, the cold air in contact with the ground flows downhill and along valley bottoms. This is opposite of anabatic wind.

Karst (Karst) A geologic formation, kind of terrain with characteristics of relief and drainage arising from a high degree of rock solubility. The majority of karst conditions occur in limestone areas but may also occur in areas of dolomite, gypsum, or salt deposits. Features associated with such a terrain may include irregular topography, abrupt ridges, sinkholes, caverns, abundant springs, disappearing streams, and a general lack of a well developed surface drainage system of tributaries and streams.

Kerma It is the sum of the initial kinetic energies of all charged particles liberated by indirectly ionizing particles in a volume, divided by the mass of matter in that volume.

Kerogen (Kerogen) The disseminated organic matter of sedimentary rocks that is insoluble in nonoxidising acids, bases, and organic solvents. Includes both marine and land-derived organic matter.

Keystone Species (Mooltatva Jeevanu) Animal or plant species whose action or pattern of living determines the survival of other living creatures.

Kilo Electron Volt One thousand electron volts or 103 eV.

Kilowatt Hour (Kilowatt Ghanta) A unit to measure the rate of electricity generation or use. Equals 1,000 watts.

Kinetic Energy (Gatik Urja) Energy which is in action. Heat, motion, and light are examples of kinetic energy.

Koeppen Climate System (Koppen Jala Vayu Yantra) A method used to classify the world climate in broad climatic regions. The regions are Tropical Humid, Tropical and Mid-Latitude Dry, Coastal, Continental and Polar. Each system is further divided into subsystems to further classify the climatic region.

L

Lab Pack Waste An overpack container. Used to consolidate waste in small quantities or if the packing of a waste is either leaking or may leak due to transportation. The overpack container is generally constructed of steel or any hard fiber. The material of the overpack must be nonreactive with the substance that it will hold.

Labelling of Containers (Dibbon Par Label Lagaanaa) All containers should be labeled for predominant hazard characteristics as per the labels prescribed under Motor Vehicles Rules, 1989.

Lagoon (Samudrataal or Lagoon) A small, shallow body of water close to or adjoining an ocean or a large lake but not connected. As they are very shallow, the water is purified naturally because of sunlight, bacterial action and oxygen. Because of these qualities, they are constructed specifically for sewage to decompose by the action of algae. It also refers to a shallow body of water separated from the sea by coral reefs or sandbars.

Laminar Flow (Stariya Pravah) A type of liquid flow in which the stream lines remain constant throughout the region. There is no mixing between the layers. Consequently, heat exchange is minimal. Groundwater flow is mostly laminar.

Land Application (Dharti or Jameen Mein Lagaanaa) When wastewater is discharged on to land with the sole purpose of using it as a fertilizer or for reuse.

Landfill A disposal facility or part of a facility where garbage is placed in layers, compacted, and generally covered with soil. Cover material is applied at the end of each operating day. It is on open land and the place of a landfill is generally not a land treatment facility, a surface impoundment. Historically, any open place which needed to be filled, became a landfill. Modern day landfills are lined with synthetic materials which will not generate leachate runoff. Along with methane, landfills generate other harmful gases from the waste. They subside in due course of time. Operations may go on for about thirty years or more.

Landfill Cell A discrete volume of a landfill which uses a liner to provide isolation of wastes from adjacent cells or wastes or trenches. A large landfill which is divided into various sections and each section is called a cell. Each cell may be designed to hold distinct types of waste.

Landfill Gas Generated by anaerobic decomposition of domestic refuse. The gas is generally colourless with an offensive odour due to the presence of traces of organosulphur compounts. The gas consists of mostly methane which is about 62%. Other gases of significant amounts include carbon dioxide which is about 33%, Nitrogen is approximately 2.5% and oxygen less than 0.2%. Other gases in trace amounts include hydrogen, carbon monoxide, saturated hydrocarbons, unsaturated hydrocarbons, halogenated compounds, organosulphur compunds, alcohols.

Landfill of Hazardous Waste A disposal facility or part of a facility where hazardous waste is placed in or on land and which is not a land treatment facility, a surface impoundment.

Land Treatment Facility (Bhoomi Upachaar Kendra) A facility or a part of a facility at which hazardous waste is applied to the soil surface; such facilities are disposal facilities if the waste will remain after closure.

Langelier Index Number indicates the equilibrium pH of water with respect to calcium and alkalinity. It is used in stabilising water to control both the corrosion and scale deposition.

Larvae (Illi or Dimbhak) Early form of animal or insect that hatches from eggs into a wormlike form and then goes through an intermediate period of development before metamorphosing in to an adult. Examples are frog tadpoles and the aquatic larvae of dragonflies.

Latency (Avyaktata) The time necessary for the effects of exposure to a hazardous or toxic substance become noticeable.

Latent Heat (Antarhit Taap) The amount of heat supplied or released during the phase changes, such as from a solid to liquid or from a liquid to a vapour. An example is water, when it changes its phase from ice to liquid water or from water to gaseous phase.

Latent Period (Aprakat Kaal or Gupt Kaal) It is the period or state of seeming inactivity between the time of exposure of tissue to an injurious agent and response. Cancer has latent period from ten to thirty years.

Lateral Dispersivity (Parshvik Visarjan) Distribution or suspension of fine particles in directions lateral to the flow path of a dispersion medium, such as contaminants in ground water.

Laterite (Makharla) A leached soil, high in iron and aluminium, that is found in many tropical areas.

Lava (Lava) Hot, molten rock that is extruded from the crust onto the earth's surface through fissures in the ground or from volcanoes. Mostly magma that has reached the surface of the earth.

LC (LC) Lethal Concentration of a chemical or substance.

LC_{10}-Low Lethal Concentration (LC 10 Kam Ghatak Sandran) The lowest lethal concentration observed in tests on lab animals or in accidental human exposure.

LC_{50}-Lethal Concentration (LC 50 Ghatak Sandran) Amount of gaseous toxic or hazardous substance necessary to kill half of a test population in a given time from inhaled concentration. The organism in which the test is being carried out should be exposed solely to the chemical being tested. This applies to airborne concentrations.

LD_{50}-Lethal Dose (LD50 Ghatak Khurak) Amount of toxic or hazardous substance necessary to kill half of a test population within a given period of time. The test population is treated with a single oral dose under the conditions of the test. The smaller LD50 value of a substance indicates that it has a higher toxic characteristics. This involves ingestion, injection or other means of applying a substance.

Leachate (Nikshalitak) Any liquid, including any suspended components in the liquid, that has percolated through or drained from any substance such as municipal waste or hazardous waste. Results when water percolates or trickles through waste materials and collects components of those wastes. Leaching may occur at landfills and may result in hazardous substances entering soil, surface water, or ground water. The depth of leachate over the liner in a leachate management system in a hazardous waste facility should not exceed 30 cm (one foot). The liner should be chemically resistant to the waste and leachate and of sufficient strength and thickness to prevent its collapse.

Leaching (Nikshalan or Vikshalan or Ghulkar Bahna) When rain water percolates through a landfill, dissolving soluble constituents of a solid material by the natural action. The water moving through the pores of the constituents will slowly dissolve or suspended constituents of chemicals or fertilizers and carry the components with it contaminating ground or surface water in the process. In landfill design, leachate collection systems are installed which are then pumped and treated before disposal.

Lead (Sisa) A known toxic heavy metal which accumulates in the body and can cause damage to internal organs such as the kidney or liver. It can also reduce mental capacity, hearing loss, blood disorders, hypertension and death at very high levels. It is a highly malleable silvery gray heavy metal and is highly corrosion-resistant. As it is not easily biodegrade, it accumulates in the environment and cause damage through bioaccumulation. Lead is used as an antiknock additive in petrol used for cars, as a paint pigment, and as solder. Atomic weight: 207.2. Symbol: Pb.

Lean-Burn Engine (Kam Indhan Vala Engine) An engine that operates on a higher air-to-fuel ratio than a standard engine does and consequently uses less fuel.

Legionella (Legionella) Bacteria which can cause a type of pneumonia called Legionnaires Disease.

LEL-Lower Explosive Limit (Nimnatar Visphotak Sima) The lowest percentage by volume of a mixture which will propagate a flame in air at 250 C or 770 F and atmospheric pressure. Expressed as percent by volume.

Levee (Tatbandh or Ghat or Bandh) Natural or human-created bank, usually of dirt, silt, rock or earth, formed parallel to a river. Rivers that continually flood will eventually deposit enough silt to form levees, which help control further flooding.

Life Cycle Assessment (Jeeven Chakra Mulyankan) Evaluation of all impacts and aspects of a product, from procurement of needed raw materials to end product waste and disposal.

Life Time Exposure (Jeevan Kal Prabhavan) Total amount of exposure to a substance that a human would receive in a lifetime. The time considered for this purpose is 70 years.

Light-Water Reactor (Halka Jal Reactor) The most common type of nuclear reactor in which water is used as a moderator and coolant.

Lignite (Bhoora Koyla) Brownish coal with low heating value. Lower heating values than sub-bituminous coal but higher than peat. Mined in Neyveli of Tamilnadu. In pelletised form, it is used as a heating fuel.

Lime Stone (Choona Patthar) Calcium carbonate. Moderately soluble in water. Mostly found in warm, shallow seas. Used in building material and also in the production of steel and fertilizer.

Liming (Choona Milaana) Addition of calcium, often calcium carbonate, to acidified waters or soils to restore pH.

Limnology (Sarovar Vigyan) The study of the physical, chemical, hydrological, and biological aspects of fresh water bodies.

Liner (Astar) A continuous layer of natural material such as impermeable soil or man-made material such as plastic. This material is placed beneath or on the sides of a surface impoundment, landfill, or landfill cell. This material restricts the downward or lateral escape of hazardous waste, hazardous waste constituents, or leachate.

Lipids (Lipid) A broad term that includes all oil-soluble, and water-insoluble substances such as fats, waxes, fatty acids, sterols, and pigments. They will very selectively disperse through the environment via uptake in living tissue.

Liquid Metal Fast Breeder Reactor (LMFBR) A breeder reactor that is cooled by a circulating liquid metal such as sodium.

Liquid Traps (Dravya Fanda or Rok) Sumps, well cellars, and other traps used in association with oil and gas production, gathering, and extraction operations for the purpose of collecting oil, water, and other liquids. These liquid traps may temporarily collect liquids for subsequent disposition or reinjection into a production or pipeline stream, or may collect and separate liquids from a gas stream.

Lithology (Ashma Vigyan or Shila Vigyan) Description of rocks based on its physical character and composition such as colour, composition, and grain size. Should imply a specific rock or soil type.

Littoral (Samudra Tat) Activities of organisms or substances that take place on or near a coastline of a river or an ocean.

Loam (Dumat) A mixture of sand, silt, clay and may include organic matter.

Local Authority (Sthaaniya Adhikari or Sanstha) 'Local Authority' defined by The Water Cess Act of 1977 means a municipal corporation of a municipal council (by whatever name called) or a cantonment board or any other body entrusted with the duty of supplying the water under the law by or under which it is constituted.

Loess (Maheen Mitti) Very fine soil or sand that has been transported by wind.

Loss or Decay (Haani or Kshay) The degradation of chemicals in any substance which results in a reduction in the concentration of contaminants in soil or ground water.

Love Canal (Love Canal) A waste dump site that was partly filled with trichlorophenol by Hooker Chemicals and Plastics Corporation of Niagara Falls, New York, in the 1950s. The effects of the chemicals became known in 1970s when it was a residential site. It was discovered in 1977 to be leaching chemicals to the surface and eventually traces of highly toxic chemiical called TCDD (2, 3, 7, 8 tetrachlorodibenzoo-dioxin) were detected.

Lower Explosive Limit (LEL) (Nimna Visphotak Seema) The minimum concentration of vapour in air below which propagation of a flame will not occur in the presence of an ignition source measured as lower explosive limit in air, percent by volume. See also LEL.

Low Level Waste (Nimna Stariya Apashisht) When a pollutant is present in very low levels. Adverse effects on the environment may be very low.

Low Level Radioactive Waste (Nimna Stariya Radiodharmi Apashisht) Any radioactive waste not classified as high-level or transuranic waste is a low-level waste. Generated in research and medical activities. The waste is usually composed of rags, papers, tools, equipments, and discarded protective clothing used with radionuclides. Most low-level radioactive waste do not require extensive protection. They will decay to harmless levels in a few years.

Luminescent Material (Prakash Sheel Padaarth) Substances that emit light upon excitation by such energy sources as photons, electrons, and applied voltage. Some of these materials include zinc sulphide, calcium halophosphate.

Lustre (Chamak or Dipti) Means of identifying rocks and minerals by the amount and angle of light deflected from it.

M

MEC Minimum explosive concentration for a dust in air.

Magma (Magma) Contained in the earth's core which is about 50 to 100 miles beneath the earth's surface. In some places, it rises to the surface through volcanoes or other geological disturbances, as it is lighter than surrounding rock. It is very hot, in the range of 3,000 to 4,000 degrees. F.

Magnetic Pole (Chumbakiya Dhruva) The two points on the earth's surface where the lines of magnetic force from the earth's magnetic field converge and become vertical to the ground. They are the North and the South Pole.

Major Accident (Badi Durghatna) 'Major Accident' means an occurrence including any particular major emission, fire or explosion involving one or more hazardous chemicals and resulting from uncontrolled developments in the course of an industrial activity or due to natural events leading to serious effects both intermediate or delayed, inside or outside the installation, and likely to cause substantial loss of life and property including adverse effects on the environment.

Malthusian Principle (Malthusian Ka Siddhant) States that the food supply is the limiting factor for population of humans as well as animals. The number of living beings that are able to survive have access to a smaller amount of the food supply. So if the food supply is increased, the number of living entities will again increase.

Man-Made Pollutants (Manav Nirmit Pradushak) When a substance is manufactured by humans for their own consumption, they are termed as man-made pollutants. Some examples include the pesticides, detergents, chlorine, and PCBs.

Man-rem A unit used in health physics to compare the effects of different amounts of radiation on groups of people. Obtained by multiplying the average dose equivalent to the whole body of a given organ or tissue (measured in rems) by the number of persons in the selected population.

Manganese (Manganese) Flammable silvery metal. Essential for plant and animal life. Mined in India. Used in the manufacture of steel, and aluminium.

Manifest (Maal Suchi) Transporting document originated and signed by the generator or occupier. An occupier who transports, or offers for transportation, hazardous waste for off-site treatment, storage or disposal should prepare a manifest as per the form included in Annexure-V of the Guidelines for Management and Handling of Hazardous Waste 1991. Six copies of the manifest containing details of hazardous waste should be prepared by the occupier/generator. The manifest must indicate a permitted primary facility and an alternate facility and which is going to handle the waste. It should contain 23 items as listed in Appendix J.

Marine Environment (Samudri Paryavaran) The nearshore coastal waters of India are extremely rich fishing grounds. The total commercial marine catch for India has stabilised over the last ten years at between 1.4 and 1.6 million tonnes. There is a wide range of coral reefs of commercial value that occur along only a few sections of the mainland, principally the Gulf of Kutch, off the southern mainland coast, and around a number of islands opposite Sri Lanka. Other notable marine areas are seagrass beds, green tiger prawn Penaeus semisulcatus. Five species of marine turtle occur in Indian waters.

Marsh (Daldal) When large quantities of grass, reeds, and other vegetation is present in a wetland covering the layer of water completely. Generally found in areas where water is shallow and is either stagnant or very slow moving. They may either be fresh or salt water, tidal or non-tidal.

Marsh Gas (Daldal se Nikli Gas) Refers to methane gas which is produced from partial decay of plants in swamps.

Mass Emission Standards For automobiles refers to the gram of emission emitter per kilometre run of the vehicle as determined by a chassis dynamometer test using the Indian Driving Cycle.

Mass Number (Pariman Matra) The number of nucleons (neutrons and protons) in an atom.

Maximum Contaminant Level (Uchchatam Sandushak Star) The maximum permissible level of a contaminant in water that is delivered to any user of a public water system.

Mean Free Path The average path distance a particle (neutron or photon) travels before undergoing a specified reaction (with a nucleus or electron) in matter.

Mechanical Ventilation (Yantrik Samvaatan) Forced movement of air by fans into and out of a building.

Medha Patkar (Medha Patkar) She was born in 1956 and is the leader of the Narmada Bachao Andolan. She has gone to jail many times for the cause of the 60,000 evacuees of the Sardar Sarovar project. She received the Right Livelihood Award, 1991. Because of her protest, the World Bank withdrew Rs. 7,000 crore loan towards building the dam. She has a doctorate from the Tata Institute of Social Sciences. She is convinced that mass mobilisation is the only way to help the tribals understand the environmental problem.

Medical Waste (Aspatal Ka Kachara) Any solid waste which is generated in the diagnosis, treatment, or immunization of human beings or animals in research, production, or testing of biological matter. This type of waste is generally produced in hospitals, and clinics. See also Infectious waste.

Megacurie (Megacurie) Ten lakhs or one million curies of radioactive substance.

Mehta, M.C. He is a lawyer, very active in challenging industries who pollute the environment. Magsaysay award winner, Mr. Mehta has won many landmark decisions from courts in this regard.

Member (Sadasya) 'Member' means a member of either a Union, State or a Union Territory Pollution Board and includes the Chairman thereof. Created under The Water Act of 1974.

Meniscus (Navachandrak or Meniscus) The curved top of a column of liquid in a small tube.

Mercaptans (Mercaptans) Organic compounds that have the general formula of R-SH. It means it is a thiol group in which –SH is attached to a radical such as CH3 or

C2H5. The simpler mercaptans have strong, repulsive, garlic-like odours. Odours become less pronounced with increasing molecular weight and higher boiling points.

Mercury (Para or Parad) One of the heaviest metal with an extremely high surface tension. A very good conductor of electricity, it is used in switches and fluorescent lamps. Silvery white in color. When swallowed, it is a highly toxic and cancer causing substance which may damage kidney and nervous system disorders. It bioaccumulates in fish and animals and thus biomagnifies the problems as they pass in the food chain and get concentrated in the process. Limit of mercury in drinking water as per the Water Act of 1975 in the final (combined) effluent is 0.01 mg/l. Atomic weight: 200.59. Chemical symbol: Hg.

Mesa (Pathirili Choras Pahadi) An isolated and elevated plateau which is flat at the top but with one steep side. Generally small in size.

Mesh (Jali) Opening of a screen. Mesh size is indicated by the number of openings per linear inch. Bu\u the size or thickness of wire is not taken into consideration, the size of the opening is not the same even for a constant mesh size.

Mesophyte (Samod Bhid) In comparison to most of the trees, a plant that requires an average amount of moisture. These trees are generally found in climates of moderate rainfall and temperatures.

Mesosaprobic Zone (Samapooti Kshetra) The area of a river which is strongly polluted but with smaller but some dissolved oxygen.

Mesosphere (Madhya Kshetra) The subdivision of the atmosphere situated between the stratosphere and an altitude of about 80 kilometres.

Mesothelioma (Mesothelioma) A type of cancer caused by exposure to asbestos.

Mesozoic (Madhya Jeevi) A geological time frame including Triaswsic, Jurassic and Cretaceous periods. It is between Paleozoic and Cenozoic period.

Metabolism (Chayaapa Chay) The sum of all physical and chemical processes by which living organized substances are produced and maintained by which energy is made available for the use of the organism. Chemicals can be metabolized and made either more or less harmful by the body.

Metabolite (Upaap Chay) Any substance produced by living organism due to exposure to a chemical substance. It is a product of metabolism.

Metabolites (Upaap Chayag or Metabolite) Substances that are produced by biological processes, such as those from pesticides.

Metal (Dhatu) Solid substances which are generally good conductors of electricity. Form positive ions in aqueous solutions. Commonly form bases with hydroxyl radicals and replace the hydrogen of an acid to form a salt. Trace amounts are essential for living organisms. Large quantities of some of the heavy metals such as cadmium, mercury, lead, and chromium are known to be carcinogens.

Metal Cladding See also Cladding.

Metalimnion (Madhya Sar) It is the middle layer of a thermally stratified lake or reservoir. In this layer there is a rapid decrease in temperature with depth. Also called thermocline.

Metamorphic Rock (Rupantarkarik Chhattan) A rock formed when a preexisting rock is subjected to high temperatures, confining pressures, and chemically active fluids deep within the earth's crust.

Methane (Methane) A colourless, odourless gaseous hydrocarbon, the principal component of natural gas. Also a strong greenhouse gas, its concentration in the atmosphere is 1.72 ppm. Animals and landfills produce large amounts of methane naturally. Naturally occurring methane in the earth is formed during anaerobic decomposition of plant and animal matter over a course of millions of years. Formula: CH4.

Methyl Isocyanate (Methyl Iso Cyanate) Methyl isocyanate (MIC) is an ester of isocyanic acid (HNCO). Highly volatile and inflammable gas; vapours are denser than air; stable under dry and neutral conditions at room temperature but can violently react in the presence of acids, alkali, and the like. MIC can be easily produced and stored at room temperature. When it comes to industrial production, three stages are involved: i) the manufacture of carbon dioxide, ii) production of phosgene and iii) the synthesis of MIC and its storage. MIC, with phosgene as one of the substances used to manufacture it, creates immediate irritation, chest pain, breathlessness, and can trigger severe asthma. If the exposure is high, as in Bhopal, it leads to severe bacterial pneumonia, tumour or laryngeal edema, and massive cardiac arrest. The real problem, however, is that it sensitises the skin and even a mild exposure proves lethal. MIC is manufactured for use as an intermediate product in a variety of pesticides.

Mhos Scale A scale used to measure the hardness of rocks and minerals. Talc is the softest and its hardness is 1 to 10 for Diamond which is considered as the hardest. See also Hardness scale.

Microbial Pesticide (Jeevanu Nashak Rasayan) Instead of a substance, when a microorganism is used to control pests. They are generally very less toxic to man.

Micron (Sukshma or Micron) A micrometre. A one-millionth part of a metre (i.e. 10-6 metre or 10-4 centimetre). Roughly four one-hundred-thousandths of an inch.

Microorganism (Sukshma Jeev) The Hazardous Micro Organisms Rules of 1989 define this as to include all the bacteria, viruses, fungi, mycoplasma, cells lines, algae, protodones, and nematotes indicated in the schedule and those that have not been presently known to exist in the country or not have been discovered so far. They are living things but microscopic in size.

Microrem (Microrem) A unit of measure of 'dose equivalence', which reflects the health risk resulting from a given absorbed dose of radiation. A microrem is one millionth (10 -9) of a rem (roentgen equivalent man).

Microsecond (Microsecond) One-millionth part of a second.

Microwave (Suksham Tarang or Microwave) A form of electromagnetic energy of relatively long wavelength that falls between infrared waves and radio waves in the electromagnetic spectrum.

Migration Pathway (Sthanantarn Path) Route (e.g., a stream or river) for potential movement of contaminants to environmental receptors (e.g., plants, animals, humans).

Milk of Lime (Dudhiya Chuna) Calcium hydroxide suspended in water.

Millimetre (Millimetre) A unit of length equal to one thousandth of a metre.

Millirad (Millirad) A one-thousandth part of a rad.

Million Electron Volt (MEV) A unit of energy used in nuclear physics. It is equivalent to 1.6 X 10-6 erg.

Millirem (Millirem) A unit of radiation dosage equal to one-thousandth of a rem. Rems are a way to measure radiation according to the ability of the specific type of radiation to do damage to biological tissue. Humans receive it from natural radiation, medical exposure, consumer products, and from nuclear industry-related activities.

Minamata Disease (Minamata Rog) A disease of the central nervous system caused by mercury poisoning.

Mineralization (Khanijikaran) The end result of biodegradation processes where a contaminant is biodegraded to its basic components. For example, petroleum hydrocarbons degraded to carbon dioxide and water.

Minimum Explosive Concentration (Nimnatam Visphotak Sandrata) See also MEC.

Mining of an Aquifer (Jaladhar Se Pani Nikalna) When ground water is pumped over an extended period of time which results in lowering of the water table. This means the recharge of the aquifer is less than the pumping rate. Cone formation takes place at the bottom of the well.

Mixed Waste (Mishrit Kuda) Where more than one contaminant is present in any substance. In case of radioactive waste, when hazardous component is also present, then it is considered to be a mixed waste.

Molasses (Sheera) After the manufacture of sugar, the thick liquid from which no more sugar can be extracted. The thick liquid will contain sucrose, ash, water, and organic nonsugars.

Molecule (Anu) The smallest unit of a particle of a substance that can keep all of its characteristics as the larger mass. Helium molecules contain only one atom, while oxygen has two, ozone has three.

Monitoring (Prabodhan or Niyantran Rakhana) The process of either continuously or at a fixed interval, monitoring the contamination at any given site. It is done by analytical means. Monitoring can be conducted of underground water, soil, plants, and other media.

Monitoring Wells (Niyantran Ke Kuan) Wells specifically drilled at precise locations on or around a site so that ground water can be sampled at selected depths and studied to determine such things as the direction in which ground water flows and the types and amounts of contaminants present. These site may be hazardous waste sites. Analysis could be either physical, chemical, or biological.

Monoclonal Antibodies (Ek Jeevi Rog Pratikari) When molecules of living organisms that selectively find and attach to other molecules to which their structure conforms exactly. Monoclonal antibodies could also be clones of a molecule produced in a lab for medical or research purposes.

Monoculture (Ek Dhan Ki Krishi or Ek Phasal) When only one crop is repeatedly harvested in a large area. Because of only one crop grown, the crops lack built-in feedback loops which are available to natural systems. For this reason, ingredients necessary for their growth may have to be supplied to keep the growth of vegetation. They are very vulnerable to diseases.

Monomer (Eklak) A compound containing carbon and a simple structure which is capable of conversion to polymers, and synthetic resins when it combines with itself or other similar compounds. Vinyl chloride, and adipic acid are monomers.

Morbidity (Rugnata) Rate at which a disease affects humans in an environment. It is also the ratio of number of sick individuals to the total population of a community.

Mulch (Ghas Paat Se Dhakna) To hold moisture around the trunk of a plant, placing of material such as straw, leaves, and wood chips. This enriches the soil.

Mutagen (Utparivartan) Agents that produce or cause permanent genetic change in a cell or genes. Also called mutations of cells. Result in alterations of genetic materials such as DNA. Carcinogens are generally mutagens. Mutagenic effects such as mental retardation, cancer, infertility could be seen after many generations also. Examples are DDT and Arsenic.

Mutation (Parivartan) Change in the structure of the reproductive DNA of an organism. Changes the characteristics of the organism's offspring. Future generations will inherit this mutation.

Mycotoxin (Kavak Vish) Produced from molds or fungi, they are highly toxic. An example is Aflotoxins which are produced from a fungus.

N

Nanogram (Nanogram) A unit of mass equal to one billionth of a gram.

Naphtha (Naphtha) Flammable liquid which is produced from the distillation of crude oil. Toxic to humans. Used in paint and varnish as thinners, solvents, and in many different types of cleaners.

Natality (Janma Dar) The rate of production of new individuals by birth, hatching, or germination.

National River Action Plan (NRAP) (Rashtriya Nadya Karya Yojana) Initiated by the Central government to save the rivers. As major rivers have been dammed at the source for much needed irrigation projects, there is not much water at the lower reaches. The pollutants that industries dump into them make things worse. To save the rivers, the Central government has started the NRAP. As per the policy, the rivers have been classified into four zones:

- A1 - point where the river originates up to its first dam or weir;
- A2 - the main stage of the river or the stretch below the first designated weir or dam;
- A3 - river water used for aquaculture; and
- A4 - that which flows into the cities and lowest plains, used mainly for agriculture and industrial cooling processes.

Criteria for siting of industries with reference to classification of river zones is given in Appendix I. See also Industrial Classification.

Natural Gas (Prakratik Gas) Colourless, odourless, flammable gas or liquid. A type of fossil fuel almost always found with petroleum deposits below ground. Under high pressure. Formed with the petroleum due to the decomposition of microorganisms. The mixture of natural gas may have mostly methane and ethane. Other gases such as butane and nitrogen may be in trace amounts.

Natural Pollutants (Prakratik Pradushak) Several substances considered by men as pollutants have been present in the earth as a part of the natural occurrence. Examples include radiation, hydrocarbons, and sulphur dioxide.

Natural Radiation (Prakratik Vikiran) Radiation that is naturally present all the time in the environment. Natural radiation is from such source as cosmic rays, and radioactive materials.

Natural Ventilation (Prakratik Samvatan) Movement of air into and out of a building through intentional openings, such as windows and vents.

Necrosis (Ootakakshyay) When plant or animal cell die. The stems of the plant or leaves may become discoloured in the process.

Negantropy (Anutkram Maap) The tendency for a system to get more organized. It is the opposite of entropy.

Negligence (Laparvahi or Asaavdhani) Failure to exercise proper care, resulting in responsibility for injury or damage to a person or thing.

Nematode (Gol Krami) Worms that are parasitic on plants and animals. Generally they are elongated and unsegmented. Commonly found in soils.

Nephelometric When light is passed through a water sample to measure the turbidity in a water sample. Measured by the amount of light that has been deflected back.

Nephrotoxicity On exposure to a substance that can cause adverse effects on the kidney, ureter, or bladder. Some examples include carbon tetrachloride and trichloroethylene, and heavy metals such as cadmium and lead.

Neon (Neon) Colourless, odourless, tasteless, Nobel and inert gas. Used in electric tubes and in lasers. Atomic weight: 20.179. Chemical symbol: Ne.

Neoplasm (Nava Dravya) An uncontrolled and progressive growth of cells. It may be benign or malignant, similar to Tumor.

Neritic Zone (Neritanchal) The region of the ocean that extends from the low tide line to the outer edge of the continental shelf.

Neuritis (Tantrika Shoth) Inflammation of a nerve.

Neurotixin A systemic poison whose target organ is the nervous system.

Neutralisation (Nishprabhavan) When acid is added to an alkaline solution or an alkali is added to an acid solution so that their pH becomes 7.0.

Neutron (Neutron) A particle which has no electrical charge in the atom's nucleus. Their Atomic mass: 1.009.

Neutron Particle (Neutron Kan) An uncharged particle found in the nucleus of all atoms which are heavier than hydrogen. A neutron is one of the three basic particles that make up the atom. Neutrons interact with matter by collisions with the nucleus, which result in secondary charged particles that cause ionization. They have very long range of several hundred feet in air but are best shielded by materials with a high hydrogen content such as water, plastic, or concrete. Effect the whole body. Sources could be from americium, plutonium, uranium.

Nitrate (Nitrate) An oxidized form of nitrogen, plant nutrient. Found in septic systems, animal feed lots, agricultural fertilisers, manure, and in sanitary landfills. Can have harmful effects on humans and animals. Nitrates in sufficient quantities in water can be harmful to infants and domestic animals.

Noble Metal (Uttam Dhatu) Very high in monetary value and have some specific quality such as resistance to corrosion. Gold, silver, and platinum are some examples.

Noise (Shor or Kolahal or Dhwani) Noise is defined as unwanted sound. Sound which pleases the listeners may be termed music and that which causes pain and annoyance can be termed as noise. Noise also increases blood pressure, especially in children, and the resulting disturbed sleep and rise in heart rate and blood pressure, may aggravate angina, congestive failure or arrhythmias, more so in the elderly cardiac patients. Noise prevention and control is important as noise affects us in hearing, ability to communicate, and behaviour. Less noise can make the environment more friendly and life pleasant. The following are the limits by the Environment (Protection) Rules of 1986 Schedule III.

Area Code	Category of Area	Limits in db(A)	
		Day Time	Night Time
A	Industrial Area	75	70
B	Commercial Area	65	55
C	Residential Area	55	45
D	Silence Zone	50	40

Note:

1. Day time is reckoned in between 6 a.m. and 9 p.m.
2. Night time is reckoned in between 9 p.m. and 6 a.m.
3. Silence zone is defined as areas upto 100 metres around such premises as hospitals, educational institutions, and courts. The Silence zones are to be declared by the competent authority.
4. Mixed categories of areas should be declared as one of the four above mentioned categories by the competent authorities and the corresponding standards shall apply.

Nonionizing Radiation Aaayanikrit Vikiran) Radiation that does not have enough energy to cause ionization to an atom with which it interacts.

Non-routine Waste Wastes produced from environmental restoration program activities, including primary and secondary wastes associated with retrieval and remediation operations. Non-routine wastes are a direct result of past operations and activities rather than current processes.

NOx Refers to nitrogen oxides, which are a major cause of acid rain. The oxides are nitric Oxide (NO) and nitrogen dioxide (NO2), collectively abbreviated NOx, where 'x' stands for 1 or 2.

Nuclear Chain Reaction (Naabhikiya Shrinkhala Pratikriya) A nuclear reaction that takes place in the nucleus of an atom and changes the atom into one or two entirely different elements. A chain reaction stimulates its own repetition.

Nuclear Energy (Nabhikiya Urja) The energy released when the nucleus of an atom splits or when two nuclei fuse or due to the radioactive decay of a nucleus.

Nuclear Fission (Nabhikiya Vikhandan) The process of dividing or splitting the nucleus of an atom.

Nuclear Fuel Cycle (Nabhikiya Urja Kram) The complete series of steps involved in supplying fuel for nuclear reactors. Includes mining, refining, enrichment, fabrication of fuel elements, and fuel use in a reactor.

Nuclear Medicine (Nabhikiya Chikitsa or Dava) When radioactive substance is used to either treat a disease or conduct a diagnostic exam. Some examples of diagnostic exam include use of Thallium-201 for stress exams to check the adequacy of blood supply to the heart muscle.

Nuclear Power (Nabhikiya Urja) Electricity generated by a nuclear reaction.

Nuclear Radiation (Nabhikiya Vikiran) Particulate and electromagnetic radiation emitted from nuclei.

Nuclear Waste (Nabhikiya Apashisht) Primarily, the radiation waste which is generated by nuclear plants. Nuclear waste, however, is also produced in hospitals and medical labs though these waste may be low level waste in nature.

Nucleus (Nabhik) The central potion of a living cell or the central mass of an atom that contains protons, neutrons, and other particles. Except for the nucleus of ordinary (light) hydrogen, which is a single proton, all atomic nuclei contain both protons and neutrons. The number of protons determines the total positive charge, or atomic number, this is the same for all the atomic nuclei of a given chemical element. The nuclei of isotopes of a given element contain the same number of protons, but different numbers of neutrons. Thus they have the same atomic number, and so are the same element, but they have different mass numbers.

Nuclide (Kendrik) An atom which is characterized by the makeup of its nucleus-namely, by the number of protons and neutrons and the energy content in the nucleus.

Nutrient Pollution (Poshak Pradushan) When presence of excessive nutrient is the cause of a major concern. In a small pond, when excess nutrients are supplied, the result is an algae growth which could kill the pond.

O

Occlusion (Avarodhan) An absorption process by which one substance is taken in and retained in the interior rather than the exterior surface of another substance. Sometimes, this occurs during co-precipitation.

Occupier (Pradhikari) The Environment Act of 1986 defines 'Occupier' as in relation to any factory or premises, means the person who has control over the affairs of the factory or the premises, and includes, in relation to any substance, the person in possession of the substance.

Ocean Power (Samudri Urja) When the temperature difference of water in the ocean is used to generate power. The temperature differential may be as much as 15 to 25 degrees centigrade. Energy can also be derived from waves. Ocean tides contain about 97% of earth's water supply. For energy generation, strong water movement is required. Wave energy is best when strong winds blow. Ocean thermal energy can also be derived where the water is very warm.

Oceanic Zone (Samudri Tat Kshetra) The region of open ocean that lies beyond the continental shelf.

Oceanographer (Samudri Vaigyanik) A person who explores and studies the ocean.

Oil of Vitriol (Sulphuric Amla) An old term for sulphuric acid.

Oil Shale (Shila Tel) Shale deposits containing Kerogen or organic materials that can produce oil when the shale is heated to high temperatures. Currently not economical to recover oil from shale.

Oil Spills (Tel Ka Fail Jana or Tel Ka Bikhar Jana) When petrol or any type of oil is spilled either on the ground or on the surface of water, the damage to the environment is significant. When spilled on the ground, the oil can pollute underground water making the water unsuitable for use of any kind. If the oil spill occurs on a water body, fishes are killed, aquatic plants seriously affected, and birds destroyed. Cleanup of spills depend on the location but the method can be mechanical, skimming, chemical dispersion. Depending on the quantity of the spill, it may take years for the environment to recover.

Oleum (Oleul Ka Tel) The solution of sulphuric acid and sulphur trioxide in the form of fuming sulphuric acid. Oleum is the name given for the stage of the mixture in the production of sulphuric acid. Latin word for oil.

Oligosaprobic Zone (Alpa Poshi Kshetra) A river when it has no contaminant of any kind. The oxidation process is in full swing.

Oligotrophic Lake (Alpa Poshi Jheel) A lake with a low rate of nutrient cycling, little organic matter, and a low level of biological productivity. However at the bottom of the lake, they have high dissolved oxygen levels. Generally deep and very cold.

Omnivore (Sarvaa Haari or Sarva Bakshi) An animal that eats both plants and other animals. Their digestive tracks are longer than those of carnivores.

Oncogenic Substance (Arbudiya Padaarth) Substance that causes the formation of tumors.

Opacity (Apaara Darshita or Dhundhalapan) Degree of emissions that reduce the transmission of light and obscure the view of an object in the background. Emission of particulate matter or radiant energy obscures the passage of light and heat. Clear indication of the air pollution due to particulate matter. Opposite of transparency. High degree of opacity is said to be opaque. Opacity of a clear glass is zero while that of a thick iron metal is 100 percent.

Open Dump (Khula Kuda) Uncontrolled or unauthorised disposal of waste material in any area. As there are no environmental controls installed in that area, may result in pollution of ground water due to formation of leachate from the waste.

Operating Procedure (Karya Paddhati) A document that describes in detail an operation, analysis or action that is commonly accepted as the preferred method for performing certain tasks that may not be routine or repetitive.

Operator (Prachaalak) Person who owns or operates facility for collection, reception, treatment, storage, and disposal of hazardous waste.

Organic Chemicals (Carbonic Rasayan) Chemical compounds that contain carbon with the usual exception of carbon dioxide.

Organic Compounds (Carbonic Yogic) Derived from plants and animals. Carbon is always one of the components. Generally combustible and support propagation of bacteria or other living organisms.

Osmosis (Parasaran or Rasakarshan or Dravya Sanskaran) When water or another pure solvent passes through a membrane. The passage occurs due to difference in the concentrations of dissolved materials on opposite sides of the membrane. The membrane must be permeable to enable the passage of molecules. Presence of the layer eliminates rapid mixing.

Outfall (Jal Nikas) The point at which a sewer or drainage channel discharges to a river or other body of water. Also a narrow part of a stream, lake, or other body of water where it drops away into a larger body. May be the place that a monitoring of any water discharge permit location.

Outgassing Emission of gases during curing, aging, and degradation of a substance.

Outlet (Nikas or Bahar Ane Ka Rasta) 'Outlet' includes any conduit pipe or channel, open or closed, carrying sewage or trade effluent or any other holding arrangement which causes or is likely to cause pollution.

Overpack A waste container used to hold waste packages which provide protection or convenience in handling, or consolidates two or more packages.

Owner (Malik) It means a person who owns, or has control over handling any hazardous substance at the time of accident and includes:

- In the case of firm, any of its partners;
- In the case of an association, any of its members; and
- In the case of a company, any of its directors, managers, secretaries or other officer who is directly in charge of, and is responsible to the company for the conduct of the business of the company.

Oxidizer (Oxikaran) A substance such as a chlorate, permanganate, inorganic peroxide, or a nitrate, that readily yields oxygen to stimulate the combustion of a matter.

Oxygen (Oxygen or Pranaa Vaayu) Necessary for all life to exist, it is one of the most abundant element on the earth. Atomic weight: 15.9994. Chemical symbol:O.

Oxygen Sag Curve A graphic representation of the characteristic decrease and subsequent increase in dissolved oxygen levels in a river downstream from a discharge of organic wastes.

Oxygen Supplementation (Oxygen Sampooran) The addition of bio-available dissolved oxygen to a groundwater system to augment the capacity of the aquifer system to aerobically biodegrade and mineralize contaminants.

Ozone (Ozone) An unstable form of oxygen which has three oxygen atoms instead of two. At ground level, it is an irritant and is a pollutant. Naturally occurring ozone is found in two layers of the atmosphere. At about 25 kilometres above the earth and extending for another 15 kilometres, there is an increased amount of ozone. But at higher levels, forms a layer in the atmosphere that screens out cell damaging harmful solar radiation. Hole in the ozone layer is the cause of increase in Ultraviolet radiation which is suspected as a primary cause for increase in skin cancer. Depletion of the ozone layer affects the photosynthesis process and thus lead to harming aquatic organisms. A one percent drop in the ozone allows 2% more ultraviolet light to reach the earth which means an increase of between 3 and 6% in the cancer rate among human beings. It also causes a one percent increase in melanoma skin cancer and a 2.6% increase in non-melanoma skin cancers.

Ozone Layer or Shield (Ozone Parat or Kavach) An area of stratosphere which is between 25 to 40 kilometres above the earth. Contains mostly naturally occurring Ozone in the atmosphere. Layer of ozone that protects the earth by absorbing Ultraviolet-B radiation from reaching the earth and also helps to hold heat around the planet.

P

Packaging Requirements The packaging should be secure enough to prevent leaks, spills, and vapourization during transportation. The hazardous wastes should be stored in 200 litres steel clamp-lid containers. The containers should be coated with black paint.

Palaeolithic (Purapashan Yug) Era when humans used primitive rock tools by chipping or flaking. Also is called Stone Age. That time is from about 25,00,000 years to about 10,300 years ago.

Palaeontology (Jeevashmiki or Jeevasham Vigyan) Science that deals with the study of fossils, both animal and vegetable.

Paraffin (Parafin) A chemical substance whose general formula is C_nH_{2n+2}. Normally, they are tasteless, odourless substances derived from petroleum. Methane is the simplest paraffin.

Parasite (Parajeevi) Organism that is dependent on another organism to maintain itself. In the process, the dependent organism is weakened and killed by the main (parasite) organism.

Parasitism (Parajeevita) An interaction in which one organism (the parasite) obtains energy and nutrients by living within or upon another organism (the host).

Particulate (Kan) Very fine particles which may be of any solid or liquid material that remain suspended in the air. Generally found in dust, smoke, mist, fumes, or smog. Adjective indicating that a material is composed of particles. When particles are suspended in air, they are also called aerosols. They hold all types of chemicals which can be toxic to both human and plant life. Very fine particulate (less than 10 microns in size) may travel long distances. When collected in large quantities, they may block sunlight. These particles are brought to earth by rain or snow. Fine particulate can cause respiratory diseases such as bronchitis and asthma by penetrating into the lungs. Dust, smoke, and mists fumes are examples of particulate matter.

Paryavaran A Hindi word for environment.

Passive Smoking Also referred to as second hand smoking. The inhalation of smoke when some one else is smoking a cigarette or pipe.

Pasteurisation (Pasturikaranor Nirjeevi Karan) A process to kill disease causing organisms in milk. The time to heat milk and to kill the bacteria varies with the temperature. If heated to 150 degrees centigrade, then milk is heated for one second.

Pathogen (Rog Janak) An organism that causes disease to other organisms such as humans, animals, and plants. Most are either viruses or bacteria. Found in sewage, in runoff from farms, or rural areas populated with animals. Some of the pathogens identified in the Hazardous Micro Organisms Rules of 1989 include salmonella, trichophyton, and hepatitis.

Pathogenic Substances (Rog Moolak Padarth) Substances capable of causing disease.

Peat (Peat or Paans) Dark brown or black, first stage of coal which is formed by decomposition of organic matter, in areas where water is also available. Generally found on surface, they are a good source for natural gas and oil. Along with lignite, peat is found in Neyveli in Tamilnadu.

Perched Groundwater (Duhsthith Bhoomi Jal) Unconfined ground water in a zone of saturation separated from an underlying saturated zone by an unsaturated zone. Perched ground water is supported by a perching bed whose permeability is so low that water percolating downward through it is not able to bring water in the underlying unsaturated zone above atmospheric pressure.

Percolation (Risan or Dhire Se Tapakna or Parishravan) The movement of water or other liquids down through the pores of rocks or soil. Movement of water underground is generally very slow. Besides gravitational, it could also be due to capillary action.

Perc Test (Perc Parikshan) Rate of movement of water underground. Expressed as centimetres per minute.

Permafrost (Sthayi Tushar Bhoomi) A permanently frozen aggregate of ice and soil occurring in very cold regions.

Permeability (Pargamyataa) A measure of soil resistance to fluid flow in a particular direction. Movement of fluid depends on the size and shapes of stones or rocks. Permeability, along with fluid viscosity and density are used to determine fluid conductivity. Unit of permeability is Darcy. See also Darcy.

Permissible Exposure Limit-PEL (Anumeya Anashrayataa Seema) The time weighted average and ceiling concentrations similar to (and in many cases derived from) the threshold limit values, specified in 29 CFR 1910, Subparts G and Z.

Person In relation to any factory or premises means a person or occupier or his agent who has control over the affairs of the factory or premises and includes in relation to any substance, the person in possession of the substance.

Personal Protective Equipment (PPE) (VaiyaktikRuraksha Saadhan) When working in a hazardous or dangerous locations or sites, chemical protective clothing or devices placed on the body to prevent contact with, and exposure to, an identified substance in the work area. Ranges from goggles for eye protection, to full protection with coveralls, gloves, shoe covers, respiratory protective equipment, and hood or skull cap. For example: chemical protective clothing, aprons, hoods, goggles, face splash shields, and various types of respirators.

Pest (Nashak Jeev) An insect, rodent, nematode, fungus, weed or any other form of aquatic or animal life or virus, bacterial organism or other microorganism which is deemed to be injurious to human health or the environment. See also Plant Pest

Pesticide (Keetnashi) Substances which are used to prevent, repel, destroy, or mitigate pests. Used on wood to prevent termites. In general, used to repel undesirable organisms and so are toxic and/or carcinogenic to that particular organism. Depending on the actual pest that they are used to kill, Pesticides are further classified as fungicide or insecticide. Generally synthetic organic chemical and are a a petroleum product. The disadvantage of extensive use is that they may get into the food chain meant for human consumption. In trace amounts, DDT has been found in mother's milk. Example of pesticides include DDT, chlordane, pentachlorophenol, and methyl bromide.

Petroleum (Petrol) Originated from plant and animal sources long ago, are naturally occurring complex mixtures containing many chemicals. Crude oil pumped from earth. May also include oils derived from shale, tar, and coal. Petroleum products are derived by refining or distilling the crude and various grades recovered are used in heating, automobile, machinery, power production, and lubricants.

pH A measure of acidity. Also called Power of Hydrogen. On the pH scale, 7 is neutral (pure water); a pH below 7 is acidic, greater than 7 is alkaline. A decrease of one pH unit represents a ten-fold increase in acidity. For example, pH 4 is one hundred times as acidic as pH 6. The Water Act limits the pH of drinking water between 5.5 to 9.0.

Phenol (Phinaile) An organic compound, it is white-to-clear crystalline solid and consists of a benzene ring with a hydroxyl group (OH-) attached to it. An extremely toxic chemical, it can be absorbed through skin. Causes nausea, vomiting and ultimately death. Used as a lab reagent, and also in the manufacture of dies, medicines, and as a solvent. Chemical formula: C6H5OH.

Phosphate (Phosphate) A salt or ester of phosphoric acid. It is a compound containing PO4 radical. Mostly used in fertilizers.

Phosphorous (Phosphorous) Crystalline transparent solid. An essential element for life, Phosphorous forms a part of the DNA molecule. Ignites spontaneously in the atmosphere at over 30 degrees centigrade. It is a component of teeth, bone, and nerve tissues. Used in the manufacture of semiconductors and fertilisers. Atomic weight: 30.97. Chemical symbol: P.

Photochemical Smog (Prakash Rasaayanik Dhoom Kohraa) A noxious, hazy mixture of aerosols and gases formed by sunlight acting on oxides of nitrogen and hydrocarbons such as nitrogen oxides. Common pollutants in urban-industrial air.

Photolysis (Prakashik Apaghatan) The decontamination or degradation of a contaminant by chemical reactions catalyzed by light.

Photon (Photon) A unit or particle of electromagnetic radiation, carrying a quantum of energy which is characteristic of the particular radiation. X-rays and gamma rays are examples of photons.

Photosynthesis (Prakash Sanshleshan) The process by which green plants use sunlight and bacteria to produce energy from carbon dioxide and water. Chlorophyll acts as a catalyst. It is ultimately responsible for all animal and plant life on earth. It is also the principal source of atmospheric oxygen.

Phototropism (Prakash Anuvartan) Growth of most of the plant is almost always towards the direction of sunlight.

Photovoltaic Cell A semiconductor device that directly converts some of the sunlight falling on it into electricity.

Photo Ionization Detector (Prakash Aayanikaran Samsoochak) A photoionization detector (PID) is an instrument of measure used to determine the presence and concentration of volatile organic chemicals and to confirm the level of protection. All surveys should be performed with a photoionization detector that has an appropriately rated lamp.

Physical Treatment of Hazardous Waste (Khatarnak Apashisht Ka Bhautikiya Upachar) Processes that include various methods of phase separation and solidification. The phase separation includes lagooning, sludge drying in beds, and prolonged storage in tanks. All these processes depend on the gravitational settlement. Lagooning and tank storage are widely used to separate oil and water from mixed wastes. Solidification or fixation processes convert the waste into an insoluble, rock-hard material and they are generally used as pre-treatment prior to landfill disposal. The conversion is achieved by blending the waste with various reactants to produce a cement-like product.

Phytoplankton (Paadap Plavak) Microscopic plants that drift in water and are the basis of the aquatic food chain. They are not truly plants but are primary producers in all the aquatic ecosystems. This in turn provides 70% of earth's atmospheric oxygen. They are algae and diatoms.

Phytotoxicity (Paadap Vishaaktata) Ability of a chemical compound to kill or seriously harm plant life.

Picocurie (pCi) A Picocurie is one billionth (10-12) of a curie, or 0.037 disintegrations per second or the quantity of radioactive material producing 2.2 nuclear transformations per minute.

Pipeline (Pipeline) 'Pipeline' means a pipe (together with any apparatus and works associated therewith) or system of pipes (together with any apparatus and work associated therewith) for the conveyance of a hazardous chemical other than a flammable gas as set out in Column 2 Part II of Schedule 3 of Manufacture, Storage and Import of Hazardous Chemical Rules, 1989 at a pressure of less than 8 bars absolute; the pipeline also includes inter-state pipelines.

Pit (Gaddha) The central core of a nuclear weapon consisting of fissile material surrounded by a sealed metal shell.

Place (Sthan or Sthal) Under The Water Act of 1974, 'Place' includes a vessel.

Place of Sample 'Place' includes a vessel, stream, well, or sample of any sewage or trade effluent which is passed from any plant or vessel or from or over any place into any such stream or well.

Placer Deposits Heavy minerals found in sand and gravel layers in streambeds or in coastal areas.

Plankton (Plavak) Small plants and animals that live in or on the surfaces of oceans or bodies of fresh water. Generally, do not swim but drift with the movement of water or lie at the bottom of the water table.

Plant Pest (Paudha Naashak Jeev) As per the Hazardous Micro Organisms Rules of 1989, this means any living stage (including active and dormant forms) of insects, mites, nematodes, slugs, snails, bacteria, fungi, protozoa, other parasitic plants or reproductive parts thereof: viruses or any organisms similar to or allied with any of the foregoing; or any infectious agents or substances, which can directly or indirectly injure or cause disease or damage in or to any plants or parts thereof, or any processed, manufactured, or other products of plants are considered plant pests.

Plasma Arc Incinerator Any enclosed device using a high intensity electrical discharge or arc as a source of heat followed by an afterburner using controlled flame combustion and which is not an industrial furnace.

Plastic (Plastic or Jhilli) A synthetic polymer, it can be shaped in any shape or form. They are now used in almost all industries. Non-metallic, but they are very hard and in many cases have replaced many metals. Used in automobile industry, pipes, chemical plants, foams, fabric, and in construction industry.

Plating (Parat or Satah) Forming a thin adherent layer of metal on an object through an electric process.

Pleistocene This is the geological period which preceeded the Halocene (or the recent) in the Quarternary period. It lasted about one and one half million years ago until ten thousand years back. During the Pleistocene epoch, four major ice ages occurred.

Plume Refers to a three dimensional area, usually on air or ground water of contamination movement. The highest concentration is closest to the source and gradually concentration decreases away from the source of contamination. The contamination spreads in the direction that the underground water moves through the pores of soil and rocks or the air in the atmosphere. The direction and concentration of the pollutant is dependent on the concentration of the receiving and emitting chemical and the location of the source. When in air, it is influenced by the movement and direction of wind. In all these, temperature is also an important factor.

Plutonium (Plutonium) First prepared in 1941, it is one of the most toxic substances known. A heavy, radioactive element which is readily fissionable and so must be handled with extreme care. As it has enormous energy, it is used as a fuel to produce nuclear energy. The atomic number is 94 and is man-made. Its most important isotope is fissionable 239Pu, which is produced by the irradiation of 238Pu. Its half-life is 24,360 years.

PM_{10} Particulate matter with an aerodynamic diameter less than or equal to a nominal 10 micrometres. Particles of such a small size can be breathed and so can get deposited in lungs.

Poise A unit of viscosity which is equal to the dynamic viscosity of a fluid in which there is a tangential force of 1 dyne per squre centimetre resisting the flow of two parallel fluid layers past each other when their differential velocity is 1 centimetre per second per centimetre of separation.

Poison (Vish or Jahar) A substance, in any form, that is harmful to humans. Once inside the body, produces chemical reactions that interfere with normal bodily functions. It may be a toxin or a carcinogen.

Pollen (Paraag) The element which fertilises a flowering plant. They can also be called as background air pollutant. If pollen count is very high in air, they are considered to be harmful to humans.

Pollutant (Pradushak) Any substance, whether it is a chemical, physical or biological, which produces or exerts an undesirable effect on human health, the environment or to any of the belongings. The effect could be caused by any form of exposure, or inhalation. Includes any element, substance, compound, or mixture thereof. It can result in disease, behavioural abnormalities, cancer, genetic mutation, physiological malfunctions, including malfunctions in reproduction, physical deformities, and even death. See also Natural Pollutants, Man-made Pollutants, and Pollution.

Pollution (Apavitrikaran or Pradushan) As per The Water Act of 1974, 'Pollution' means such contamination of water or such alteration of the physical, chemical or biological properties of water or such discharge of any sewage or trade effluent or of any other liquid, gaseous or solid substance into water (whether directly or indirectly) as may, or is likely to, create a nuisance or render such water harmful or injurious to public health or safety, or to domestic, commercial, industrial, agricultural or other legitimate uses, or to the life and health of animals or plants or of aquatic organisms. In Hindi, *Pradushan*.

Pollution Prevention (Pradushan Nivaran or Rok Tham) The use of materials, processes, and practices that reduce or eliminate the generation and release of pollutants, contaminants, hazardous substances, and wastes into land, water, and air. Pollution prevention includes practices that reduce the use of hazardous materials, energy, water, and other resources along with practices that protect natural resources through conservation or more efficient use.

Pollution Prevention Opportunity Assessment (Pradushan Nivaran Avasar or Nirdharan) A systematic, planned approach used to evaluate input materials and parameters of a process, identify pollution and waste exiting the process, and generate and evaluate options for pollution prevention.

Polychlorinated Biphenyls (PCBs) A group of commercially produced organic chemicals used since 1940s in industrial applications. Most notably, they are found in large electrical transformers, and capacitors. Proven to be toxic to both humans and laboratory animals.

Polymer (Bahulak) A natural or synthetic compound of unusually high molecular weight that consists of many repeated links, each link being a relatively light and simple molecule. In synthetic polymers, the number of monomer could be controlled. Rayon, nylon, and polyvinyl chloride are examples of polymer.

Polysaprobic Zone (Bahuputik Kshetra) A part of the river or water bed which has a very high contamination level of organic material. This zone is characterized by the presence of blood worms.

Porosity (Chidrilataa or Sukshma Randhrataa) The volume percentage of the total soil bulk not occupied by solid particles or open space in a soil or rock layer.

Positron (Dhananu) A positively charged particle having the same mass and magnitude of charge as the electron.

Potential Energy (Sambhavit Urja) The capability to produce energy. Coal has potential energy as it can be used as a fuel.

Pour Point (Bahaav Bindu) Under specified conditions, the lowest temperature at which a given substance will flow.

Powder Snow (Barf Ke Churan) Formed during cold snowfalls, it is composed of very small, separate crystailine flakes. Behaves similar to sand.

Powered Air Purifying Respirator-PAPR Used at installations unsafe for workers to go without a respirator. Almost always required whenever working in any hazardous area or during friable asbestos removal work.

Pozzolonic Materials Cement kiln flyash or flyash from fossil fuel power plants, and other such materials. Often used in combination with portland cement as a stabilization technique.

ppm Abbreviation for Parts Per Million.

Pradushan Hindi word for pollution.

Predation (Parbhakshan) An interaction in which one organism (the predator) kills and eats another organism (the prey).

Predator (Parbhakshi) An organism that captures and kills to eat another organism.

Prefilter (Pratham Chanan) An initial filter that removes the largest particles at the beginning.

Preliminary Assessment (Prarambhik Vichar Nirdharan) The process of collecting and reviewing available information about a known or suspected hazardous waste site or release. The extent of release and degree of threat to human health and the environment are evaluated to determine whether further study is needed and whether the release meets the criteria for a CERCLA
funded removal.

Preliminary Risk Assessment (Prarambhik Jokhim Nirdharan) A risk assessment conducted using a simplified and not necessarily appropriate scenario and assuming no mitigating or corrective measures beyond those already in place is required.

Premises (Sthal or Kshetra) 'Premises' means any building structure or load used for industrial or commercial purposes where pollution occurs.

Prescribed (Nirdharit Karna) In The Water Act of 1974, 'Prescribed' means prescribed by rules made any Act by the Central Government or, as the case may be, the State Government. See also Standard.

Priority Pollutant (Purva Pradushak or Prathamik Pradushak) Pollutants listed in regulations and whose emissions are controlled to limits set by them.

Process Wastewater (Samsadhit Jal or Udyogic Kriya Ka Vyarth Pani) Any water that comes into contact with or results from the production of any product, raw material, product, or process waste. May also be from washdown from equipments, vehicles, pipelines, vessels, storage tanks, process, floor drains, sump drains, cooling water. Independent of the level and/or the nature of the contaminants.

Program Warning Signs (Chetaavani Sanket) Generic warning signs installed at the entrances of any hazardous site. Example: "Hazardous site: Approval required prior to disturbing posted sites Contact: ."

Prohibited Substance (Nishiddha Vastu) The Environment Act of 1986 defines it as when the substance is prohibited for handling.

Protein (Protein - Bhojan Ka Ek Rasayan Tatva) Primary component of a living tissue. They are complex high polymer organic molecules and are mostly amino acids but may carry other components such as oxygen, hydrogen, nitrogen, and carbon attached to them.

Proton (Proton) An extremely small positively charged particle. A proton is found in the nucleus and is one of the three particles that make up an atom. They are identical to an hydrogen ion.

Protozoan (Ek Koshika Jeev) One-celled organism found commonly in water and soil. It is an algae. A few classes of them may cause sickness such as dysentery but are actually an important part of the food chain.

Pu It is the symbol for Plutonium, a radioactive substance.

Public Liability Insurance Act, 1991 (Sarvajanik Deyta Beema Adhiniyam) An Act to provide for public liability insurance for the purpose of providing immediate relief to the persons affected by accident occurring while handling any hazardous substance and for matters connected therewith or incidental thereto. By this Act, not only companies but also individual supervisors may be subjected to face any criminal and monetary penalties. 179 hazardous, toxic and explosive chemical and compounds with quantities and flammable substances characteristics for application of this act have been specified.

Public Liability Insurance Advisory Committee (Sarvajanik Deyta Beema

Salaahkaar Samiti) A committee constituted by the Central government in accordance with section 21 of the Act of 1991.

Pumice (Jhanva) Igneous rock which during formation had air trapped inside. For this reason, they are very light. Generally used as a cement filler, heat and sound insulation, and paint filler.

Putrescible Waste (Sadaa Kuda or Kachara or Sadiyal Kachara) Solid waste containing organic matter which can be decomposed by microorganisms and of such a character and proportion as to be capable of attracting or providing food for birds.

Pyrolysis (Taap Apaghatan) A conversion technique whereby organic substances such as garbage, wood, or coal are broken down by intense heat applied in the absence of oxygen. Products include oils and combustible gases.

Pyrolytic Gas and Oil (Taap Apaghatan Gas Aur Tel) Gas or liquid products that possess useable heating value that is recovered from the heating of organic material, usually in an essentially oxygen-free atmospheres.

Pyrometer (Taap Mapi Yantra) An instrument to measure very high temperatures. They are used to measure where there is an oil or natural gas fire as a normal thermometer may not be able to read such high temperatures.

Pyrophoric (Swatah Jalansheel) Chemical material so reactive that when exposed to air, they spontaneously burst into flame because of oxidation or hydrolysis. These may occur at temperatures below 130 degrees F, no ignition source needed. It is any solid material, other than one classed as an explosive, which under normal conditions is liable to cause fires through friction, retained heat from manufacturing or processing, or which can be ignited readily and when ignited burns so vigorously and persistently as to create a serious transportation, handling or disposal hazard. Included are spontaneous combustible and water-reactive materials.

Q

Quality Factor (Guna Vakta Karak or Ghatak) In radiation technology, the linear-energy transfer dependent factor by which absorbed doses are multiplied to obtain (for radiation protection purposes) a quantity that expresses-on a common scale for all ionizing radiations-the effectiveness of the absorbed dose. They take into account the chronic low-level exposures from natural sources.

Quarry (Khuli Khan or Khadaan) A small-scale surface mine or pit used for the recovery of rock or building stone.

Quartz (Sfatik) A colourless rock containing mostly silica or silicon dioxide (SiO_2). An inert and extremely stable material in wide ranges of temperatures. Capable of constantly emitting very stable high-frequency electrical pulses. Used primarily in glass, and electronic equipment.

Quarternary Era (Quarternary Kaal) The geologic period succeeding the Tertiary era and extending to the present time.

Quench Station (Bujhane Ka Sthan) A place where hot metal is cooled through the use of a suitable coolant, usually water. An essential part of the tempering process. Mostly used in the metallurgical industry.

R

Rad (Rad) A unit of absorbed dose of radiation in any material. Absorbed dose results from energy being deposited by the radiation. Represents the absorption of 100 ergs of nuclear (or ionizing) radiation per gram of absorbing material, such as body tissue. SI unit for rad is gray (Gy). 100 rad equals 1 gray (Gy).

Radiant Exposure (Vikirak Anaasrayata) The total amount of thermal radiation energy received per unit area of exposed surface. Usually expressed in calories per square centimetre.

Radiant Heat (Vikiran Ushma) Heat radiated by the sun. It is transmitted in all directions.

Radiation (Vikiran) Emission of atomic particles from the nucleus of an atom. Energy is in the form of alpha and beta electromagnetic waves. Fast particles emitting electromagnetic rays or waves. The electromagnetic waves are emitted from the center of an atom during radioactive disintegration. It can be nonionizing which is not harmful to living creatures or ionizing which is harmful to living tissue. Some substances are naturally radioactive but others may become radioactive on contact.

Radiation Dose (Vikiran Maatraa) Amount of radiation received during a given amount of time. Measured by an electronic instrument called a Geiger Counter.

Radiation Sickness (Vikaran Se Utpanna Rog) Sickness that results from exposure to excessive amounts of radiation. Symptoms may include nausea, fatigue, vomiting, and loss of teeth and hair. In severe cases, can include damage to blood-forming tissues, and decrease in red and white blood cells. Immediate medical care is essential to restore patient's health.

Radioactive Material (Vighatanaatmik or Radiodharmi Padaarth) Any material that contains unstable, or radioactive atoms that emits radiation.

Radioactive Decay (Vighatanaabhik Sadaav or Kshay) Spontaneous changing or transformation of an atom into a different atom or a different state of the same atom. Results in the emission of radiation and a decrease, over time, of the original radioactive atoms, also known as disintegration.

Radioactive Isotope (Vighatanaabhik Samasthakin) An unstable isotope of an element that will eventually undergo radioactive decay by spontaneous emission of charged particles, photons, or both.

Radioactive Tracer A radioactive material which is either added or induced in to a sample for the purpose of monitoring chemical or physical losses of the target analytes. The tracer is assumed to behave in the same manner as that of the target analytes. Tracers can also be added to check for leaks.

Radioactivity (Vighatanaabhiktaa) Giving off radiant energy in the form of particles and rays by the disintegration of atomic nuclei of an unstable isotope. As a result of this emission, the radioactive isotope is converted (or decays) into the isotope of a different (daughter) element which may or may not be radioactive. Ultimately, as a result of one or more stages of radioactive decay, a stable and non-radioactive end product is formed. Release of a beta particle converts one neutron in the nucleus into a proton, raising the atomic number by one while keeping the atomic weight the same. Release of an alpha particle converts two protons and two neutrons out of the nucleus, lowering the atomic number by two and the atomic weight by four. During the release of these particles, there is generally a release of energy in the form of heat. When such a substance is undergoing spontaneous radioactive decay, it can also induce decay in nonradioactive substances by physically knocking protons or neutrons out of its nucleus. The common unit of radioactivity is the curie (Ci), which measures the number of disintegrations in one second of one gram of radium.

Radioisotopes (Vikaran Samasthaanik) Atoms of an element that have the same number of protons and a different number of neutrons that emit ionizing radiation when they decay.

Radioactivity (Vighatanaabhikta) Nuclear transformation of elements, such as uranium, of spontaneously emitting alpha or beta particles or gamma rays from the nucleus of an atom.

Radionuclides (Radio Naabhik) Radioactive particles. Nuclides that emit radiation and are thus radioactive.

Radon (Radon) A colorless, odourless, naturally occurring, radioactive gaseous element formed by radioactive decay of radium atoms. This is the only naturally occurring radioactive element which is a gas. As radon further breaks down, polonium, bismuth, and lead are formed. Radon itself is not harmful, but its decaying products, when inhaled or ingested, attach to humans which may lead to lung cancer. Radon itself comes from the radioactive decay of uranium and thorium. Chemical symbol: Rn. Atomic weight: 222. Half life: 3.82 days.

Radon Progeny/Daughters (Radon Utpad) As the half life of radon is short, it decays into products which have longer life or which can attach themselves to airborne dust and other particles. If inhaled, these particles damage the linings of the lungs. The four radioactive elements which immediately follow radon-222 in the decay chain. Polonium-218, Lead-214, Bismuth-214, Polonium-214. These elements have such short life that they exist only in the presence of radon.

Raman, Sir C.V. Indian physicist who discovered the analytical technique called as Raman Spectroscopy. He won the Nobel Prize.

Random It relates to a member of a set whose members have equal probability of occurring or from which each member has equal probability of being selected. Frequently applied to selection of sampling points.

Ranking of a Hazardous Waste Site (Khatarnaak Apashisht Sthal Ka Shreni Karan) Based on an objective evaluation of receptor pathway, waste characteristics, and waste management related attributes based on scaling-weighing technique which involves aggregation, importance and sensitivity of the attributes.

Raptors (Shikari Pakshi) Birds which feed on large rodents, reptiles and other birds. They catch their prey with their legs. Examples include vultures, hawks, and eagles.

Rare Earth Metals Any of the series of very similar metals ranging in atomic number from 57 through 71. See Appendix B.

Rare Species (Durlabh Jeev Jati) Species which are in very small numbers in a particular region. They may be abundant in another region which is not contagious to this region where this species is rare.

Reactivity (Pratikriya Kshamataa) Any substance:

- That is normally unstable and readily undergoes violent changes with detonations;
- Reacts violently with water;
- Generates toxic gases, vapours, or fumes; or
- All explosive materials.

Reactor (Pratikriya Ka Sadhan) The part of a process where a reaction or chemical change takes place. In a plant, this may be one of the important operations.

Reagent (Abhikarmak or Abhikarak) Chemicals which are primarily used to cause a chemical reaction to occur or used for the purpose of detecting and analysing other substances. High purity is essential.

Receptor (Abhigrahi or Abhigraahak) A human individual or individuals, plant, animal, or geographical location that is exposed to or potentially subject to exposure of a hazardous chemical or physical agent released to the environment by human activities.

Recharge (Punah Bharan Karna) The process by which water is added to the zone of saturation, either directly into a geologic information or indirectly by way of another formation or through unconsolidated sediments.

Recipient System 'Recipient System' as per The Environment Act of 1986 means the part of the environment such as soil, water, air, or other which receives the pollutants.

Reclamation (Sudhar) The process of regenerating or recovering a usable product from a material. The restoration of air, land, or water to a better or more useful state, such as reclamation of strip-mined land by sanitary landfilling or reclamation of abandoned landfills by creating recreational park land. It is also when a previously contaminated site is cleaned so that it could be used again.

Recommended Exposure Limit (REL) (Sanstut Vigopan Seema) Time weighed averages and ceiling concentrations on lab evaluations. These are recommended values only.

Record Keeping (Abhilekh) An occupier shall keep a copy of each manifest signed until he receives a signed copy from the designated facility which received the waste. The occupier should keep the signed copy as a record for at least three years from date the waste was accepted by the waste disposer. The record should contain:

- Date, quantity and source of generation;

- Physical state/consistency of waste;
- Type of waste category as per Schedule of Hazardous Wastes (management and Handling) Rules, 1989;
- Chemical constituents of waste;
- Hazardous class of waste as per Motor Vehicles Rules, 1989.

Recycling (Punah Istemal Karna or Prayog Karna) When a substance is diverted a waste stream into a beneficial use, the material is considered to have been recycled. This is generally achieved by collection, separation, and reuse as a raw material in the process. Indirect recycling occurs when a substance which has become a waste is burned to extract heating value out of it. This is called Refuse Derived Fuel.

Red Tide When the marine plankton which are mostly toxic and often fatal to fish as they proliferate. Generally occurs due to significant addition of nutrients. The colour of the tide depends on the colour of the plankton and so could be red, green, or brown.

Redox (Redox) In a chemical reaction, when reduction and oxidation reaction occurs simultaneously. Decomposition of the chemical could be very violent. Examples are hydrazine and hydroxylamine.

Reference Dose (Niedeshit Maatraa) An estimated daily exposure level of a contaminant to a human population below which no adverse noncancer health effects are anticipated.

Refinery (Parishkaran Shaalaa) A plant where crude oil is refined and thus separated into various distillation products.

Refining (Parishkaran) Process by which undesirable elements or substances are removed from the desired substance.

Reforestation (Punah Vanaropan) Process of growing trees and other vegetation in an area which was once a forest. First step towards wild growth of vegetation again in that region.

Reformulated Gasoline (Punar Sutrit Gasoline) Newly developed gasoline blends that produce less air pollution than older gasoline formulae. Reformulated gasolines of different oil companies are not necessarily the same.

Refuse Derived Fuel (Kachare Se Bana Indhan) When fuel is produced from waste. It is generally by incineration of the waste. Also solid in the form of pellets from municipal waste. When the fuel generated from waste is in the form of steam or electricity, the use has to be close to the generation plant itself. In this case, the waste must have high Btu value and must burn relatively easily. Fly ash may pass through the chimney as an air pollutant while the bottom ash from the incinerator is sent to the landfills. See also waste-to-energy plants.

Relative Humidity (Aapekshik Aadrata) Amount of moisture present in air divided by the maximum amount of moisture that air can hold in similar conditions. During rainfall, relative humidity can be 100% as the air may be fully saturated with moisture or water. Air is capable of holding less moisture at lower temperatures.

Relative Risk (Aapekshik Khatraa) The grouping of sites in high, medium, or low categories based on an evaluation of site information using three key factors: the contaminant hazard factor, the migration pathway factor, and the receptor factor.

Release (Chodna or Mukt Hona) An unintentional or unplanned release of any substance through spilling, leaking, pumping or leaching into the atmosphere. Release is generally associated when the substance involved is harmful to the environment and so is hazardous or toxic in nature. See also Spills.

Rem (Roentgen Equivalent Man) A unit of absorbed dose of ionizing radiation and the biological effects on the human body. The rem takes into account the absorbed dose and the biological effects of different types of radiation. Each type of radiation affects the body differently. Therefore, each type has been assigned a quality factor based on how much injury it causes to the body. Rem is the rad times the quality factor. Quality factor of beta, gamma, or X-Ray is one while that of Alpha radiation and is 20. The measurement of biological dose equivalence. The SI unit is the sievert (Sv). 100 rem equals 1 sievert (Sv).

Remedial Action (Upachari Karya) Becomes necessary when a release at any time in the past has occurred. The hazardous or toxic substance has to be removed from the environment so that they do not migrate and cause substantial danger to present or future public health or welfare or the environment. The term includes such actions at the location of the release as storage, confinement, perimeter protection using dikes, trenches, or ditches, clay cover, neutralization, cleanup of released hazardous substances and associated contaminated materials, recycling or reuse, diversion, destruction, segregation of reactive wastes, dredging or excavations, repair or replacement of leaking containers, collection of leachate and run off, on site treatment or incineration, provision of alternative water supplies, and any monitoring reasonably required to assure that such actions protect the public health and welfare and the environment.

Remedial Design (Upachari Ruprekha) A site where a release has occurred and an investigative study has been completed. This phase includes the development of engineering drawings and specifications for a site cleanup.

Remedial Investigation (Upachari Jaanch Padtaal) A process undertaken to determine the nature and extent of the problem presented by a release. The remedial investigation emphasizes data collection and site characterization, and is generally performed concurrently and in an interactive fashion with the feasibility study. Includes sampling and monitoring, as necessary, and the gathering of sufficient information to determine the necessity for remedial action and to support the evaluation of remedial alternatives.

Remedial Investigation/Feasibility Study (Upchaari Jaanch Padtaal/Auchitya Adhyayan) Investigative and analytical studies performed in an interactive, iterative process. Intended to study the cost/benefits of treating, transporting, storing, and disposing of hazardous substances.

Renewable (Navinikaran Yogya) The capability of being replenished quicker than the supply is being depleted to meet present, near-term, or future demand. Time and quantity are the critical elements in measures of renewability.

Replicate Measurement Measurement carried out one more time of a prepared sample.

Repository (Bhandar or Godam) A place where nuclear waste, both high level and low lével are placed for permanent storage. Generally underground.

Reprocessing (Punaha Samsaadhan or Dubara Prakriya) When a substance is processed again, in order to concentrate it further or recover a useful component from a compound. It could be a form of recycling, reusing of a material which, otherwise may have no use.

Resistivity (Pratirodh Prakriya) The amount of corrosion that may occur to a metal due to the stray-current in the soil. The higher the resistivity, the lower the corrosion of the metal.

Resolving Time Counter The minimum time interval between two distinct events which will permit both to be counted. It may refer to an electronic circuit, to a mechanical indicating device, or to a counter tube. In a gas Chromatograph, indication of two distinct elements will come out in distinct time frame for ease in identification.

Respirable Particles (Shwasaniya Kan) Particles that penetrate to the lungs when inhaled; usually particles smaller than five micrometres.

Response Action (Anukul Pratikriya) An action taken at a hazardous waste site involving either a short term removal action or a long term remedial response that may include, but is not limited to, the following activities:

- Removing hazardous materials from a site to an approved, licensed hazardous waste facility for treatment, containment, or destruction;
- Containing the waste safely on site to eliminate further problems;
- Destroying or treating the waste on site using incineration or other technologies; and
- Identifying and removing the source of groundwater contamination and halting further movement of the contaminants.

Restricted Access to Hazardous Waste Site (Khatarnaak Sthal Par Pratibandhit Pravesh) A site which, without disturbing the soil, could present a threat to the on site individuals. Restricted access sites are fenced and require a Health and Safety Plan before entry is permitted. Individuals entering that site need to have received some hazardous waste training.

Restricted Substance (Pratibandhit Padaarth) 'Restricted Substance' means the substance restricted for handling.

Retardation (Vilamban) The act or process that reduces the rate of movement of a chemical substance in a water stream relative to the average velocity of the water. The movement of the chemical substance in the water can be retarded by sorption and desorption reactions, by precipitation and dissolution reactions, and by diffusion into the pore water of the rock matrix.

Reverse Osmosis (Vipareet Paraasaran or Rasaa Karshan or Ulta Dravya Sanskaran) Removal of dissolved pollutants from water by forcing liquid through a semi-permeable membrane which has holes large enough to pass water molecules but small enough to block the passage of the pollutant molecules. Very high energy consuming process and so is resorted to only when very pure water is a requirement. An example is desalination of sea water.

Ribonucleic Acid or RNA Similar to DNAs, they are a class of organic acids found in living cells.

Richter Scale (Richter Maap) Based on seismograph readings, it is a scale to measure earthquakes. It is on a logarithmic scale. Ranges from one to ten.

Rill (Choti Nadi or Nadika) A very small continuously free flowing water stream generally found close to springs or water falls. Occurs naturally due to surface runoff and may also disappear through natural causes.

Ringlemann Chart A chart which is used to measure the opacity of air pollution emissions. Varies from light gray to black.

Riparian Areas (Nadi Tatiya Kshetra or Tatavarti Kshetra) Vegetated ecosystems along a water body through which energy, materials, and water pass. Areas characteristically have a high water table, are subject to periodic flooding from the adjacent water body. These systems are comprised of wetlands, uplands, or some combination of these two land forms. They will not have all the characteristics necessary for them to be classified as wetlands.

Riprap (Patthar Bharaav) Protective covering, often stone or coarse gravel, for earthen slopes to prevent erosion.

Risk (Khatra or Jokhim) A measure of a negative or undesirable impact associated with an event. Also the probability of developing a disease as a result of exposure to a contaminant. Site risk may include the contaminant concentrations in a given environmental medium, movement or potential movement of the contamination away from the original source, and an indication of the potential for human or ecological contact with site contaminants. Views of the community of potential impact must also be taken into consideration.

Risk Assessment (Khatra Nirdharan) A balancing or trading off process in which various combinations of environmental risks are compared and evaluated against particular social or economic gains. Serves as an effective tool in the Hazardous Waste Management Programme for evaluation of various risks involved so as to prevent, mitigate, and compensate risks. The uncertain nature of consequences of Hazardous Waste Management Programme are analysed in this process. A risk assessment is generated by collecting, analyzing, and synthesizing scientific data to determine the potential human health or environmental risk associated with contamination of environmental media. Risk assessment includes hazard identification, exposure assessment, and dose response analysis. For human health risk assessments, two end points are generally estimated:

(1) Excess lifetime cancer risk; and
(2) Noncarcinogenic toxicological impacts.

Rodenticide (Kritanknashi or Stan Vale Jeev Nashi) A chemical directed at killing rats, mice and other rodent pests. They must be used with extreme care as these are also extremely toxic to humans.

Roentgen A unit for measuring ionizations caused by gamma/X-Ray radiation. It is defined as the quantity of gamma (or X) rays that will produce electrons with a total charge of 2.58 X 10 -4 coulomb in 1 kilogram of dry air. An exposure of 1 roentgen is approximately equivalent to an absorbed dose of 1 rad in soft tissue. It is a measurement of exposure and does not relate to the biological effects of radiation on the human body. The SI unit is the coulomb/kilogram (C/kg) of air. 1 roentgen (R) is equal to 1,000 milliroentgen (mR).

Rugosity (Jhurridari or Jhurri) The degree of roughness or irregularity of the borehole wall. This may affect some log types in drilling of wells.

Run-off (Baha Jaanaa) Any rain water, leachate, or other liquid that drains over land from any part of a facility. When the rain water run off takes place from agricultural land, the fertilizers and pesticides applied to the soil may wash off into other areas with the moving water. This is a very serious form of non-point source of pollution.

Run-on (Bahanaa) Any rain water, leachate, or other liquid that drains over land onto any part of a facility.

Rut (Madkaal) The period when a male animal is sexually active.

S

Dr. Salim Ali (1896-1987) Known as the 'The Great Bird Man' all over the world, he was born on November 12, 1896. He was associated with BNHS from 1944 to 1987. He dedicated his lifetime for the study of birds. He was a father figure for BNHS, the institution that he nurtured. Dr. Salim Ali's pioneering work in the field of ornithology was of great importance. Indian birds got recognition under his studies. He surveyed India as well as the neighbouring countries and wrote innumerable books on birds. The "Book of Indian Birds" and "The Pictorial Guide to The Birds of The Indian Sub-continent" are two vital books which can enable any amateur bird watcher to study birds.

Saline Intrusion (Khare Jal Ka Pravesh or Lavaniiya) When salt water intrudes into fresh water aquifers or areas. Occurs when the use of fresh water is very heavy. In urban area such as Chennai and Mumbai, there is very heavy pumping of fresh water by wells for human consumption which forms a cone and lets the saline ocean water to seep in. A common occurrence in urban coastal areas.

Salinity (Lavanataa) Amount of dissolved salt or minerals in any liquid or soil. Sea water is saline water.

Sanitary Landfill A facility for the disposal of solid waste and municipal waste such as garbage that are generated by normal household activities and that are not hazardous or radioactive in nature. Made up of small cells, modern sanitary landfills are designed in such a way so as to control further contamination which may be present in the waste deposited in any location. These landfills are lined with synthetic material and are so designed to recover gas which may be produced in due course of time. Generally, the primary constituent of this gas is methane and so after purification can be used as a heating source. After a landfill area is full, it is then closed by applying a cover to it. The cover may be made up of a synthetic liner and a foot layer of earth on top of it. By taking proper precautions for gas control and subsidence, a covered landfill can be put to other uses such as parks.

Sanitary Sewer (Swasthyakar Mal Pranaal or Naali) A sewer which carries only sanitary waste waters from residential and commercial buildings. Does not contain any runoff water from rain or any industrial pollutant.

Sanitary Waste (Ghar Ka Kudhaa or Kachara) Solid or liquid sanitary waste such as garage or sewage. Generally non-hazardous in nature.

Saprobic Index An index which indicates the degree of pollution stress present in that water bed.

Saprophytes (Mrita Jeevi) Living or dead organisms which help in the natural decomposition of organic matter in water. Also includes decaying organic matter.

Saturated Zone (Santrapt Kshetra) That part of a zone in which the pore spaces or fractures are also completely is filled with water.

Schedule I of The Water Cess Act of 1977 Fifteen industries are listed in the Schedule. They are:

1. Ferrous Metallurgical Industry
2. Non-ferrous Metallurgical Industry
3. Mining Industry
4. Ore Processing Industry
5. Petroleum Industry
6. Petro-chemical Industry
7. Chemical Industry
8. Ceramic Industry
9. Cement Industry
10. Textile Industry (including cotton synthetic and semi-synthetic fibres manufactured from these fibres)
11. Paper Industry
12. Fertilizer Industry
13. Coal (including Coke) Industry
14. Power (Thermal and Diesel) Generating Industry
15. Processing of animal or vegetable products industry (including processing of milk, meat, hides, and skins, all agricultural products and their wastes).

Scrubber (Maarjak or Ghisne Vaalaa) An industrial air pollution control device that removes soluble gases from effluents by spraying water through the effluent stream or by bubbling waste gases through water.

Sea Level (Samudra Tal) Average level of the sea when it is calm.

Sediment (Talchat) Solid particles that settle at the bottom of a water tank. Particles of solid matter that move from their original site to settle on a land surface or at the bottom of a waterway or body of water. Pile up in reservoirs, rivers, and harbours damaging aquatic life in the process.

Sedimentation (Avasaadan) Natural process in which silt, sand, rocks, organic matter, and soils are carried by running water, wind, glaciers, or seas and deposited elsewhere. Also the settling of particles by gravity to the bottom of a water source. Process is used extensively in water purification. In turbulent streams, the sedimentation process slows down as particulate matters travel a longer distance. Careless farming, mining, and building habits may result in excessive sedimentation to occur and thus damage aquatic life in rivers and harbours.

Seismograph (Bhikamp Maapi Yantra) A device to measure earthquake or vibrations of the earth's crust.

Self Contained Breathing Apparatus (SCBA) When a person working in a hazardous or oxygen deficient area carries breathing air with him. The oxygen container along with complete breathing apparatus is attached in such a way that the person can work unhindered, generally as a backpack. Supply of air is only for a limited time. Some devices use oxygen from the exhaled air while others do not.

Septage (Mal Jal) The liquid and/or solid material which is periodically pumped from a septic tank, cesspool, or similar domestic sewage treatment system or a holding tank when the system is cleaned for maintenance purposes. Generally nonhazardous in nature as it is derived from sewage system.

Septic System (Mal Jal Saaf Karne Ka Sthal) A water-tight covered receptacle designed to receive and/or process sewage. The system is composed of both a septic tank and a septic field. The tank is an underground container through which sewage flows very slowly and in which solids separate from the liquid to be decomposed or broken down by anaerobic bacterial action. The septic field is the area through which the sewage liquid passes and in which it is cleaned through physical filtering by soils, biodegradation, and evaporation. The effluent from such a system is distributed for disposal through the soil and settled solids and scum from the tank are pumped out periodically. These are primarily used for residential sewage treatment only.

Servant (Naukar or Sewak) The Water Act defines a 'Servant' as person who is not a member of the family.

Sewage Effluent (Mal Jal Pravaahi) The Water Act of 1974 defines affluent from any sewerage system or sewage disposal works and includes sullage from open drains. It is domestic wastewater. It may carry both living and dead bacteria. In 1996, Class I and II cities in India generated around 2,000 crore litres of sewage wastewater daily, but only a tenth of it was treated.

Sewer (Mal Jal Ki Mori or Naali) As per The Water Act of 1974, any conduit pipe or channel, open or closed, carrying sewage or trade effluent.

Shock Load Sudden release of water containing unusual amounts of algae or colloidal matter into a treatment plant. This sudden influx of material may upset the operation of the plant.

Sick Building Syndrome Indoor illness that includes headaches, nausea, breathing difficulties, fatigue, difficulty in concentrating, dry cough, eye irritations, and skin rashes. It may be caused by bad ventilation, poor building maintenance, and by the presence of indoor toxic substances. Indoor pollutants could include smoke from cigarettes, asbestos dust, lead paint dust, and fumes from any machinery such as copying and printing.

Silica (Baalu or Ret) Silicon dioxide. Used in industries. Chemical formula: SiO2.

Silt (Gaad) When the sedimentary material is composed of fine or intermediate-sized mineral particles.

Silviculture (Vana Vriksha Vigyan) Branch of forestry concerned with the development and care of forests, often used for growing trees as commercial crops.

Site (Sthal or Kshetra) Any location where hazardous chemicals are manufactured or processed, stored, handled, used, disposed of, and includes the whole of an area under the control of an occupier and includes pier, jetty, or similar structure whether floating or not.

Siting of Hazardous Waste Treatment and Disposal Facility Requires the synthesis of two distinct selection procedures, viz., a technical screening process based upon economic, engineering, and environmental suitability and a public approval process. Appendix K lists the factors that need to be considered. The goal of siting a facility should consider the following:

- Minimise health Risks;
- Minimise adverse environmental impacts;
- Minimise costs; and
- Maximise public acceptability.

Skimmer (Kalchi or Pauni or Dravya Ke Upar Se utarne Ka Yantra) A device used to separate or collect the top layer of any liquid. Used to recover oil spills over water. The layer to be collected must not be miscible in the liquid it is floating on. Skimmers are generally mechanical devices. If oil is to be skimmed, first it is controlled in place by placing booms around the oil and then skimmers are used to remove the same.

Slimicides Substances used to control or inhibit the growth of biological slimes which is composed of algae, bacteria, or fungi. Used in industrial water cooling systems and other industries where water is extensively used.

Slope Factor Estimate of the probability of a response per unit intake of a chemical over a lifetime. The slope factor is used to estimate an upper-bound probability of an individual developing cancer as a result of a lifetime of exposure to a particular level of a carcinogen. Lifetime considered is 70 years with 365 days in a year, drink 2 litres of water, and inhalation of 23 cubic metres of air per day. In case of a 15 kg. child, ingestion is 200 milligrams of soil per day. On the other hand, an average adult of 70 kilogram ingests 100 milligrams of soil per day for carcinogenic constituents.

Sludge (Keechad) Any solid, semi solid, or liquid waste generated from a wastewater treatment facility. Also generated at water treatment facility. The solids that settle on the bottom of any body of water or the impurities at the bottom of fractionation of crude oil. Generally considered to be a waste product, in some cases, it may also be hazardous.

Sludge Requirements (Keechad Ki Aavashyaktayen) The sludge should be dewatered prior to disposal by an appropriate dewatering system and handled like semi-solid and/or solid hazardous wastes.

Slurry (Gaaraa) A watery mixture of insoluble matter. Also when small fragments of solid particles combined with water flow like a liquid. Liquid containing nondissolving solid particles.

Smog (Dhoom Kohraa or Kohra Dhuan Mishrit) Occurs when multitude fine organic chemical particulates join together to form smog. Chemicals can be those emitted by industries or by automobile. Toxicity of the smog depends on its chemical composition. Some of them may include VOCs, lead, benzene, heavy metals, carbon monoxide, and sulphur dioxide. Smog could be either brown yellow or gray and are usually found over large cities. Generally very toxic and may cause or aggravate respiratory problems, asthma, cancer, chest pains and heart diseases. Over four thousand people died due to the December 1952 smog over London. The 1997 fire in South-East Asia -- Malaysia, Singapore, Brunei, the Philippines, and Indonesia created such a smog that pilots were unable to fly to some airports in the south Philippines. The crash of an Indonesian airliner during this time in Sumatra that killed all 234 passengers on board has been attributed to smog.

Smoke (Dhuan) Mixture of gases and small particles generated by incomplete combustion. The gas would be from incomplete combustion of wood, coal, or smoke from chemical industries. See also Smog.

Snag (Thunth) A dead tree which has lost all its leaves but is still standing in place.

SO_2 Sulphur dioxide, a major cause of acid rain and smog. A heavy colourless gas with a pungent odour. Produced during the burning of fuels containing Sulphur. A highly irritating compound, it is toxic to plants and causes lung damage in humans. Extensively used in paper, metal refining, disinfectants, and reducing agents.

Soft Water (Mridu Jal) Water which does not contain hardening materials such as calcium. It has low mineral content. With soap, will form lather.

Soil Degradation (Mrida Avakraman or Mitti Ka Nimnikaran) Overgrazing of fertile land may eventually remove so much plant material as to render the soil without any plant cover to hold water. Further drying of the soil makes it harder to retain any moisture further destroying its ability to retain any nutrients for further plant growth. This results in the deserts that are formed by lack of water in soil and erosion of land.

Soil Gas (Mrida Gas or Mitti Se utpat Gas) Gaseous elements and compounds that occur in the small spaces between particles of the earth or soil. Rock can also contain gas.

Soil Washing (Mitti Ki Safai) In this process, soil is excavated and scrubbed to remove contaminants in one of two ways, by dissolving or suspending the contaminant in a water-based wash, or by concentrating them into a smaller volume of soil through particle size separation, gravity separation, and attrition scrubbing. Soil washing is done to reduce the volume of waste requiring disposal.

Solar Cells (Solar Cell) Process of converting sun rays into electrical energy by means of semiconductors. See also Photovoltaic Cell.

Solar Energy (Saur Urja) Energy derived from the sun. It can be stored as heat or electricity. Low-wavelength energy greter than 0.7 micrometres is known as infrared and is felt as heat but is not visible. Intermediate-wavelength energy of wavelengthbetween 0.4 and 0.7 micrometres is visible as light and felt as heat. Short-wave energy of less than 0.4 micrometres is known as ultraviolet. This is not visible but is felt as it causes subburn. Collector panels placed strategically track the sun and concentrates towards its heat and light. Solar cooking is being encouraged by the government so as to cut down on the use of natural gas as well as pollution through the burning of woods used for cooking. It is a clean energy without producing any type of pollution.

Solar Ponds (Saur Talab) Ponds that receive water to be evaporated by the sun.

Solid Waste (Koodha Karkat) Any household waste, garbage, refuse, or sludge which is solid in nature and is non hazardous.

Solid Waste Derived Fuel(Koodha Karkat Se Banaa Indhan) Fuel generated from solid waste. The fuel generated could be natural gas, solid fuel pellets, or liquid fuel which can be used as a useful fuel supplement.

Solvent (Vilaayak) Any liquid capable of dissolving or dispersing one or more substances.

Solvent Recovery (Vilaayak Nikaasan) When a useful solvent is recovered from any substance through any process such as condensation, filtration, adsorption, or vapourisation.

Somatic Cell A body cell other than germ cell.

Somatic Effect (Kayik Prabhaav) An effect that appears in an individual exposed to radiation.

Sonic Boom (Dhwani Garjan or Gunjan) A shock wave created by an aircraft flying faster than the speed of sound which is about 760 miles per hour.

Soot (Kaalikh or Kajal) Formation of carbon dust due to incomplete combustion.

Sorbent (Avashoshak or Sukhane Vali Vastu) Any material which is used to absorb another liquid (sorbed). This is one of the methods to collect spilled oil or any liquid substance.

Sound (Dhwani or Aawaz) Various sources of sound are: industry, road traffic, rail traffic, air traffic, construction and public works, and indoor sources such as air conditioners, air coolers. In Indian conditions, indiscriminate use of public address system and diesel generator sets have added a new dimension to the noise pollution problem. The Central Pollution Control Board constituted a Committee on Noise Pollution Control. The Committee recommended noise standards for ambient air and for automobiles, domestic appliances and construction equipment, which were later notified in Environment (Protection) Rules, 1986 and as amended on May 19, 1993.

Sound Level (Dhwani Stir) Measurement of sound pressure by use of metering devices. Measured in decibels as dB and measured in A, B, or C weighed sound pressure. The most common being the A-weighed sound pressure.

Source (Strot or Udgam Sthal) An area where hazardous substances or products have been deposited, stored, released, disposed of, or placed. Object or process that releases pollutants into the atmosphere.

Source Reduction (Udgam Sthal Mein Bachav) Any practice that reduces the amount of hazardous substances, pollutants or contaminants entering any waste stream or other wise released into the environment before recycling, treatment, or disposal.

Span Gas A gas of known concentration which is used routinely to set the output level of any analyzer.

Specific Conductivity (Vishisht Chalakta) Capacity of water supply to carry an electric current. Gives an estimate of ions or dissolved solid content of a water supply and thus an indication of pollutants present in water.

Specific Gravity (Vishisht Ghanatva) Ratio of density of a substance to the density of a known or specific substance. The specific substance for liquids is generally distilled water and for gases it is either hydrogen, oxygen, or air.

Specific Heat Capacity (Vishisht Ushma Kshamata) The quantity of heat required to raise the temperature of a unit mass of a substance by one degree Celsius.

Specified Industry (Vishesh Udyog) Any industry specified in Schedule I of The Water (Prevention and Control of Pollution) Cess Act, 1977 or any in any other Act or Rules.

Spent Nuclear Fuel Nuclear reactor fuel that has been irradiated to the extent that it can no longer effectively sustain a chain reaction. Fuel becomes spent when its fissionable isotopes have been partially consumed and fission-products have accumulated in it.

Spill (Girana) An unintended release or discharge of a substance, generally hazardous or toxic in the environment. The impact on the environment depends on the substance, quantity, and the area where the release has occurred.

Spill Prevention Control and Countermeasures Plan-SPCC Generally required for each location where any hazardous substance is stored and where a spill could possibly occur. See also Emergency Plan.

Spray Boom (Fuhara Sanchalan) Equipment that is used to distribute water or chemical agents over a wide area in order to either control an oil spill or to control a chemical fire on a water surface.

Stabilization (Sthayikaran or Dradikaran) Conversion of the active organic matter in sludge into inert, harmless material.

Standards (Maan Dand) Parameters that are prescribed or laid down by any of the Acts or rules for compliance by industries or any operation.

State Board (Rajya Board) The Water Act of 1974 defines the 'State Board' as a State Pollution Control Board constituted under government authority. The Board shall consist of a Chairman to be nominated by the State Government; such number of officials, but not exceeding five, to be nominated by the State Government to represent that Government; such number of persons, but not exceeding five, to be nominated by the State Government from amongst the members of the local authorities functioning within the State; such number of non-officials, not exceeding three, to be nominated by the State Government to represent the interest of agriculture, fishery or industry or trade or any other interest; two persons to represent the companies or corporations owned, controlled, or managed by the State Government, to be nominated by that Government; and a full-time member-secretary.

State Government (Rajya Sarkar) 'State Government' in relation to a Union Territory means the Administrator thereof appointed under the articles of the Constitution.

State Air Laboratory (Rajya Vaayu Prayog Shaalaa) By notification in the Official Gazette, the State may establish a laboratory for analysis of air components, similar to State Water Laboratories. See also State Water Laboratory.

State Water laboratory (Rajya Jal Prayog Shaalaa) By notification in the Official Gazette, the State may:

- establish a State Water Laboratory;
- or specify any State laboratory or institute as a State Water Laboratory, to carry out the functions entrusted to the State Water laboratory under any of its Pollution Acts.

Storage (Godam or Bhandar) The holding of hazardous waste for a temporary period, at the end of which the hazardous waste is treated, disposed of, or stored elsewhere. Generally, there is a limit of 90 days.

Storage of Ignitable or Reactive Waste (Dahaniiya or Abhikriya Sheel Apashisht Ka Bhandaar) Containers holding ignitable or reactive waste should be stored at least 15 metres (50 feet) away from the plant operational area. 'No Smoking' signs should be placed conspicuously wherever ignitable or reactive waste is stored.

Stratification (Starvinyaas) A separation in horizontal layers. It could be temperature or mineral stratification.

Stratosphere (Sama Taap Mandal) A relatively stable layer of the atmosphere between the troposphere and ionosphere and is from 15 kilometres to a height of about 50 kilometres in which temperature changes very little (in polar and temperate zones) or increases (in the tropics with increasing altitude. In the stratosphere clouds of water never form and there is practically no movement or convection.

Stratum (Stir) A single sedimentary bed or layer, regardless of thickness, that consists of generally the same kind of rock material.

Stream (Dhara or Nadi) The Water Act of 1974 defines 'Stream' to include:

- river;
- water course (whether flowing or for the time being dry);
- inland water (whether natural or artificial);
- sub-terranean waters;
- sea or tidal waters to such extent or, as the case may be, to such point as the State Government may, by notification in the Official Gazette, specify in this behalf.

Strict Liability (Sakht Jimmedari or Sunishchit Dayitva) Responsibility for injury or damage in spite of the fact that the terms of the contract or warranty have been fulfilled.

Strontium A metallic element chemically similar to calcium that occurs as a soft, flammable, pale-yellow solid. Soluble in alcohol and acid, decomposes in water, melts at 770 degrees C and boils at 1380 degrees C. Strontium-90 is a radioactive isotope. Its half-life is about 30 years. Chemical symbol: Sr.

Sublimation (Urdhwa Paatan) The process whereby a solid such as ice is transformed directly into the vapour state without going through the intervening liquid state. This phenomena occurs when the bonds joining the molecules into solid form are weak enough to allow some of those on the surface to escape. Odour of solids is due to the sublimation process occurring.

Subsidence (Khisakana or Utarna) Unevenly distributed settlement after closure. May threaten the integrity of a cover by creating cracks and depressions. All municipal landfills show signs of subsidence after a few years of its closure.

Sulphur Dioxide A colourless gas with a distinct odour. Power plants are one of the largest emitters of this gas into the atmosphere. When in the atmosphere, it results in acid rain and causes damage to plant and wildlife. It is one of the greenhouse gas causing the ozone depletion. This gas causes respiratory problems such as bronchitis, and asthma among others. See also SO2.

Sunderlal Bahuguna Attired in a green bandana, crumpled kurta and a prophet's beard, his name is synonymous with the "CHIPKO" Andolan (Hug the tree movement). He assisted the women from the Tehri region of Uttar Pradesh in their battle to save trees from the mafia. They hugged the trees and thus protected them from being cut down, and hence the name "Chipko Andolan". During the Chinese invasion, he visited the frontier villages. From 1965 to 1971, he mobilised the hill women of Uttar Pradesh in an anti-liquor campaign.

Supercooled Water (Ati Sheetal Jal) Water that remains in the liquid state when cooled below its normal freezing point.

Superheat (Ati Ushma or Garam) Heating a substance to a temperature above the level that normally would cause it to change its state, without the change occurring.

Supertanker (Badaa Tanker) Ships of very large size used to transport liquid cargo. Most of the time, the cargo is petroleum oil. As they are economical to transport huge quantities at a very low cost, they are getting bigger. But if an accident occurs, the environmental problems are severe. One of them exemplified by the Exxon Valdez oil spill in Alaska.

Surface Impoundment (Sataha Avarodhan) A facility or part of a facility which is a natural topographic depression, man-made excavation, or diked area formed primarily of earthen materials (although it may be lined with man-made materials), which is designed to hold an accumulation of liquid wastes or wastes containing free liquid wastes or wastes containing free liquids, and which is not an injection well.

Surfactant (Prasht Sakriya) A soluble compound that reduces the surface tension of liquids or reduces the tension at interfaces between two liquids or between a liquid and a solid. Also, an agent used in detergents to cause lathering.

Suspended Particles (Nilambit Kan or Latke Hue Kan) Particles (usually smaller than 100 micrometres) that are small enough to remain in the air and settle out slowly under the force of gravity. As per the Water Act of 1975, the limit for suspended solids in drinking water is 250 mg/l.

Swamp (Dal Dal) A low land saturated with water but unsuitable for agricultural purposes. May be fresh or sea water. See Wetland

Symbiosis (Sahajeevan) A relationship between two organisms in which both derive some benefit from such a relationship. Bees and flowers are an example of this.

Synergy (Sahakriyaa) The combined action or effects that are generally greater than the sum of their individual effects.

Synthetic Fuels (Sanshleshit Indhan) When petroleum and natural gas is produced from sources other than crude oil. Sources could be coal, shale, wood, waste.

Synthetic Organic Chemical (Sanshleshit Carbonic Rasaayan) They all contain carbon in them. Some well known names include DDT, chlorofluoro carbons (CFCs), polychlorinated biphenyls (PCBs), polyvinyl chloride (PVC), volatile organic compounds (VOCs) dioxins, and petrochemicals. As these chemicals do not break down very easily, they are harmful to humans, wildlife and plants in one form or the other. Many of these chemicals are also the cause of greenhouse effect.

Systemic Effects A chemical or substance that requires adsorption and distribution of the toxicant to a site distant from its entry point where adverse effects are noticed. Most chemicals that produce systemic toxicity do not cause a similar degree of toxicity in all organs. These are referred to as the target organs of toxicity for that chemical.

T

Tailings (Pachodan or Avashisht) Solid wastes produced from primary processing of ores. Also low-level radioactive sandy residues of Uranium mining. Sand-like waste resulting from uranium production and so are radioactive. Also waste rock produced by a mine, smelter or other mineral extraction industry. Generally pebble-sized rock chunks but may vary from powder to large boulders. Tailings from coal mines may be highly acidic in nature. Tailings dumped on land may adversely affect the vegetation and the environment.

Tannic Acid (Tannic Amla) Organic acids formed on leaves and plants. Contribute to the acidity of humus and of bog water. Used to tan leather and in the production of rubber and some inks. As they have the ability to bind metals, used as antidote for heavy metal poisoning. Poisonous in nature.

Target Organ Chemical (Lakshya Avayav Rasasyan) Health hazard that enters the bloodstream and damages specific internal organs or body systems; effects can be delayed.

Target Species (Lakshya Jeev Jaati) When a specific species of any animal is targeted until it is close to extinction. Generally these types of species are of exotic types and found in very specific areas.

TC_{LO} Lowest published toxic concentration.

Tectonic Activity (Vivartanik Kriya) Results due to the movement of earth's crust. Noticed after earthquakes, volcanic intrusions.

Temporary Board Members (Board Ke Asthaayi Sadasya) The Central Board may invite any persons, whose assistance of advice it considers useful to obtain in performing any of its functions, to participate in the deliberations of any of its meetings.

Tenor (Ausat Pratishat) The percentage of a metal in an ore or in an impure metal.

Teratogen A substance or a compound that causes birth defects in a developing fetus.

Teratogenic (Veerupjanan Or Veerotpadan) When physical or chemical agents tend to produce anomalies of formation in an embryo or effect the unborn children. Produces reproductive hazards that damage the fetus during development thus resulting in functional defects in birth. Example of such chemical is mercury.

Terminal Electron Acceptor Chemicals necessary for electron transfer during the metabolic processes in which microorganisms biodegrade contaminants. Biodegradation will not occur in the absence of necessary terminal electron acceptors. Oxygen is the acceptor during aerobic biodegradation of petroleum hydrocarbons and iron, sulphate, and nitrate are acceptors during anaerobic biodegradation.

Thallium Soft malleable gray heavy metal with a low melting point. The metal is highly toxic. Used in making night-time devices. Atomic weight: 204.37. Chemical symbol: Tl.

Thermal Inversion (Taapiya Viparivartan) Weather condition where air is held in by a larger air mass, becoming stale and contaminated. Common in valleys and during winter months.

Thermal Oxidation (Tapiya Oxikaran) When heat is used to break down toxic substances.

Thermal Pollution (Tapiya Pradushan) Release of a substance, often liquid or air, that changes the temperature in the area where it is released. For example: when hot water is released from a plant in to a cold river or lake, the surrounding area may see increase of species dependent on that heat. And when that heat is stopped even for a short time, the species dies or may suffer severe consequences. A rise in temperature increases the solubility of solids and therefore the ability of the water body to carry more amount of pollutant load while decreasing the solubility of gases and thus causing Dissolved oxygen content to fall. With the fall in dissolved oxygen, the biological oxygen demand increases. This substantially increases the use of oxygen use by fish and other water dwelling organisms. Change in temperature results in thermal pollution and the effect is generally not positive on the receiving water. As per the Water Act of 975, the temperature of discharge water shall not exceed 5 degrees centigrade above the receiving body.

Thermal Treatment (Tapiya Abhikriya) The treatment of hazardous waste in a device which uses elevated temperature as the primary means to change the chemical, physical, or biological character or composition of the hazardous waste.

Thermocline (Taap Pravanata) The transition zone in a stratified lake between the upper warm layer and the lower cold layer. Characterised by a rapid temperature decline as depth increases. The decrease is about one degrees C per metre. This may act as a barrier and thus inhibit natural mixing of water and thus the nutrients for fish may not be available at that layer. This is characteristic in ocean waters.

Thermodynamic Laws (Ushmagatik Niyam)

- First Law: Energy may neither be created nor destroyed. It is also called the Law of Conservation.
- Second Law: All systems tend to move from order to disorder. It is also called as the Law of Entropy.
- Third Law: The Entropy of a crystalline substance at a temperature of absolute zero is also zero. It means that at absolute zero temperature, there are no molecular movements.
- Zeroth Law: If two bodies are each at the same temperature as a third body, they are also at the same temperature as each other. It is called as the Law of Equivalency of Temperature.

Thermosphere (Tap Mandal or Bahya Vayumandal) The uppermost subdivision of the atmosphere, characterised by a continuous increase of temperature with height.

Threat to the On Site Individual An exceedence of a permissible exposure limit, or a published exposure limit of the specified contamination levels.

Threatened Species 172 species of animal considered globally threatened are in India. These include 53 species of mammal, 69 birds, 23 reptiles and 3 amphibians. Some of them are the Bengal Fox, Asiatic Cheetah, Marbled Cat, Asiatic Lion, Indian Elephant, Asiatic Wild Ass, Indian Rhinoceros, Markhor, Gaur, and wild Asiatic Water Buffalo. See also Wild Life Act.

Threshold Dosage (Avaseemit Khuraak) The minimum harmful dosage of a substance.

Threshold Limit Value (TLV) (Dehalij Seemant Maan) Time weighed averages which are based on the supposition of the condition workers may be repeatedly exposed to a particular chemical or substance. They are only guides indicating the point at which a substance may prove to be dangerous to the worker.

Threshold Limit Value-Time Weighed Average-TLV-TWA Concentration of a normal 8 hour workday and 40 hour work week to which nearly all workers may be repeatedly exposed without any adverse affect. This value should be used as a guide only. It should not be used as an absolute threshold.

Threshold Limit Value Short Term Exposure TLV-STEL Defined as a 15 minute TWA (Time Weighed Average) exposure which should not be exceeded at any time during a work day even if the 8 hour TWA is within the TLV-TWA. Exposures above the TLV-TWA up to the STEL should not be longer than 15 minute and should not occur more than four times per day. There should be at least 60 minutes between successive exposures in this range. An average period other than 15 minutes may be recommended when this is warranted by observed biological effects.

Threshold Limit Value Ceiling TLV-C The concentration that should not be exceeded during any part of the working exposure at any time. This should both be exceeded even instantaneously.

Threshold Quantity (Dehalij Maatraa) 'Threshold Quantity' refers to them Manufacture, Storage and Import of Hazardous Chemical Rules, 1989 and means:

- in the case of a hazardous chemical specified in Column 2 of Schedule 2, the quantity of that chemical specified in the corresponding entry in Columns 3 & 4;
- in the case of hazardous chemical specified in Column 2 of Part I of Schedule 3, the quantity of that chemical specified in the corresponding entry in Columns 3 & 4 of that part; and ,
- in the case of substances of a class specified in Column 2 of Part II of Schedule 3, he total quantity of all substances of that class specified in the corresponding entry in Column 3 & 4 of that part.

Time Weighed Average (TWA) In air sampling, this refers to the average air concentration of contaminants during a particular sampling period.

TNT A flammable, toxic, and very high explosive used in the manufacture of bombs.

Tolerance Level (Sahansheeltaa Stir or Sahishnutaa Stir) Legal residual amount of substance or chemical that is allowed to be in food which will not cause any kind of undue harm to humans.

Toluene A colourless, volatile liquid. An aromatic hydrocarbon consisting of a benzene ring. A good solvent with a low flash point. Used to make food extracts as it is less toxic than Benzene. Toluene can cause headache, and nausea. Chemical symbol: C6H5CH3.

Topography (Sthalaa Krati) Physical features or shape of land with regards to elevation. A map shows the contours of the area with respect to elevation.

Total Coliform Count (Sampoorna Coliform Gananaa) An indicator of fecal pathogens in drinking water.

Total Dissolved Solids (Sampoorna Ghule Huye Thos Padaartha) All solids dissolved in a water sample, including salts and minerals. This term indicates salinity.

Total Organic Carbon (Sampoorna Carbonic Rasayan) The amount of total carbon in any substance. Measured by burning the substance completely and measuring the amount of carbon dioxide released.

Total Solids (Sampoorna Thos Padarth) Amount of solids present in wastewater. Includes both dissolved and suspended solids.

Total Suspended Particulates (Sampoorna Nilambit Kan or Latke Hue Kan) Total number of particulate matter, both solid and liquid, which are suspended in air at any given time. They can be suspended pollutants from industries or vehicular emissions. Higher the number means that they are very harmful to humans. High air particulates found in cities such as Delhi.

Toxic Chemicals (Vishaile Rasayan) Toxic chemicals include chemicals that are poisonous, carcinogenic, mutagenic, teratogenic, phytotoxic, or toxic to aquatic species. Carcinogenic chemicals have been shown to cause cancer. Mutagenic chemicals cause mutations or changes in the genes. Teratogenic chemicals affect unborn children. Phytotoxic chemicals affect plants. Toxic chemicals and waste can come from industries involved in or manufacturing batteries, electroplating, paint and related products, pharmaceuticals, textile dyeing and finishing, rubber and plastics, paper printing, paper manufacturing and finishing, and metal mining and machinery manufacturing, among many others.

Toxic Emissions (Vishailaa Utsarjan) Harmful gases or particles released into the air, soil, or water.

Toxic Precipitation (Vishaila Padarth Ka Girana or Patan) Presence of toxic substances in rainfall or other forms of precipitation. Due to the presence of toxic substances suspended in the atmosphere and rain drops which act as the carrier of the pollutant. One way a pollutant may travel a good distance before coming down. Though the presence of toxic substance in rainfall is very small, their effects on the environment are significant.

Toxicity (Vishailapan or Vishaaktataa) A substance that has the natural and inherent property of producing injury, illness, damage, and/or harm to any part of human being or a living tissue in any way under the circumstances of exposure or contact, then it is termed as a toxic substance. Produces adverse health effects after physical contact, ingestion, or inhalation. The substance can produce fumes, vapours, or dust and pass into the bloodstream. All chemicals are harmful if consumed by human beings in sufficient quantities. For this reason, level of toxicity has been defined for all chemicals.

Toxicity Characteristic Leaching Procedure (TCLP) Test to determine toxicity and mobility characteristics of hazardous waste.

Toxicity Curve (Vishaaktataa Vakra) The curve produced from toxicity tests when LC50 values are plotted against duration of exposure.

Toxin (Jeev Vish) A poisonous substance which is produced by plants or animals.

Toxicological Profile (Vish Vigyani Roop Rekha) An examination, summary, and interpretation of a hazardous substance to determine levels of exposure and associated health effects.

Toxic Pollutant (Vishaila Pradshan) Any substance when discharged into water, air or on land can directly or indirectly cause adverse effects or death to aquatic organisms or human beings.

Trade Effluent (Udyog Se Apagaami Dhaaraa) The Water Act of 1974 states that 'Trade Effluent' includes any liquid, gaseous or solid substance which is discharged from any premises used for carrying on any industry, operation or process, or treatment and disposal system, other than domestic sewage.

Transboundary Movement As per the Hazardous Wastes Rules of 1989, 'Transboundary Movement' means any movement of hazardous wastes or other wastes from an area under the national jurisdiction of one country to or through an area under the national jurisdiction of another country or to or through an area not under the national jurisdiction of any country, provided at least two countries are involved in the movement.

Transmissivity (Paaragamyata) A measure of the amount of water that can be transmitted horizontally by the full saturated thickness of the aquifer under a hydraulic gradient of 1.

Transparency (Paaradarshita) The amount of light that is able to penetrate a body of water. A good indication of the amount of plants and autotrophs it can support. Presence of large amounts of autotrophs may lower the transparency of the body of water. Oligotrophic bodies of water are much more transparent than eutrophic.

Transpiration (Vaashpotsarjan) The loss of water vapour from plants through leaves. Due to constant evaporation, leaves constantly lose water. This is essential for the exchange of carbon dioxide into the atmosphere.

Transportation of Hazardous Waste (Khatarnaak Apashisht Ko Le Jaanaa) The driver of the vehicle should receive special training and should carry the Transport Emergency (TREM) card with him. The driver should carry sufficient equipments such as fire extinguisher, gas mask, and first aid kit. In case of a spill, should take proper steps to contain/clean it and report to proper authorities.

Transported Waste (Kachare Ka Parivahan) Industrial emissions from air stacks move along with the movement of the wind until it is brought down by rain, snow, or other natural causes. As the direction and distance depends on the direction of the wind blowing at any time, pollutants can be transported long distances and in any direction.

Transuranic (Paraauranium) Waste that is contaminated with alpha emitting transuranium nuclides (atomic number greater than 92) with half lives greater than 20 years and concentrations greater than 100 nano-curies per gram of waste (excluding natural and depleted uranium). They are all manmade.

Treatment (Upchaar) Any method, technique, or process, including neutralization, designed to change the physical, chemical, or biological character or composition of any hazardous waste so as to neutralize such waste or so as to render such waste non-hazardous, safer for transport, amenable for recovery, amenable for storage, or reduced in volume. Treatment includes any activity or processing designed to change the physical form or chemical composition of hazardous waste so as to render it non-hazardous.

Treatment Methods for Hazardous Waste (Vishaile Tatvon Ke Upchaar Ke Tarike or Vidhiyaan) The aim of treatment is to modify the physical and/or chemical properties of the waste. The choice of the best practicable way of treating the waste depends on the availability and suitability of treatment or disposal facilities, discharge standards, and cost considerations. Some of the types of treatment are physical treatment, chemical treatment, and biological treatment. Disposal methods include landfill and incineration of the waste.

Treatment for Drinking Water When water is treated with activated alumina (granulated form of aluminium oxide), it removes arsenic and fluoride. Treatment by activated carbon removes hydrogen sulphide, chlorine, volative organic compounds, pesticides, benzene, colours and odours. When water is passed through air filled chamber for aeration, it removes hydrogen sulphide. Anion exchange units (a resin that exchanges chloride or in some cases hydroxides) remove nitrates, silphates, and fluorides. During the anion exchange process, chloride content of water may increase. Chlorination of water (continuous dispensation of chlorine in water) removes bacteria, iron, hydrogen sulphides, and some viruses. Distillation of water (vapourisation of water) removes bacteria, lead, nitrate, sodium, chloride, organic chemicals and many pesticides. Ion exchange process removes the minerals such as calcium, magnesium, iron, manganese. Mechanical filteration of water is done to remove sediments that may be present. Reverse osmosis process removes lead, sulphate, calcium, magnesium, sodium, potassium, manganese, aluminium, chloride, nitrate, flouride, many microorganisms, and organic chemicals.

Trees of India (Bharat Ke Ped) ASUPALAV OR THE MAST TREE: Mast Tree is the English name for this tree and is also called the False Ashoka Tree. It is a tall, handsome, straight growing, evergreen tree growing to about 15 metres. It has short, slender branches growing horizontally to the main stem with small greenish flowers. The fruit is small, round and green initially and purple when ripe and are food for squirrels, bats, and birds. Being evergreen and thickly foliaged from top to almost ground level, this tree is planted on the periphery of gardens, parks, open grounds and compounds to prevent dust, heat and sound pollution.

NEEM OR MARGOSA: This is an Indian tree and is also found commonly in Sri Lanka, Burma, Malaysia and other tropical countries. It is a large, elegant, evergreen tree with a large trunk, widely-spaced branches, a brownish-gray bark and graceful leaves. All the parts of the tree are bitter in taste. A gum exudes from the trunk when wounded. The leaves are compound comprising of leaflets that are narrow, long, pointed at the tip, serrated at the margins, deep green in colour, and shiny on the surface. Its flowers are tiny, creamy-white, honey-scented, and are visited by bees for the nectar. The main flowering season is from March to May, and a second flush of blooms may be seen in the rainy season. The flowers are considered sacred and are a must for Gudi Padva. Its fruit is oblong, one-seeded, smooth, yellow when ripe with a juicy pulp, on which birds and animals feed. Neem wood is used in the construction of houses and in making boats. The leaves are used as fodder and as green manure, as pesticide to protect grains, crops, books, clothes and as a mosquito repellent, and to treat boils and ulcers. The twigs are used to clean the teeth and strengthen the gums. Toothpaste is prepared using its leaves. The flowers are taken as tonic. The most important medicinal product is the margosa oil obtained from its seeds. It is used in treating skin-diseases and even leprosy. Soaps are also manufactured using the margosa oil. The oil is used for rheumatism. The tree is planted near houses, places of worship, and along highways to keep the environment healthy. It is supposed to absorb more carbon dioxide and other atmospheric pollutants.

Copper Pod Tree: This species is native to Sri Lanka, Andamans, Malaya, and North Australia. It was first introduced into India along its eastern coast about a century ago. The tree is called Copper Pod as it bears copper-coloured fruit (pods), when still immature which ultimately turn black on maturity. On account of its striking mass of golden-yellow flowers, its shade-giving foliage and its ability to grow fast in almost all types of soils and climates, it is popular in both urban and rural areas. It grows up to 15m in height and develops spreading branches. Although it sheds leaves for a very short time in winter, it is never completely without leaves. A semi-evergreen tree, the leaves are compound and parrot green in colour. In March, sprays of golden-yellow flowers are issued at the ends of the branches.

Bhendi/Portia: It is commonly found along the sea-coast of India, Burma, and the islands of the Pacific and East Africa. The vernacular name of the tree is Palav. This is a moderate-sized evergreen tree with a dense crown. The heart-shaped leaves are dark green and glossy. It flowers throughout the year but is at its peak in winter. The flowers are showy, large, funnel-shaped, yellowish on the upper portions and deep red in the centre, and turn pinkish on withering. This is a fast growing tree and comes up in almost all types of soils including saline soil.

Trichloroethylene An organic chemical composed of hydrogen, carbon, and chlorine. A heavy, stable, toxic, volatile organic compound. Commonly used in metal degreasing, solvent extraction, and dry cleaning.

Trickling Filter (Alpa Matra Ka Chhanana) Bed of stone or other material through which wastewater is tricked. During the process, organic waste breaks down to produce clean water.

Trinitro Toluene See TNT.

Triple Point (Tri Bindu) A specific temperature and pressure at which an element or compound is present in all three phases of solid, liquid, and gas.

Tritium Radiotoxic material emitting beta particles. A radioactive isotope of Hydrogen. It has a mass of 3 units and is produced in nuclear reactors. Half life 12.26 years.

Tropopause (Kshobh Seema) Boundry between the Troposphere and the Stratosphere. It is about 16 kilometres over the equator.

Troposphere (Kshobh Mandal) Region of the atmosphere closest to the earth's surface and up to the Tropopause whis is about 9 to 15 kilometres. In this region, the temperature falls fairly regularly with increasing altitude, clouds form convection is active, and mixing is continuous and more or less complete. The area is estimated to contain about 75% of the atmospheric mass. Stratosphere is between 15 to 50 kilometres.

Tsunami (Bhukamp Dwara Bani Samudri Tarang) A giant sea wave triggered by an earthquake. In mid-ocean, they show up as a long swell 1 to 2 metres high and move extremely rapidly.

Tundra (Tundra or Uttar Dhruvi Anaurvar Pradesh) A treeless, circumpolar biome characterised by a permanently frozen subsoil. Found at high altitude.

Turbidity (Gadalaapan) Cloudiness in untreated or contaminated drinking water caused by suspended sediment or colloidal matter. Turbidity may prevent effective disinfection of water as light cannot penetrate the same. It increases human health risks. Turbidity may hide the presence of pollution in water.

Turbine (Turbine) A device driven by a wheel connected to a drive shaft with many blades. Pressure from steam, air, or water turns the wheel. This converts kinetic energy into a mechanical energy.

Two-Stroke Engine (Do Stroke Ka Engine) Lighter, smaller and more efficient than a standard four-stroke engine. This type is traditionally associated with pollution.

Typhoon (Prachanda Toofaan) Cyclone or hurricane.

U

Ultraviolet Rays (Paraa Baingani Kirane) Radiation from the sun which can be both useful or potentially harmful. Ozone layer above the earth's surface shield us from these harmful rays. They are electromagnetic radiation of wave length between the shortest visible violet (about 3,850 Angstroms) and soft X-rays (about 100 Angstroms). Dangerous to eyes and exposure may cause skin cancer.

Umbrella Species Often a large predator that requires a large range of land for survival, saving it also ensures the continued survival of all the smaller species in the same area.

UN Class Number Hazardous Materials Class Numbers associated with Hazard Classes designated by the United Nations Organization used in international shipping of hazardous materials. They appear at the bottom point of most diamond labels and placards placed on the packages to be transported.

Unstable Isotopes (Asthayee Isotope) Isotopes that are likely to change.

Upper Explosive Limit (UEL) (Sarvoccha Visphotak Seema) The maximum amount of airborne chemical that can be present in an air-chemical mixture and still have it to be explosive.

Upwelling The upward movement of cold bottom water in the sea, which occurs when winds or currents displace the lighter surface water. In this process, surface water moves away from the coast.

Uranium (Uranium) An electropositive, heavy, hard, shiny, and naturally occurring metallic element that is radioactive. Highly toxic radioactive material. Atomic number 92, atomic weight 238.04. Two fissionable isotopes are the fissionable uranium-235 and uranium 238 which is most abundant naturally. Used to generate electricity in nuclear power plants.

Uranium-234 An isotope of uranium with an atomic mass number of 234.

Uranium-235 An isotope of uranium with an atomic mass number of 235. Capable of undergoing rapid fission, and releasing a large amount of atomic energy. For this reason, it is used as a fuel in nuclear power plants.

Uranium-238 An isotope of uranium with an atomic mass number of 238.

Uranium Dioxide The chemical form of uranium when it is made into fuel pellets. Chemical formula: UO2.

Uranium Enrichment (Uranium Samvriddhi) The process that increases the percentage of the Uranium-235 isotope in uranium fuel from less than 1 to 3 percent.

Uranium Hexafluoride A gaseous form of uranium that is made from yellow cake and fluoride. The gas is made and purified by a conversion plant and then shipped to a gaseous diffusion plant for enrichment.

Uranium Milling The process of removing uranium from uranium ore. Milling produces a substance called yellow cake.

V

Vadose Zone (Aadhibhouma Jal Kshetra) The portion of a porous medium above the water table within which the capillary pressure is less than atmospheric and the moisture content is usually less than saturation. The vadose zone includes the capillary fringe.

Vagility (Prakeernataa) The capacity of an organism for sustained free movement.

Valence (Sanyojakataa) It is the number which represents the combining or displacing power of an atom. It is also the number of electrons lost, gained, or shared by an atom in a compound. It is the number of hydrogen atoms with which an atom will combine, or which it will displace.

Vapour (Vaashp) Gaseous phase of a substance that is predominantly a liquid or solid at room temperature.

Vapourization (Vaashpan) When a substance changes its physical state-from liquid to gaseous form.

Vapour Pressure (Vaashp Daab) It is the pressure exerted when a solid or a liquid is in equilibrium with its own vapour. It is a function of the chemical and the temperature. Chemicals with a vapour pressure of over 100 mm mercury evaporate quickly.

Vapour Recovery System (Punar Vaashpan Tantra) A system which is installed in any process to capture or collect all or most of the vapours which may be exhausted by the process. These vapours are generally hazardous in nature and so are to be captured or recovered by a system. Generally vapours are hydrocarbons that are being emitted.

Vector (Rog Vaahak) An organism such as an insect or rodent which is capable of transmitting a pathogen from one organism to another. Other organisms include flies, and other insects, birds and vermin. Wind and water also serve as a vector.

Vegetated Buffer (Vanaspatik Pratirodhak) Strips of vegetation separating a water body from a land use that could act as a non point pollution source. Vegetated buffers are variable in width and can range in function from a vegetated filter strip to a wetland or riparian area.

Vegetated Filter Strips Created areas of vegetation designed to remove sediment and other pollutants from surface water runoff by filtration, deposition, infiltration, adsorption, absorption, decomposition, and volatilization. A vegetated filter strip is an area that maintains soil aeration as opposed to a wetland that, at times, exhibits anaerobic soil conditions.

Vehicle (Vaahan) It means any mode of surface transport other than railways.

Venom (Vish or Jahar) Poison excreted by animals and passed on to victims through bites or stings.

Ventilation (Samvaatan) Controlled movement of air into and out of a building.

Venturi Scrubber Removal of particulate matter from air emissions by using water in the pollution control devices.

Vermiculite (Vermiculite) It is a light weight water-absorbent clay mineral.

Virus (Vishanu) Smallest infectious particle consisting of protein and nucleic acids. They generally replicate only in a host's cells by directing a host cell to create material required to produce more virus. They cause most infectious diseases, reduce plant growth.

Viscosity (Viskaasitaa) It is a measure of resistance to flow of a substance which is a liquid. It is the friction that exists between solids.

Viscous (Viskaasi) A substance which is highly resistant to flow. It may be due to its adhesive or sticky qualities.

Vitrification (Kaanch Ka Bananaa) The process of converting waste into an immobile solid. From radioactive waste, glassy material is produced which can then be stored permanently.

Vitrified (Kaanch Bananaa) Describes material already heated into a glasslike substance so it is largely inert. The process produces a glass-like solid that captures the radioactive materials.

Viviparous (Sajiv Prajak) An animal that produces living offspring instead of eggs. Examples include all mammals. Examples in plants include those that produce bulbils or small plants instead of, or in addition to, seeds.

Volatile Organic Chemical (VOC) (Vashpasheel Carbonic Rasayan) A carbon-containing compound that tends to evaporate rapidly under normal atmospheric conditions. They are generally hydrocarbons and are known to be the principle cause of smog, and danger to the atmospheric ozone. VOCs may cause damage to many human organs. Examples are benzene, toluene, xylene.

W

Waste Reduction (Kachara Kam Karna) A change in process, operation or activity that results in the economically and efficient reduction in generation of waste per unit of production of the material without reducing the output in any way. In the changed process, the health of the environment should not decrease in any way.

Waste-to-Energy Plants (Apashisht Urja Samyantra or Kachade Se Urja Udyog) Waste which has very high Btu content in it, can be burned and in the process, and the heat generated can be used as an energy source. The ash resulting from burning of waste which may be hazardous in nature, is landfilled. Because of burning, heavy metals such as lead are emitted into the atmosphere.

Water (Prevention and Control of Pollution) Act of 1974 This Act provides for the prevention and control of water pollution and the maintaining or restoring of wholesomeness of water, for the establishment, with a view to carrying out the purposes aforesaid, of Boards for the prevention and control of water pollution, for conferring on and assigning to such Boards powers and functions relating thereto and for matters connected therewith. It is expedient to provide for the prevention and control of water pollution and the maintaining or restoring of wholesomeness of water.

Water (Prevention & Control of Pollution) Cess Act of 1977 This Act provided for the levy and collection of a Cess (fee) on water consumed by persons carrying on certain industries and by local authorities with a view to augment the resources of the Central Board and the State Boards. A rebate is available for a person or any local authority which installs a plant for the treatment of sewage or trade effluents to remove contaminants.

Water Contaminants Contaminants found in agricultural water include detergents, coliform bacterial, erosion and sedimentation, and total dissolved solids. In residential water, the contaminants include alkalinity, detergents, coliform bacterial, and total dissolved solids. In natural water, they may contain coliform bacteria, hardness, radium,metals such as arsenic, barium, copper, iron, lead, aluminium, mercury, manganese, silver, sodium, zinc, and total dissolved solids. Industrial water may include any contaminants including alkalinity, radium, total dissolved solids and the chemicals from the industry.

Water Cycle (Jal Chakra) Natural process of the atmosphere through which water recycles by itself through evaporation and condensation.

Water Pollution Control Areas (Jala Pradushan Niyantran Kshetra) A State Government may, by notification in the Official Gazette, declare a specific area of the state by reference to the line of any watershed or the boundary of any district or any parts thereof for any specific purposes. They may survey any aarea and gauge and keep records of the flow or volume and other characteristics of an stream or well in such area.

Water Quality Criteria (Jala Guna Vaktaa Maap Dand) Levels of pollutants as specified by law to be suitable for a specific use. For use as drinking water, the level of pollution must be minimal.

Water-Reactive Chemical material that reacts with water or moist air to produce or release a hazard.

Watershed (Jal Sambhaar) Natural area that funnels into water bodies such as rivers and lakes.

Water Table (Bhoomi Mein Jal Stir) The upper most level of water found in ground. It could be on the surface or under the ground. When found underground, the water must be moist enough to be extractable.

Weathering (Apakshayan) The process where a complex compound is reduced to its simpler component parts, transported through physical processes, or biodegraded over time.

Weighed Network Decibels See dBA-A.

Well Casing (Koop Aavaran) Materials such as concrete, piping, metal, and stone that line and support a well and prevent it from collapsing.

Western Ghats (Pashchimei Ghat) Covring an area of about 159,000 sq. kn, they are a chain of highlands running along the western edge of the Indian subcontinent, from Mumbai south to the southern tip of the peninsula, through the states of Maharashtra, Karnataka, Kerala and Tamil Nadu. There are currently seven national parks in the Western Ghats and 39 wildlife sanctuaries.

Wetland (Daldal) Land or area, such as tidal flats, swamps, marshes, and bogs which contain much soil moisture. Animal as well as plant habitat in these areas is distinct as they support vegetation typically adapted for life in saturated soil conditions. An area is generally self sufficient for all the habitat of that wetland as the area is generally inundated or saturated at a frequency and duration which is substantially more than normal in other areas. India has 1,193 wetland areas, most important being the Chilka Lake in Orissa and and Keoladeo National Park (Bharatpur) in Rajasthan.

Wild Life (Protection) Act, 1972 (Vanya Prani Sanrakshan Adhiniyam) The purpose of this Act is to provide protection for wild animals and birds. It places ban on hunting for commerce and pleasure. National Policy for Wildlife Conservation was adopted in 1970.

Wind Energy (Vaayu Urja) One of the cleanest forms of energy which produces no pollution. Electricity can be produced when naturally blowing wind passes over rotating turbine blades that drive generators to generate electricity. Wind power has still not become a very large energy producer.

WL Working Level (WL Kaarya Star) Abbreviation for working level; a measure radon progeny concentration; any combination of radon progeny in one litre of air whose radioactive decay will result in the release of 130,000 million electron volts (MeV) of alpha-particle energy.

World Environment Day (Paryavaran Divas) It is observed on June 5. See also Earth Day.

X

X-Rays (X Kiranen) Electromagnetic radiations of high energy having wavelengths shorter than those in the ultraviolet region, i.e. less than 10 -6 cm or 100 Angstroms. Materials at very high temperatures (millions of degrees) emit such radiations. They are then called thermal X-rays.

Xenobiote Any biotum that has been displaced from its normal habitat. It indicates a chemical which is foreign to a specific biological system or body.

Xeriscape Use of local native plants and vegetation in gardens and lawns.

Xerophyte (Marud Bhid) Plant that can grow in arid or semiarid climates.

Xylene (Xylene) A clear flammable and toxic liquid solvent. Used in paints, solvents, and in the manufacture of rubber cements.

Y

Year (Varsh or Saal) The Government of India, under the various regulations considers 'Year' that means the financial year commencing on the first day of April.

Yellow Cake A yellow powder that is mostly uranium oxide. Produced by pouring crushed uranium ore into an acid which dissolves the uranium. The acid is then drained from the crushed ore and dried, leaving a yellow powder called yellow cake.

Z

Zeolites (Zeolite) A naturally hydrated silicate of aluminium and either sodium, calcium, barium or strontium. They are characterised by easy and reversible loss of electron-pair bonded water and the property of swelling when heated. Used as ion-exchangers in water softening. Also used as absorbents.

Zero Air Atmospheric air purified to contain less than 0.1 ppm total hydrocarbons.

Zinc (Jast or Jastaa) Shining, silvery moderately reactive metal. It has low melting point. Used in galvanizing of metals. In trace amounts, it is a necessary element for humans. Also used in dry cell batteries. Atomic weight: 65.38. Chemical symbol: Zn.

Zircaloy A strong alloy of Zirconium and tin used to make the fuel rods in a nuclear power plant.

Zirconium (Zirconium) Lustrous steel-gray, strong metallic element. It has a high melting point and is very resistant to corrosion. Used in coating of nuclear fuel rods.

Zone of Aeration (Vaatan Kshetra or Mandal) The layer of soil or rock in which pore spaces are partially filled with both air and water.

Zone of Saturation (Santrapti Kshetra) The layer of soil or rock in which pore spaces are completely filled with water.

Zooplankton (Prani Plavak) Free floating small animals, mainly crustaceans, in the surface waters of the oceans that feed primarily on Phytoplankton. In turn, Zooplankton are fed on by many fish and other animals.

APPENDIX A

HALF LIFE OF SOME RADIONUCLIDES (In Years):

Americium-241	458 years
Barium-133	7.2 years
Bismuth-207	30 years
Carbon-14	5730 years
Cesium-137	30 years
Chlorine-36	310,000 years
Cobalt-60	5.26 years
DDT	15 years
Europium-152	12
Europium-154	16
Europium-155	1.81
Hydrogen-3 or (Tritium)	12.3
Iodine-129	1.7x107
Krypton-85	10.76
Lead-210	21
Nickel-63	92
Plutonium-239	24,600
Radon-222	3.28 days
Samarium-151	87 years
Strontium-90	28.1 years
Technetium-99	2.12x105 years
Thallium-204	3.8 years
Uranium-238	4.51x109 years

APPENDIX B

SYMBOL, ATOMIC NUMBER AND NAME OF ELEMENTS:

Atomic Number	Symbol	Name
0	n	Neutron
1	H	Hydrogen
2	He	Helium
3	Li	Lithium
4	Be	Beryllium
5	B	Boron
6	C	Carbon
7	N	Nitrogen
8	O	Oxygen
9	F	Fluorine
10	Ne	Neon
11	Na	Sodium
12	Mg	Magnesium
13	Al	Aluminium
14	Si	Silicon
15	P	Phosphorous
16	S	Sulphur
17	Cl	Chlorine
18	Ar	Argon
19	K	Potassium
20	Ca	Calcium
21	Sc	Scandium
22	Ti	Titanium
23	V	Vanadium
24	Cr	Chromium
25	Mn	Manganese
26	Fe	Iron
27	Co	Cobalt
28	Ni	Nickel
29	Cu	Copper
30	Zn	Zinc
31	Ga	Gallium
32	Ge	Germanium
33	As	Arsenic
34	Se	Selenium

35	Br	Bromine
36	Kr	Krypton
37	Rb	Rubidium
38	Sr	Strontium
39	Y	Yttrium
40	Zr	Zirconium
41	Nb	Niobium
42	Mo	Molybdenum
43	Tc	Technetium
44	Ru	Ruthenium
45	Rh	Rhodium
46	Pd	Palladium
47	Ag	Silver
48	Cd	Cadmium
49	In	Indium
50	Sn	Tin
51	Sb	Antimony
52	Te	Tellerium
53	I	Iodine
54	Xe	Xenon
55	Cs	Cesium
56	Ba	Barium
57	La	Lanthanum
58	Ce	Cerium
59	Pr	Praseodymium
60	Nd	Neodymium
61	Pm	Promethium
62	Sm	Samarium
63	Eu	Europium
64	Gd	Gadolinium
65	Tb	Terbium
66	Dy	Dysprosium
67	Ho	Holmium
68	Er	Erbium
69	Tm	Thulium
70	Yb	Ytterbium
71	Lu	Lutetium
72	Hf	Hafnium
73	Ta	Tantalum
74	W	Tungsten
75	Re	Rhenium
76	Os	Osmium

77	Ir	Iridium
78	Pt	Platinum
79	Au	Gold
80	Hg	Mercury
81	Tl	Thallium
82	Pb	Lead
83	Bi	Bismuth
84	Po	Polonium
85	At	Astatine
86	Rn	Radon
87	Fr	Francium
88	Ra	Radium
89	Ac	Actinium
90	Th	Thorium
91	Pa	Protactinium
92	U	Uranium
93	Np	Neptunium
94	Pu	Plutonium
95	Am	Americium
96	Cm	Curium
97	Bk	Berkelium
98	Cf	Californium
99	Es	Einstenium
100	Fm	Fermium
101	Md	Mendelevium
102	No	Nobelium
103	Lw	Lawrencium

APPENDIX C

Guidelines To Set Up Industry:

To help the authorities concerned and entrepreneurs, it is necessary to frame certain broad guidelines for setting up an industry. It is also necessary to identify the parameters that should be taken into account when setting up an industry. With this in view, the following environmental guidelines have been recommended by the Government of India for setting up industries to ensure optimum use of natural and man-made resources in a sustainable manner with minimal depletion, degradation and/or destruction of environment. These are in addition to those directives that are already in existence under the Industries (Development and Regulation) Act.

AREAS TO BE AVOIDED:
Care should be taken to minimise the adverse impact of the industries on the immediate neighbourhood as well as distant places. Some of the natural life sustaining systems and some specific land uses are sensitive to industrial impacts because of the nature and extent of fragility. Industrial sites shall maintain the following distances from the areas listed:

Ecologically and/or otherwise sensitive areas: At least 25 km; depending on the geo-clmatic conditions the requisite distance has to be increased by the appropriate agency.

- Coastal areas: at least 1/2 km from High Tide Line;
- Flood Plain of the Riverine Systems: at least 1/2 km from flood plain or modified flood plain affected by dam in the upstream or by flood control systems;
- Transport/Communication System: at least 1/2 km from highway and railway.

Major settlements (3,00,000 population): distance from settlements is difficult to maintain because of urban sprawl. At the time of siting of the industry if any major settlement's notified limit is within 50 km, the spatial direction of growth of the settlement for at least a decade must be assessed and the industry shall be sited at least 25 km from the projected growth boundary of the settlement.

Pre-requisite: State and Central Governments are required to identify such areas on a priority basis.

Ecological and/or otherwise sensitive areas include Religious and Historic Places; (ii) Archaeological Monuments (e.g. identified zone around the Taj Mahal); (iii) Scenic Areas; (iv) Hill Resorts; (v) Beach Resorts; (vi) Health Resorts; (vii) Coastal Areas rich in Coral, Mangroves, Breeding Grounds of Specific Species; (viii) Estuaries rich in

Mangroves, Breeding Ground of Specific Species; (ix) Gulf Areas; (x) Biosphere Reserves; (xi) National Parks and Sanctuaries; (xii) Natural Lakes, Swamps; (xiii) Seismic Zones; (xiv) Tribal Settlements; (xv) Areas of Scientific and Geological interest; (xvi) Defence Installations, specially those of security importance and sensitive to pollution; (xvii) Border Areas (International) and (xviii) Airports.

CRITERIA:
Economic and social factors are recognized and assessed when siting an industry. Environmental factors must be taken into consideration in industrial siting. Proximity of water sources, highway, major settlements, markets for products and raw material resources is desired for economy of production, but all the above listed systems must be away for environmental protection. Industries are, therefore, required to be sited, striking a balance between economic and environmental considerations. In such a selected site, the following factors must be recognized.

No forest land shall be converted into non-forest activity for the sustenance of the industry (Ref: Forest Conservation Act, 1980).

No prime agricultural land shall be converted into industrial site.

Within the acquired site the industry must locate itself at the lowest location to remain obscured from general sight.
Land acquired shall be sufficiently large to provide space for appropriate treatment of waste water still left for treatment after maximum possible reuse and recycle. Reclaimed(treated) wastewater shall be used to raise green belt and to create water body for aesthetics, recreation and if possible, for aquaculture. The green belt shall be 1/2 km wide around the battery limit of the industry. For industry having odour problem it shall be a kilometre wide.

The green belt between two adjoining large scale industries shall be one kilometre.

Enough space should be provided for storage of solid wastes so that these could be available for possible reuse.

Lay out and form of the industry that may come up in the area must conform to the landscape of the area without affecting the scenic features of that place. Associated township of the industry must be created at a space having physiographic barrier between the industry and the township.

Each industry is required to maintain three ambient air quality measuring stations within 120 degree angle between stations.

APPENDIX D

Classification of Hazardous Waste Categories for Labelling:

S. No.	Waste Categories	Types of Wastes	Hazardous Class Label As per Motor Vehicle Act
1.	Waste Category No. 1	Cyanide Waste	Poison
2.	Waste Category No. 2,3 & 4	Heavy Metal Bearing Waste	Poison, Corrosives, Oxidising Substance
3.	Waste Category No. 5	Non-Halogenated Hydrocarbon including Solvents	Combustible, Poison Flammable Liquid, Corrosives
4.	Waste Category No. 6	Halogenated Hydrocarbons including Solvents	Combustible, Poison Flammable Liquid
5.	Waste Category No. 7	Waste from Paint Pigment, glue, varnish, & Printing Inks	Flammable Solids Combustibles
6.	Waste Category No. 8	Waste from Dyes & Dye intermediate containing inorganic chemical compounds	Poison, Flammable Solids, Corrosives
7.	Waste Category No. 9	Waste from Dyes & Dye intermediate containing organic chemical compounds	Poison, Flammable Solids, Dangerous when wet
8.	Waste Category No. 10	Waste Oil & oil emulsions	Flammable Liquids

9. Waste Category No. 11	Tarry waste from refining & tar residues from distillation or pyrolytic treatment	Flammable Solids/ Liquid, Combustible
10. Waste Category No. 12	Sludges from waste water treatment incl. incineration ash	Poison, dangerous when wet
11. Waste Category No. 13	Phenols	Poison
12. Waste Category No. 14	Asbestos	Poison
13. Waste Category No. 15	Waste from manuf. of pesticide, herbicide & residues from formulating units	Flammable Solids/ Liquid, Poison, Combustible
14. Waste Category No. 16	Acid/Alkaline/ Slurry wastes	Corrosive, Oxidising substance
15. Waste Category No. 17	Off-specification & discarded products	Poison
16. Waste Category No. 18	Discarded containers & liners of hazardous & toxic chemical & wastes	Dangerous (Label as given in Annexure-IV of Hazardous Waste)

APPENDIX E

List of Hazardous and Toxic Chemicals

Acetone
Acetone Cynohydride
Acetyl Chloride
Acetylene (Ethyne)
Acrolein (2-Propenal)
Acrylonitrile
Aldicarb
Aldrin
Alkyl Phthalate
Allyl Alcohol
Allylamine
Alpha Naththyl Thiourea (Antu)
Aminodiphenyl-4
Aminophenol-2
Amiton
Ammonia
Ammonium Nitrate
Ammonium Nitrates in Fertilizers
Ammonium Sulfamate
Anabasine
Aniline
Anisidine-p
Antiminy and Compounds
Antimony Hydride (Stibine)
Arseni Hydride (Arsine)
Arsenic Pentoxide, Arseine (v) Acid, and Salts
Arsenic Trioxide, Arsenious (iii) Acids and Salts
Asbestos
azinophos-Ethyl
Azinphos-Methyl
Barium Azide
Benzene
benzidine
Benzidine Salts
Benzoquinone
Benzoyl Chloride
Benzoyl Peroxide

Benzyl Chloride
Benzyl Cynide
Beryllium (Powders Compound)
Biphenyl
Bis (2-Chloromethyl) Ketone
Bis (2,4,6-Trinitrophynile) Amine
Bis (2,Chloroethyle Sulphide)
Bis (Chloromethyl) ether
Bis (tert-Butylperoxy) Butane-2,2
Bis (tert-Butyl peroxy) Cyclohexane-11
Bis-1,2 Tribromophenoxy Ethane
Bis phenol
Boron and Compounds
Bromine
Bromine Pentafluoride
Bromoform
Butoadine
Butane
Butanethiol
Butanone-2
Butoxy Ethanol
Butyl Glycidal Ether
Butyl Peroxy acetate, tert
Butyl Peroxyisobutyrate, tert
Butyl Peroxyiropropyl Carbonae, tert
Butyl Peroxymaleate, tert
Butyl Peroxypivalate, tert
Butyl Vinyl Ether
Buty-n-Mercaptan
Butylamine
C-9, Aromatic Hydrocarbon Fraction
Cadmium and Compounds
cadmium Oxide (fumes)
Calcium Cynide
Captan
Captofol
Carbaryl (Sevin)
Carbofuran
Carbon Disulphide
Carbon Monoxide
Carbon Tetrachloride
Carbophenothion

Cellulose Nitrate
Chlorats (used in explosives)
Chlordane
Chlorfenvinphos
Chlorinated Benzenes
Chlorine
Chlorine Di Oxide
Chlorine Oxide
Chlorine Trifluoride
Chloromequal Chloride
Chloroacetalchloride
Chloroacetaldehyde
Chloroanilin-2
Chloroaniline-4
Chlorobenzene
Chlorodiphenyl
Chloropoxypropane
Chloroethanol
Chloroethyl Chloroformate
Chlorofluorocarbons
Chloroform
Chloformyl-4, Merpholine
Chloromethane
Chloromethyl Ether
Chloromethyl Methyl Ether
Chloronitrobenzene
Chloroprene
Chlorosulphonic Acid
Chlorotrinitro benzene
Chloroxuron
Chromium and Compounds
Cobalt and Compounds
Copper and Compounds
Coumafuryl
Coumaphos
Coumateralyl
Cresols
Cumidine
Cumene
Cynophos
Cynothoate
Cyanuric Fluoride

Cyclohexane
Cyclohexanol
Cyclohexene
Cycloheximide
Cyclopentadinene
Cyclopentene
Cyclotetramethylenetrinitramine
Cyclotriethylene Trinitramine
DDT
Dicarbomodiphenyl Oxide
Demeton
Di-Isobutyl Peroxide
Di n-Propyl Peroxydicarbonate
Di-sed-Butyl Peroxydicarbonate
Dalifos
Diazodinitrophenol
Diszomethane
Dibenzyl Peroxydicarbonate
Dichloroacetylene
Dichlorobenzene-O
Dichlorobenzene-2
Di-chloroethane
Dichloroethyl Ether
Dichlorophenol-2,4
Dichlorophenol-2,6
Dichlorohenoxy Acetic Acid, -2 4(2,4-D)
Dichloropropane-1,2
Dichlorosalicylic Acid,-3,5
Dichlorovos (DDVP)
Dicrotophos
Dieldrin
Diepoxybutane
Diethyl Peroxydicarbonate
Diethyl Peroxydicarbonate
Diethylene Triamine
Diethyleneglycol Butyl Ether/Diethyleneglycol Butyl Acetate
Diethylenetriamine (DETA)
Diglycidyl Ether
Dihydroperoxypropane,-2,2
Diisobutyryl Peroxide
Dimethoate
Dimet

Dimethyl Phosphoramidocynidic Acid
Dimethyl Phthalate
Dimethylcarbonyl
Dimethylnitrosamine
Dinitrophenol, Salts
Dinitrotoluene
Dinitro-o-Cresol
Dioxane
Dioxathion
Dioxalane
Diphacinone
Diphosphoramide Octamethyl
Dipropylene Glycolmethylether
Disulfoton
Endosulfan
Endrin
Epichlorohydrine
EPN
Epoxypropane,1,2
Ehion
Ethyl Carbamate
Ethyl Ether
Ethyl Hexanol,-2
Ethyl Mercaptan
Ethyl Methacrylate
Ethyl Nitrate
Ethyl Amine
Ethylene
Ethylene Chlorohydrine
Ethylene Diamine
Ethylene Dibromide
Ethylene Dichloride
Ethylene Glycol Dinitrate
Ethylene Oxide
Ethyleneimine
Ethylthiocyanate
Fensulphothion
Fluenetil
Fluoro,-4,2-Hydroxybutyric Acid and Salts,Esters, Amides
Fluoroacetic Acid and Salts, Esters, Amides
Fluorobutyric Acid,-4, and Salts, Esters, Amides
Fluorocrotonic Acid,-4, and Salts, Esters, Amides

Formaldehyde
Glyconitrile (Hydroxyacetonitrile)
Guanyl, -1, -4 Nitrosaminoguanyl-1-Tetrazene
Heptachlor
Hexachloro Cyclopentadiene
Hexachlorocyclohexane
Hexachlorocycloamethane
Hexachlorodibenzo-p-Dioxin, -1,2,3,7,8,9
Hexafluoropropene
Hexamethylphosphoramide
Hexamethyl,-3,3,6,6,9,9,-1,2,4,5-Tetroxacyclononane
Hexamethylenediamine
Hexane
Hexanitrosstibene,-2,2,4,4,6,6
Hexavalent Chromium
Hydrazine
Hydrazine Nitrate
Hydrochloric Acid
Hydrogen
Hydrogen Bromide (Hydrobromic Acid)
Hydrogen Chloride (Liquified Gas)
Hydrogen Cynide
Hydrogen Fluoride
Hydrogen Selenide
Hydrogen Sulphide
Hydroquinone
Iodine
Isobenzene
Isodrin
Isophorone Diisocynate
Isoprophyl Ether
Juglone(5-Hydroxynapthalene-1,2-Dione)
Lead (Inorganic fumes and dusts)
Lead 2,4,6-Trinitroresorcinoxide (Lead Sulphonate)
Lead Azide
Leptophos
Lindane
Liquified Petroleum Gas (LPG)
Maleic Anhydride
Manganese and Compounds
Mercapto Benzothiazole
Mercury Alkyl

Mercury Fulminate
Mercury Methyl
Methacrylic Anhydride
Methacrylonitrile
Methacrylolyl Chloride
Methamidophos
Methanesuphonyl Fluoride
Methanethiol
Methoxy Ethanol (2-Methyl Cellosive)
Methoxy ethyl mercuric Acetate
Methyl Acrylate
Methyl Alcohol
Methyl Amylketone
Methyl Bromide (Bromomethane)
Methyl Chloride
Methyl Chloroform
Methyl Cyclohexane
Methyl Ethyl Ketone Peroxide
Methyl Hydrazine
Methyl Isobutyl Ketone
Methyl Isobutyl Ketpone Peroxide
Methyl Isocyanate
Methyl Isothiocynate
Methyl Mercaptian
Methyl Methacrylate
Methyl Parathiol
Methyl Phosphonic Dichloride
Methyl-N,2,4,5,-Trinitroaniline
Methylene Chloride
Methylenebis,-4,4, (2-Chloroaniline)
Methyltrichlcrosilane
Mevinphos
Molybdenum and Compounds
N-Methyl-N,2,4,6-N-Tetranitroanilin
Naptha (Coal Tar)
Napthylamine,2
Nickel and Compounds
Nickel Tetracarbonyl
Nitroaniline-O
Nitroaniline-P
Nitrobenzene
Nitrochlorobenzene-P

Nitrocyclohexane
Nitroethane
Nitrogen Dioxide
Nitrogen Oxide
Nitrogen Trifluoride
Nitroglycerine
Nitrophenol-P
Nitropropane-1
Nitropropane-2
Nitrosodimethylamine
Nitrotoluene
Octabromophenyl Oxide
Oleum
Oleylamine
OO-Diethyl S-Ethylsulphonylmethyl phosphorothioate
OO-Diethyl S-Ethylthiomethyl Phosphorothioate
OO-Diethyl S-Ethiomethyl Phosphorathioate
OO-Diethyl S-Isopropyliniomethyl Phosphorolithioate
OO-diethyl S-Propylthiomethyl Phosphorodithioage
Oxyamyl
Oxydisulioton
Oxygen (liquid)
Oxygen Difluoride
Ozone
Paraoxon (Diethyl 4-Nitrophenyl Phosphate)
Paraquat
Parathion
Parathion Methyl
Paris Green (Bis Aceto Hexametaatsinito Tetracopper)
Pentaborane
Pentabromodiphenyl Oxide
Pentabromophenol
Pentachloro Naphthalene
Pentachloroethane
Pentachlorophenol
Pentacrythritol Tetranitrate
Pentane
Peracetic Acid
Perchloroethylene
Perchloromethyl Mercaptan
Pentanone,2,4-Methyl
Phenol

Phenyl Glycidal Ether
Phenylene p-Diamine
Phenylmercury Acetate
Phorate
Phosacetim
Phosalone
Phosfolan
Phosgene (Carabonyl Chloride)
Phosmet
Phospamidon
Phosphine (Hydrogen Phosphide)
Phosphoric Acid and Esters
Phosphoric Acid, Bromethyl Bromo(2,2-dimethylpropyl) Bromoethyl Ester
Phosphoric Acid, Bromoethyl Bromo (2,2-Dimethylpropyl) Chlorethyethyl Ester
Phosphoric Acid, Chloroethyl Bromo (2,2-Dimethoxylpropyl) Chloroethyl Ester
Phosphorous and Compounds
Phostalan
Picric Acid (2,4,6-Trinitrophenol)
Polybrominated Biphenyl
Potassium Arsenite
Potassium Chlorate
Promurit (1-(3,4-Dichlorophenyl)-3-Triazenethiocarboxamide)
Propanesultone-1,3
Propen,-1,2 Chloro-1,3-Diol-Diacetate
Propylene Dichloride
Propylene Oxide
Propyleneimine
Pyrazoxon
Selenium Hexafluoride
Semicarbazide Hydrochloride
Sodium Arsenite
Sodium Azide
Sodium Chlorate
Sodium Cynide
Sodium Picramate
Sodium Selenite
Styrene,1,1,2,2-Tetrachloroethane
Sulfotep
Sulphur Dichloride
Sulphur Dioxide
Sulphur Trioxide
Sulphuric Acid

Sulphoxide,3-Chloropropyloctyl
Tellurium
Tellurium Hexafluoride
Tepp
Terbufos
Tetrabromobisphenol-A
Tetrachloro,2,2,5,6,2,5-Cyclohexadiene-1,4-Dione
Tetrachlorodibenzo-p Dioxin,2,3,7,8 (TCDD)
Tetraethyl Lead
Tetrafluoroethane
Tetramethylenedisulphotetramine
Tetramethyl Lead
Tetramnitromethane
Thalium and Compounds
Thionzin
Thionyl Chloride
Tirpate
Toluene
Toluidien-2,4 Diisocynate
Toluidiene-O
Toluene 2,6-Diisocynate
Trans-1,4-Chlorobutene
Tri,-1(Cyclohexyl)Stannyl-1H,1,2,4-Trazole
Triamino,1,3,5,2,4,6-Trinitrobenzene
Tribromophenol,2,4,6
TrichloroAcetyl Chloride
Trichloro Ethane
Trichloro Naphthalene
Trichloro (chloromethyl) Silane
Trichlorodichlorophenylsilane
Trichloroethane,1,1,1
Trichloroethyl Silane
Trichloroethylene
Trichloromethanesulphenyl Chloride
Trichlorophenol,2,2,6
Trichlorophenol,2,2,5
Triethylamine
Triethylenemelamine
Trimethyl Chlorosilane
Trimethylopropane Phosphite
Trinitroaniline
Trinitroanisole,2,2,4,6

Trinitrobenzene
Trinitrobenzoic Acid
Trinitrocresol
Trinitrophenetole,2,4,6
Trinitroesorcinol,2,4,6 (Styphnic Acid)
Trinitrotoluene
Triorthocressyl Phosphate
Triphenylin Chloride
Turpentine
Uranium and Compounds
Vanadium and Compounds
Vinyl Chloride
Vinyl Fluoride
Vinyl Iodide
Warfarin
Xylene
Xylidine
Zinc and Compounds
Zirconium and Compounds

APPENDIX F

Guidelines for Occupier/Generator of Hazardous Waste:

In crder to have a proper control over hazardous waste management, the regulatory authorities should specify the occupier or generator of hazardous waste:

To keep a complete record of the types, quantities and characteristics of hazardous waste.

To segregate hazardous waste at source from non-hazardous waste.

To transport hazardous waste only through the specified and registered transporters.

To fulfill the pre-transport requirements before transporting hazardous waste.

To dispose of hazardous waste only at the notified disposable facilities.

The regulatory authorities shall ask the occupier or generator to submit quarterly reports.

The authorities should ensure that the occupier/generator sends a copy of the manifest to them as soon as the hazardous wastes is shipped for ultimate disposal.

The regulatory authorities may allow the occupier/generator to store his hazardous waste on-site provided that:

The waste is stored in the specified containers and occupier/generator follows the requirements for storing in the containers.

The date upon which each period of storage begins is clearly marked and visible on each container.

While being stored on-site, each container is labelled or marked with the words "HAZARDOUS WASTE", both in English and respective local language.

The regulatory authorities may allow the occupier/generator to store his hazardous waste on-site a maximum quantity of 10,000 kgs or a truckload whichever is less for a maximum period of 90 days.

If an occupier/generator generates less than 1,000 kgs of hazardous waste in a month, he may be considered as a small quantity generator. Such types of generators may be allowed to store their waste on-site for a maximum period of 180 days. In any case, the quantity of waste should not exceed 6,000 kgs at any given point of time.

The regulatory authorities may provide an extension in the storage period to the occupier, on case-by-case basis, provided that:

An occupier/generator who generates less than 1000 kgs of hazardous waste in a month and who transports his waste more than a distance of 500 kms for off-site storage, treatment and/or disposal may be allowed to store hazardous waste on-site for a maximum period of 270 days at the discretion of regulatory authorities. In any case the quantity of waste should not exceed 10,000 kgs at any given point of time.

To ensure that the occupier/generator disposes their waste only in the notified disposal facilities.

In case of any unforeseen, temporary, and uncontrollable circumstances, the regulatory authorities may grant an extension to 90-day or 180-day or 270-day in the on-site period upto a maximum period of 30 days, after receiving written application from the occupier/generator.

An occupier/generator who generates less than 1000 kgs of hazardous waste more than 10,000 kgs or store hazardous waste more than 90 days or 180 days or 270 days, as the case may be, should be considered as an operator of a storage facility, unless an extension has been provided by the regulatory authorities.

An occupier may be allowed to store not more than one day's quantity of semi-solid hazardous waste at a time in containers near the source/point of generation, which is under the control of the operator generating the waste. In any case, the container should have marking of the words "HAZARDOUS WASTE" both in English and respective local language.

At all times there must be at least responsibility of one employee either on the premises or on call with the responsibilities for co-ordinating all emergency response measures.

The owner must inspect the on-site storage areas for proper storage at all times.. In order to track the hazardous waste from the source of generation to the final disposal points, the regulatory authorities should introduce the manifest system. This system should not only help the regulatory authorities in tracking the hazardous waste but also ensure the safe disposal of the waste. The manifest system would serve as a "chain of custody" document. Every time the shipment changes hands, the responsible person must sign the manifest.

APPENDIX G

Guidelines for Transportation of Hazardous Waste:

Transportation of hazardous waste is the important link in hazardous waste management system, and it requires precise control to ensure safe disposal of such wastes. Therefore, it would be prudent to consider registering the transporters of hazardous waste with the Department of Environment & Forests in addition to the Department of Transport. This would enable the Ministry of Environment and Forests/respective State Pollution Control Boards to ensure safe and secured transport of hazardous wastes.

To ensure that the occupier/generator transport their hazardous waste only in the specified transport vehicles.

The transporters should be asked to train the drivers and helpers of hazardous waste transport vehicles to handle the wastes under emergency situations.

APPENDIX H

Guidelines for Owner/Operator of Hazardous Waste Storage, Treatment and Disposal Facility:

Licensing system:
The regulatory authorities may issue a consent to an owner/operator of a facility who can demonstrate his technical, financial and managerial competence, and that his staff are properly trained. The authorities shall specify in the consent, the wastes which a facility can receive, the operational conditions which must be met, the monitoring and control procedures to be carried out and the records which must be kept. Along with the application for consent, the following information should be furnished by the owner/operator of a facility:

Area required for the facility.

Types of wastes to be handled, stored, treated and/or disposed.

Facilities available for managing these wastes.

Environment Impact Assessment of the area where the activity has been proposed.

Contingency plan of the facility.

The regulatory authorities should ensure that the owner/operator of a facility has all necessary equipment such as fire control equipment, decontamination equipment, water spray system and internal communication or alarm systems capable of meeting any emergency situation at the facility.

Establishment of standards: The regulatory authorities should identify the Principal Organic Hazardous Constituents(POHC) in the waste and set standards for stack emission for POHC from the incinerator.

Also the effluent and ground water quality should be monitored regularly. The records of the facility should be checked regularly.

Post-closure care and use of property: The post closure-care for each hazardous waste storage, treatment, and/or disposal facility should begin after closure of the facility and regulatory authorities must ensure that post-closure activities continue for 30 days from the date of closure. The local or state administrative body should be made responsible for the post-closure care.

To ensure that the copy of the manifest reaches the authorities after receiving the hazardous waste from the occupier/generator. The owner/operator should indicate the proposed treatment and disposal scheme to be followed for the hazardous waste. The copy of the manifest should be linked with the copy of the manifest sent by the occupier/generator.

APPENDIX I

CRITERIA FOR SITING OF INDUSTRIES WITH REFENENCE TO CLASSIFICATION OF RIVER ZONES:

A-I

a. 3 Kms. On the either side of the river

No development zone for any type of industries. Only specified non-industrial listed activities are allowed.

b. From 3 Kms to 8 Kms. From river (H.F.L.) on either side

Classified Green and Orange category of industries irrespective of investment with requisite pollution control devices.

c. Beyond 8 Kms. From river (H.F.L.) on either side.

Any type of industry with requisite pollution control devices.

A-II

a. 1 Km on either side of river (H.F.L.)

No development zone. Only specified non-industrial listed activities are allowed.

b. 1 Km to 2 Kms. on either side.

Classified Green and Orange category of industries irrespective of investment, with requisite pollution control devices are allowed.

c. Beyond 2 Kms.

Any type of industry with requisite pollution control devices are allowed.

A-III

a. Upto 1/2 Km on either side.

No development zones for any type of industries. Only specified non-industrial listed activities are allowed.

A-IV

a. Between ½ to 1 Km on either side of river

Classified Green and Orange category of industries irrespective of investment, with requisite pollution control devices are allowed.

b. Beyond 1 Km.

Any type of industry with requisite pollution control devices are allowed.

Note:

1. Distances mentioned in the policy note above are shortest distances measured as the crow flies.
2. High Flood Level (H.F.L.) of river will be considered as bank of the river for measuring the distances.
3. If the ridge line is nearer than prescribed zone boundary, restrictions apply to the ridge line.
4. Arrangement for pollution control shall be foolproof irrespective of the location.
5. In "No Development Zone", the permissible activities and non-permissible activities are separately prescribed.
6. Categorisation of industries is suggestive in nature and may be reviewed and modified by the Board from time to time.
7. Existing industries in "Non-Confirming Zone" will be allowed to continue with adequate pollution control arrangements.
8. Expansion, diversification, modernisation, and substitution shall be allowed subject to reduction in pollution load at source.
9. This does not absolve the Project Proponent from observing any other Rules/Regulations applicable in specific areas like Coastal Regulation Zone/Bhatsa River Basin etc.
10. Cases in pipe line would be dealt on merits of each case and would be considered beyond a distance of 500 m from H.F.L. as per the prevailing policy.
11. The above classification also covers lakes and other water bodies, excluding underground water sources.
12. Development activities in coastal areas will continue to be regulated by Ministry of Environment & Forest's notification (CRZ Notification) dated February 2, 1991.

APPENDIX J

Essential Items in a Hazardous Waste manifest:

Occupiers:

1. Occupiers' Name and Mailing Address
2. Occupier's Registration No.
3. Manifest Document No.
4. Transporter's name and Address
5. Type of Vehicle
6. Transporter's Registration No.
7. Vehicle Registration Number Transporting the Waste
8. Designated Facility Name and Site Address
9. Facility Registration No.
10. Facility Phone
11. Waste Description
12. Total Quantity of Waste
13. Consistency
14. Transport Description of Waste
15. Containers (No. and Type)

    Type of Containers
    DM-Metal Drums, barrels, kegs
    DW-Wooden drums, barrels, kegs
    DF-Fiberboard or plastic drums, barrels, kegs
    TP-Tanks portable
    TC-Tank cars
    DT-Dump trucks
    CM-Metal boxes, cartons, cases(including roll-offs)
    CY-Cylinders
    CF-Fiber or plastic boxes, cartons, cases

16. Total Quantity
17. Unit (Wt./Vol.)

    Units of Measure
    T-Tons
    Y-Cubic Yards

K-Kilograms
M-Metric Tones
N-Cubic Metres

18. Waste Category No.
19. Special Handling Instructions & Additional Information
20. Occupier's Certificate
21. Transporter's acknowledgment of receipt of Materials
22. Discrepancy Note Space
23. Facility Owner or Operator's Certification of Receipt of Hazardous Waste

APPENDIX K

Consideration in Siting of Hazardous Waste Disposal Facility

Physical Features
- Topography
- Land Stability
- Seismic Stability
- Surface Soils
- Surface Water and Streams
- Subsurface Geology and Aquifers
- Wind Direction

Ecological Features
- Flora and Fauna
- Conservation Value
- Habitat

Land Use Features
- Development Potential
- Land Use Designation (Residential/Industrial)
- Agricultural Value
- Transportation Corridor
- Extractive Industry/Mining

Logistics
- Proximity to Users
- Transport Access
- Availability of Utilities and Services (Hospital, fire)
- Adjacent Land Use/Zoning

Human Values
- Landscape
- Recreation
- Historical and Archeological
- Population Density and Health Status
- Employment Opportunities

BIBLIOGRAPHY

Ashworth, William, 'The Encyclopedia Of Environmental Studies,' Facts On File, New York, NY. 1991.

Bahri, Hardev, 'Rajpal English-Hindi Dictionary', Rajpal and Sons, New Delhi, India. 3rd Edition. 1990.

Bahri, Hardev, 'Learners' Hindi-English Dictionary', Rajpal and Sons, New Delhi, India. 1992.

Brauer, L. Roger, 'Safety and Health for Engineers', John Wiley & Sons, Inc. New York. 1994.

Bretherick, L, 'Hazards In The Chemical Laboratory', The Royal Society of Chemistry, London. 1981.

Central Pollution Control Board, 'Pollution Control Acts, Rules and Notifications Issued Thereunder', Delhi.

Committee on Environmental Improvement, 'Cleaning Our Environment-A Chemical Perspective', A Report by the American Chemical Society, Washington, DC. 2nd Edition. 1978.

Corbitt, Robert A., 'Standard Handbook of Environmental Engineering', McGraw Hill Publishing Company, New York. 1990.

Dean, John H. (ed.), 'Lange's Handbook Of Chemistry', 12th Edition, McGraw Hill Company, New York, NY. 1979.

Department of Education, 'Comprehensive Glossary Of Technical Terms-Science', Vol I and II, Government of India, New Delhi, India. 1990.

Dolan, Edward F. and Scariano, Margaret M., 'Nuclear Waste', Franklin Watts, New York. 1990.

Garell, Dale C., General Editor, 'Environmental Health', Chelsea House Publishers, New York. 1994.

Gay, Kathlyn, 'Water Pollution', Franklin Watts, New York. 1990.

Gould, Roy, 'Going Sour', Birkhauser, Boston. 1985.

Greenfield, Ellen J., 'House Dangerous', Vintage Books, New York. First Edition. 1987.

Gregory, Shaun, 'The Hidden Cost Of Deterrence-Nuclear Weapons Accidents', Brassey's (UK), London. 1990.

Halliday David, Reskick Robert, Walker Jearl, 'Fundamentals Of Physics', Fifth Edition. John Wiley & Sons, Inc. New York, NY. 1997.

Hazardous Substances Management Division, 'Guidelines For Management And Handling Of Hazardous Wastes', Ministry of Environment and Forests, Government of India, New Delhi. 1991.

Hung, John M., 'Petroleum Geochemistry And Geology', w.h. Freeman & Company, San Francisco. 1979.

Hunt, John M., 'Petroleum Geochemistry And Geology', W.H. Freeman and Company, San Francisco. 1979.

Kannan, Krishnan, 'Fundamentals Of Environmental Pollution', S. Chand & Company, New Delhi. 1991.

Kusinitz, Marc, 'Poisons And Toxins', Chelsea House Publishers, New York. 1993.

Lippmann, Morton and Schlesinger, Richard B., 'Chemical Contamination in the Human Environment', Oxford University Press, New York. 1979.

McCabe, Warren L., and Smith, Julian C. 'Unit Operations Of Chemical Engineeering', McGraw Hill, New York. 3rd Edition. 1990.

Millichap, Gordon J., 'Is Our Water Safe To Drink?', PNB Publishers, Chicago. 1995.

Nadis, Steve and MacKenzie, James J., 'Car Trouble', Beacon Press, Boston. 1993.

Saign, Geoffrey C., 'Green Essentials', Mercury House, San Francisco, CA. 1994.

Sax, Irving N. and Lewis, Richard J., 'Hawley's Condensed Chemical Dictionary', Eleventh Edition, Van Nostrand Reinhold Company, New York. 1987.

Sharma, Harish C., 'Environmental Pollution Compliance', CBS Publishers, New Delhi. 1994.

Sharma, Harish C., 'Pollution Definitions And Terminology For Chemical And Physical Hazards', Indian Journal of Env. Protection, Varanasi. Jan. 1992. Pages 8-11.

Shulman, Seth, 'The Threat At Home', Beacon Press, Boston. 1992.

U.S. Department of Energy, Office of Environmental Guidance, 'CERCLA Information Bried', EH-231-005/0991. Washington, DC. Sept. 1991.

U.S. Department of Energy, Office of Environmental Restoration and Waste Management, 'Federal Facilities And RCRA: An Orientation For DOE, EPA, And State Employees And Contractors, Appendix A', Washington, DC. Oct. 1992.

U.S. Department of Energy, 'EM Orientation Manual, Appendix G: EM Quick Reference Terms', Washington, DC. Feb. 1993.

U.S. Department of Energy, 'Committed To Results', DOE/EM-0152p. Washington, DC. April 1994.

U.S. Department of Energy, 'Environmental Management Fact Sheets', DOE/EM-0071P. Washington, DC. Aug. 1994.

U.S. Department of Energy, 'Environmental Management-1996', DOE/EM-0317. Washington, DC. Nov. 1996.

U.S. Environmental Protection Agency, Office of Emergency and Remedial Response, 'Superfund Removal Procedures' Revision No. 3. Document #9360.0-03b. Washington DC. Feb. 1988.

U.S. Environmental Protection Agency, Office of Emergency and Remedial Response, 'Technological Approaches To The Cleanup Of Radiologically Contaminated Superfund Sites', Doc. #9380.0-21. Washington, DC. Feb. 1988.

U.S. Environmental Protection Agency, Office of Emergency and Remedial Response, 'Community Relations in Superfund, Interim Version', Doc. # 9230.3B. Washington, DC. June 1988.

U.S. Environmental Protection Agency, Office of Solid Waste and Emergency Response, 'RCRA ARARs: Focus On Closure Requirements', Doc. #9234.2-04FS. Washington, DC. Oct. 1988.

U.S. Environmental Protection Agency, Office of Emergency and Remedial Response, 'Guidance On Remedial Actions For Contaminated Ground Water At Superfund Sites', Doc. #9283.1-2 Washington, DC. Dec. 1988.

U.S. Environmental Protection Agency, Office of Solid Waste and Emergency Response, 'Determining Soil Response Action Levels Based On Potential Contaminant Migration To Ground Water: A Compendium Of Examples', EPA/540/2-89/057. Washington, DC. Oct. 1989.

U.S. Environmental Protection Agency, Office of Solid Waste and Emergency Response, 'CERCLA Compliance With Other Laws Manual: CERCLA Compliance With The CWA And SDWA', Doc. # 9234.2-06/FS. Washington, DC. Feb. 1990.

U.S. Environmental Protection Agency, 'Ground Water, VOL. I: Ground Water And Contamination', EPA/625/6-90/016a. Washington, DC. 1990.

U.S. Environmental Protection Agency, Solid and Emergency Response, Office of Solid waste and Emergency Response, 'The Superfund Program: Ten Years Of Progress', EPA/540/8-91/003. Washington, DC. June 1991.

U.S. Environmental Protection Agency, Office of Emergency and Remedial Response, 'Guidance For Performing Preliminary Assessments Under CERCLA', EPA/540/G-91/013. Washington, DC. Sept. 1991.

Van Wylen and Sonntag Richard, 'Fundamentals Of Classical Thermodynamics', 3rd Edition. John Wiley & Sons, New York. 1985.